IMAGES
of America

NEW BALTIMORE

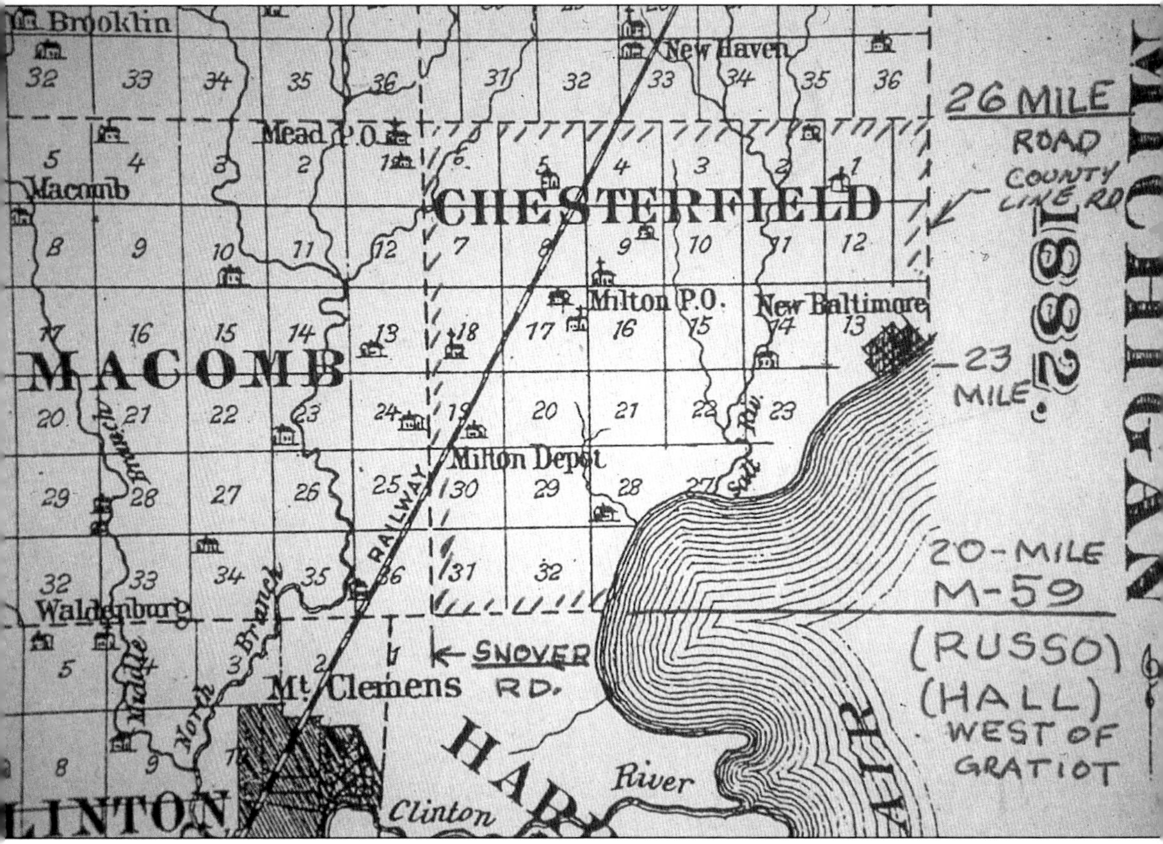

This 1882 map of Chesterfield Township shows the train and interurban tracks. Goods were shipped via the Great Lakes and the Erie Canal to the docks of New Baltimore, and from there by plank road to the Grand Trunk Railroad station, located at the end of the plank road in neighboring Lenox Township. New Baltimore's influence in the area was so strong that the railroad depot there was initially called the New Baltimore station. It was later renamed the New Haven station for the prospering village growing up around the depot. (Courtesy of Bob Mack.)

On the Cover: The Chesterfield Hotel was just one of the major hotels during New Baltimore's period as a renowned tourist destination. (Courtesy of Bob Mack.)

IMAGES
of America

NEW BALTIMORE

Richard Gonyeau, Bob Mack,
and Alan Naldrett

ARCADIA
PUBLISHING

ISBN 978-0-7385-9984-7

Published by Arcadia Publishing
Charleston, South Carolina

Printed in the United States of America

Library of Congress Control Number: 2013940626

For all general information, please contact Arcadia Publishing:
Telephone 843-853-2070
Fax 843-853-0044
E-mail sales@arcadiapublishing.com
For customer service and orders:
Toll-Free 1-888-313-2665

Visit us on the Internet at www.arcadiapublishing.com

This book is dedicated to Mary Gonyeau, Geraldine Mack, and Charles and Phyllis Maddix, as well as to the founders of our city and the people of New Baltimore, who know the meaning of the word community.

Contents

Acknowledgments		6
Introduction		7
1.	The First Settlers	9
2.	Alfred Ashley Plats a Village	17
3.	The Manufacturing Days	21
4.	Tourist Days	57
5.	Washington Street	77
6.	People of New Baltimore	91
7.	Schools and Libraries	99
8.	Notable Buildings and Businesses	107
9.	Floods, Great Fires, and the Fire Department	119
Bibliography		127

ACKNOWLEDGMENTS

There are many predecessors who have provided information on the history of New Baltimore. Foremost among them are Elmer and Grace Skinner, who wrote *History Stories of New Baltimore*, a history of New Baltimore's early days, and early history writer Stephen Rose. Bernard Trinity also chronicled many historical items about New Baltimore and Chesterfield Township, and Richard Gonyeau has long used original source materials, including old issues of the town's various newspapers, to write his history columns in local newspapers the *Anchor Bay Beacon* and the *Bay Voice*.

Bob Mack's photographic archive is unsurpassed, and his research has provided a wealth of knowledge about the details of the photographs. All the photographs not otherwise credited are from Mack's collection, including nearly every photograph in the book.

Thanks to Bette Carrothers, Shirley Hageman, Evelyn Rose Milham, Paul Torney, Milt Wolschon, Gail Zabowski, and everybody else who donated photographs and valuable information or time. Thanks to Dave Castle and Bette Carrothers, who helped with the editing.

Introduction

The first settlers in the New Baltimore area were Native Americans who most likely arrived in the area by crossing one of the many lakes or rivers. They were woodland tribes, chiefly the Chippewa and Ojibwa, and mostly lived near the shores of Lake St. Clair's Anchor Bay, Swan Creek, and near the banks of other rivers and streams in the area.

French explorer Pierre Yax was the first recorded non–Native American in the New Baltimore area. He came in 1796 and subsequently obtained a land grant signed by Pres. John Quincy Adams on July 3, 1826. The land grant tracked back to a land patent Yax had in 1812, when Michigan was still part of the Northwest Territory. Yax's land was at the mouth of the French-named Crappeau Creek. Fabian Robertjean made the first government purchase of land in the New Baltimore area in 1820.

Pierre Yax and the other French settlers got along quite well with the original natives, trapping and trading furs, and gathering salt from the Salt River. Some settlers married Native American women. When the French settlers began to farm the area, they divided the land into "strip farms," which were long, narrow portions of land platted so that a narrow end was on Anchor Bay or the Salt River, allowing many settlers to have access to the water they needed for farming.

In 1845, businessman Alfred Ashley came from neighboring Mt. Clemens and purchased 60 acres on either side of Washington Street, an area that became known as the village of Ashley. In 1851, Ashley platted the village and founded the village's first post office. The post office was christened Ashleyville instead of Ashley, in order to avoid confusion with other Ashley municipal units in Michigan. However, other areas continued to get the village's mail, so residents changed the name of the village to New Baltimore when it was officially incorporated in 1867. The original area encompassed the central part of what is now New Baltimore, extending northwest along Base, Clay, and Maria Streets down to Anchor Bay.

Alfred Ashley opened a sawmill in the village, as he had 25 years earlier in Mt. Clemens. He was a member of the company that built the plank road to Romeo, and he also built the first dock and the first steamboat in the village, the *Lady of the Lake*. He was a member of the Michigan state legislature in 1828 and was one of the founders of the village's First Congregational Church, at Base and Alfred Streets.

The village took advantage of its close proximity to the water to develop manufacturing and agricultural businesses whose wares were conveniently shipped to surrounding areas via Anchor Bay and the St. Clair and Detroit Rivers. Some of these businesses were factories that produced bricks, brooms, coffins, corsets, and creamery products. New Baltimore's largest industry was staves, which were used to construct barrels. Barrels, a valuable commodity of the day, were used to ship everything from sawdust to pickles. With three stave mills in the village, it was estimated that staves from New Baltimore made up 95 percent of the barrels used in the New England whaling industry in 1862.

From the docks of New Baltimore, lumber and other building materials were shipped to outlying areas from piers that extended more than 100 feet from the shore. As goods were shipped by water to Ashley/New Baltimore, they could be transported along the plank road that led to the New Baltimore station, the name of the Grand Trunk Railway depot in nearby New Haven. The Grand Trunk shipped goods to other parts of the state and the nation from there.

Beginning in 1878, the Detroit United Railroad had a branch that ran from Detroit to Port Huron until about 1930. The interurban train ran through New Baltimore, and because the village was in the middle of the route, the power plant for the train was built in New Baltimore on Highview Avenue, now a subdivision. The interurban trains ran along Gratiot Turnpike, down 23 Mile Road into New Baltimore, and out along M-29 to Anchorville, Fair Haven, and onward to Port Huron. The depot for New Baltimore was across the street from Hatheway Institute, the present location of the New Baltimore municipal offices.

The Hatheway Institute was a school built in 1876 with money left to the village by local tycoon Gilbert Hatheway in 1871. Hatheway owned a stave factory, commercial docks, and a shipping business. Due to prolonged litigation regarding the estate and its interest, the money left to the city had grown considerably by the time the school was built. A beautiful three-story building with a gymnasium on the top floor was built, which served as a high school and a teacher-training institute for many decades.

From the 1880s on, New Baltimore's manufacturing base began to take second place to its burgeoning status as a tourist center. With resort ships and the interurban trains bringing people from Detroit and other environs, New Baltimore became home to a mineral bathhouse, an opera house, a brewery, taverns, boating marinas and piers, luxury hotels, and other social and recreational amenities catering to the tourist trade. Undaunted by the rise of the Great Depression, New Baltimore was incorporated as a city in 1931.

During Prohibition in the 1920s, New Baltimore was an important port for the illegal liquor trade due to its proximity to Canada. There were many "blind pigs" and hidden speakeasies in the area near the docks.

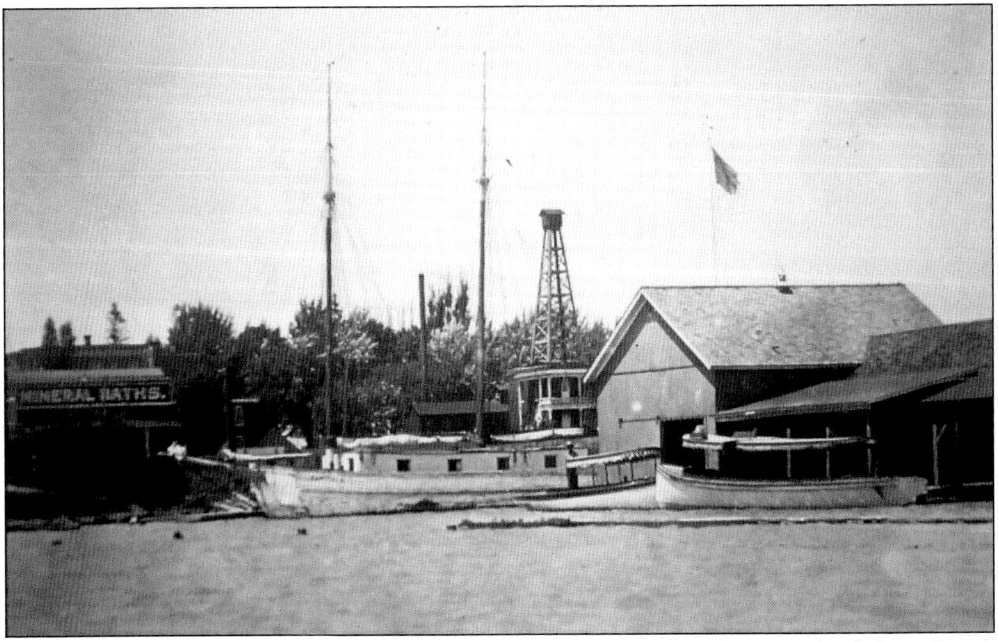

The early commerce of New Baltimore is illustrated in this 1910 photograph of the village's busy waterfront.

One

The First Settlers

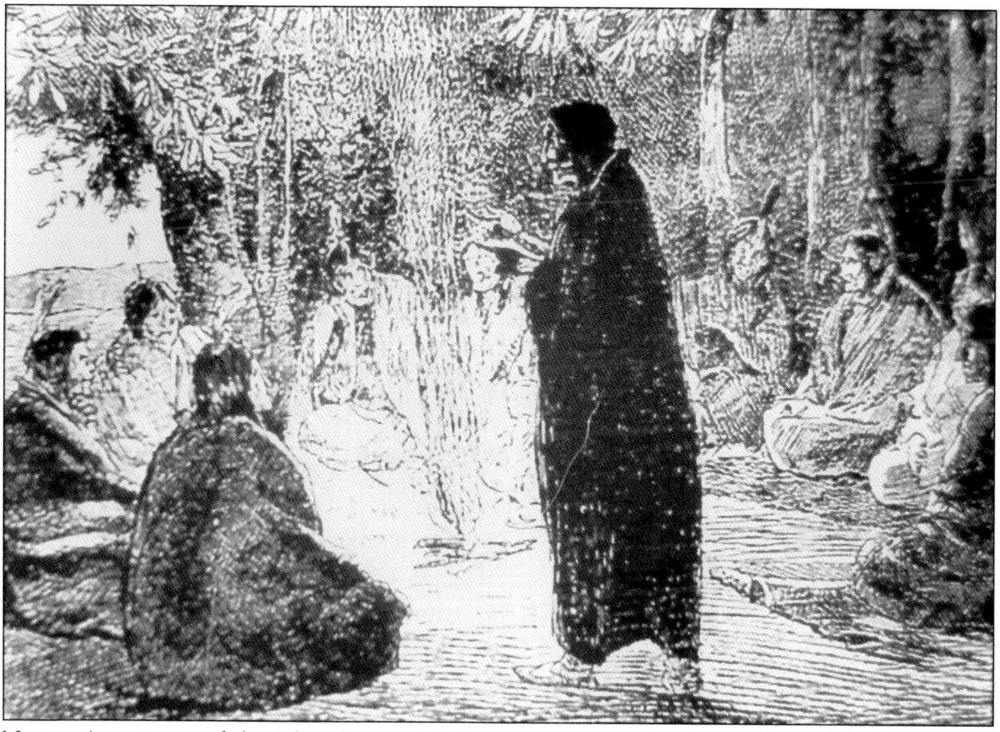

Native Americans of the Cherokee and Ojibwa tribes were the first settlers of the area, likely making the trek between 5,000 and 10,000 years ago. There were also some members of the Ottawa tribe in the area. One of the first trails in the area—more than 5,000 years old—was the ridge of a glacier. Now called Sugarbush Road, it was at one time the main road from New Baltimore to the county seat of Mt. Clemens.

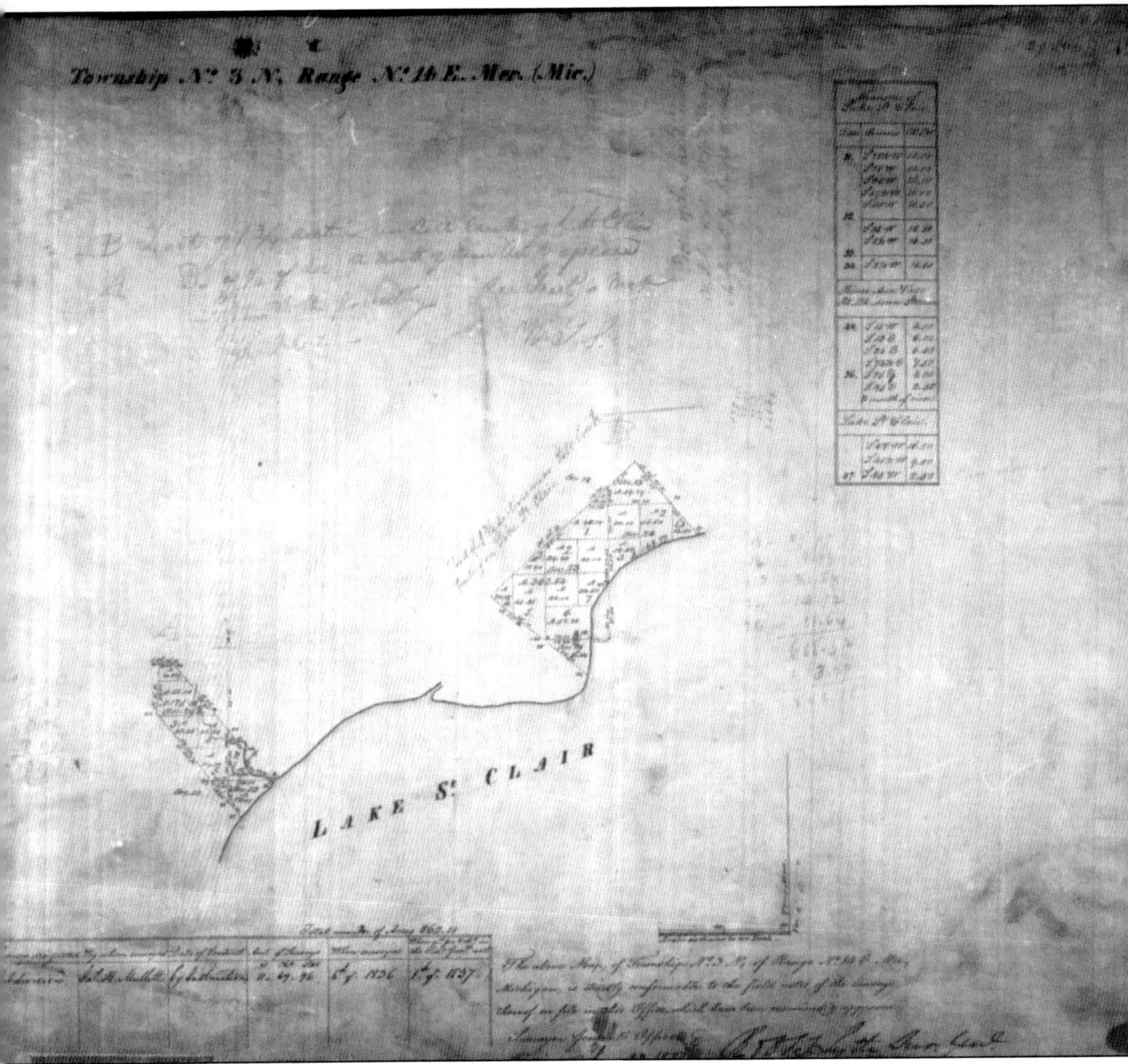

In 1807, most of the Native Americans in the area signed the Treaty of Detroit, relinquishing their claim to most of the land. Although it was highly questionable since the Native Americans did not understand the "treaty"—much less the concept of owning land—the trading of alcohol smoothed the way to having the Native American chiefs give up the land for about $10,000. There are maps in the National Archives showing the Native American reservations established in Chesterfield Township in 1807 under the Treaty of Detroit.

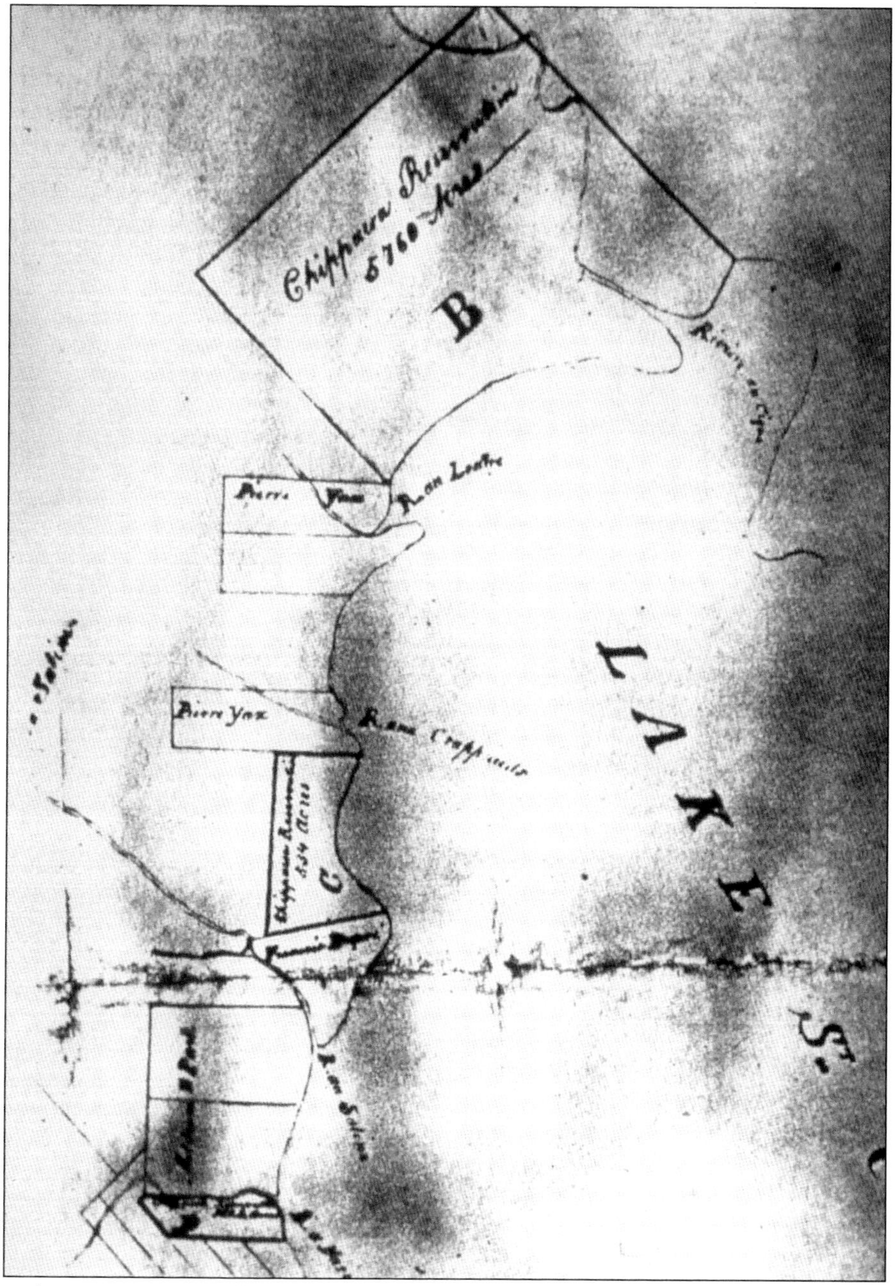

Native Americans occupied two reservations in Chesterfield Township and one in nearby Ira Township until about 1830. One of the reservations in Chesterfield, on the Aux Vasse River, had earlier been the site of a Chippewa village. After 1830, most of them were encouraged to move from the area. In 1838, those still in the area were physically taken by ship via Port Huron to Fort Dearborn (now Chicago). From there, they went farther west, on foot, to what is now Kansas. Many escaped being moved by relocating to the nearby Canadian-owned Walpole Island. Others did not move because the French had long intermarried with the Native Americans, making questions of ancestry indeterminable in some cases. This map shows the land of Pierre Yax, first non–Native American in New Baltimore.

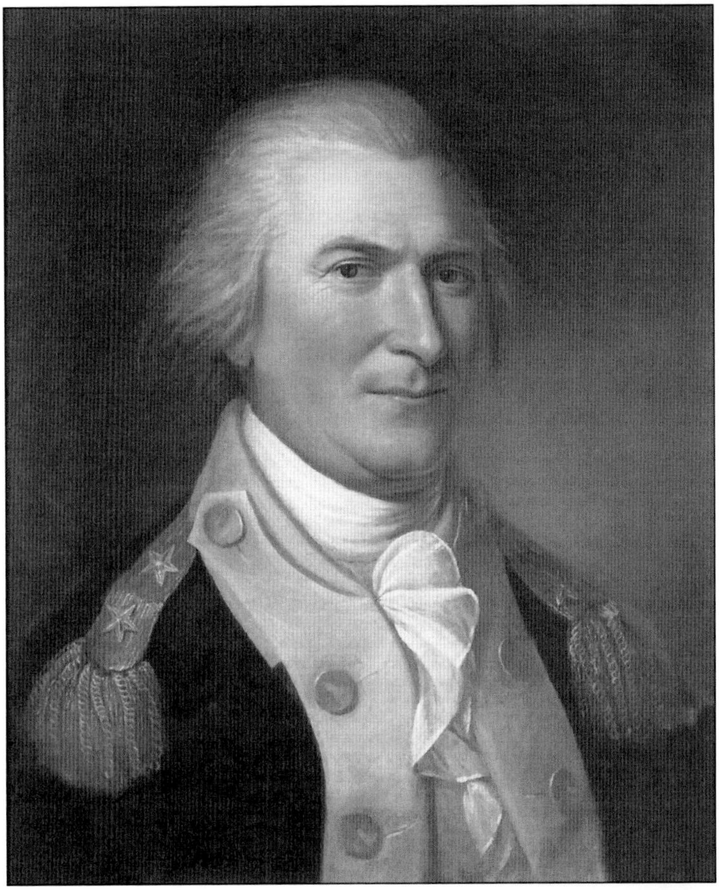

The first French explorers and missionaries came to the area around 1611, and named the dominant waterway Luc Ste. Claire on August 12, 1687. The Native American name had been Otsi-keta. Accounts vary as to whom this body of water was named for, but most say that it was Gen. Arthur St. Clair, the first governor of the Northwest Territory. The most widely known image of him is the painting at left, by Charles W. Peale in 1782. Other missives say that French explorer Sieur de La Salle and his crew sailed their ship, the *Griffin*, into the lake on Ste. Claire's Day, therefore christening the lake for the saint.

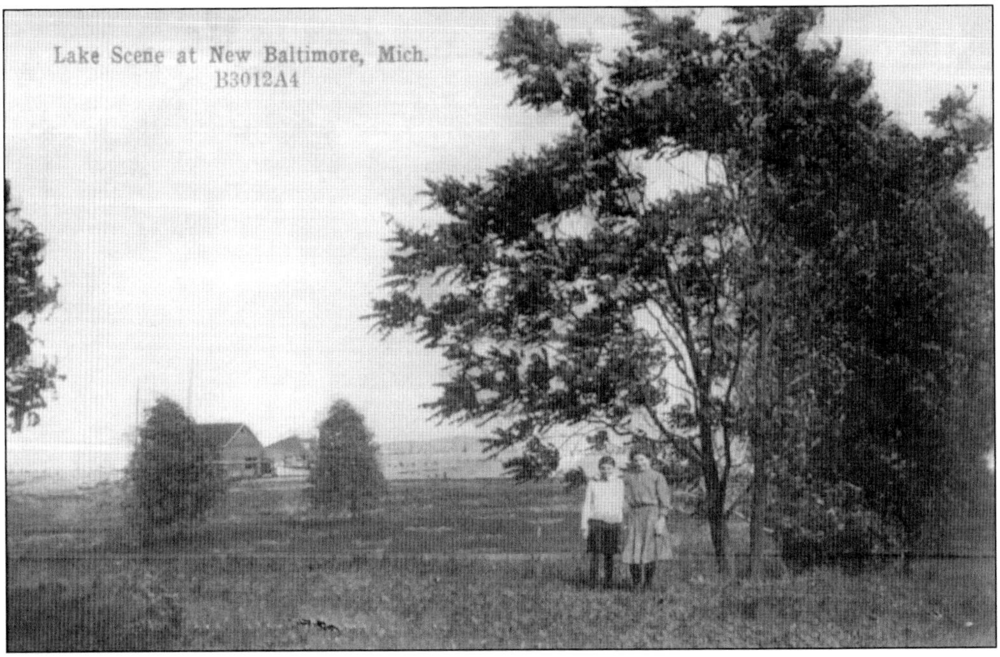

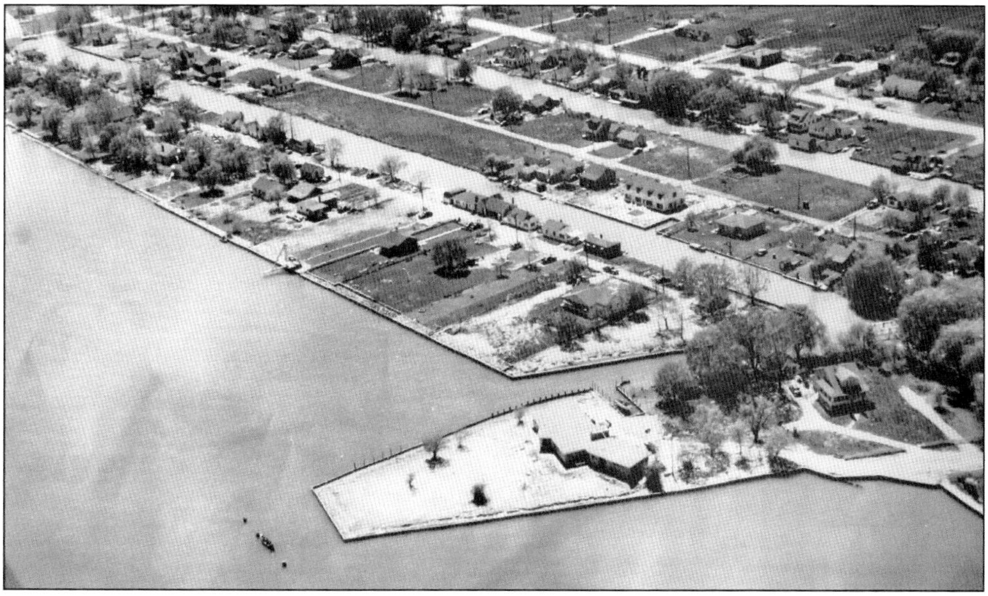

Antoine de la Mothe Cadillac settled Detroit in 1701, and French pioneers ventured forth from that point onward. Pierre Yax, born of French settlers Michel and Catherine Yax in 1763 in Grosse Pointe, came to the New Baltimore area in 1796 and staked a claim for much of the surrounding area. He was given a land grant signed by Pres. John Quincy Adams in 1826, which traced back to a land patent of his from 1812, when Michigan was still part of the Northwest Territory. Other settlers also ventured into the area; a French settlement called La Saline grew around a peninsula of the nearby Salt River.

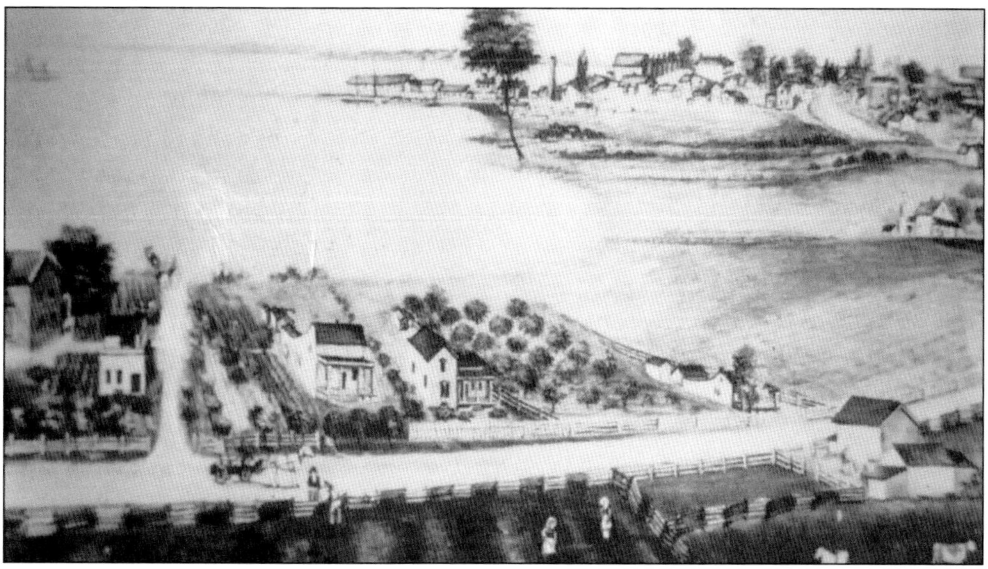

The explanations given for how Anchor Bay received its name vary. One of the most repeated involves the St. Clair River, which divides in two as it approaches the city of Algonac. Of the two divisions, or channels, the North Channel was used the most for shipping because it was wider and deeper. However, there was a sandbar at the mouth of the channel. Ships would drop their anchor before reaching the entrance of the bay and then figure out where to navigate to avoid the sandbar. Hence, it became known as Anchor Bay.

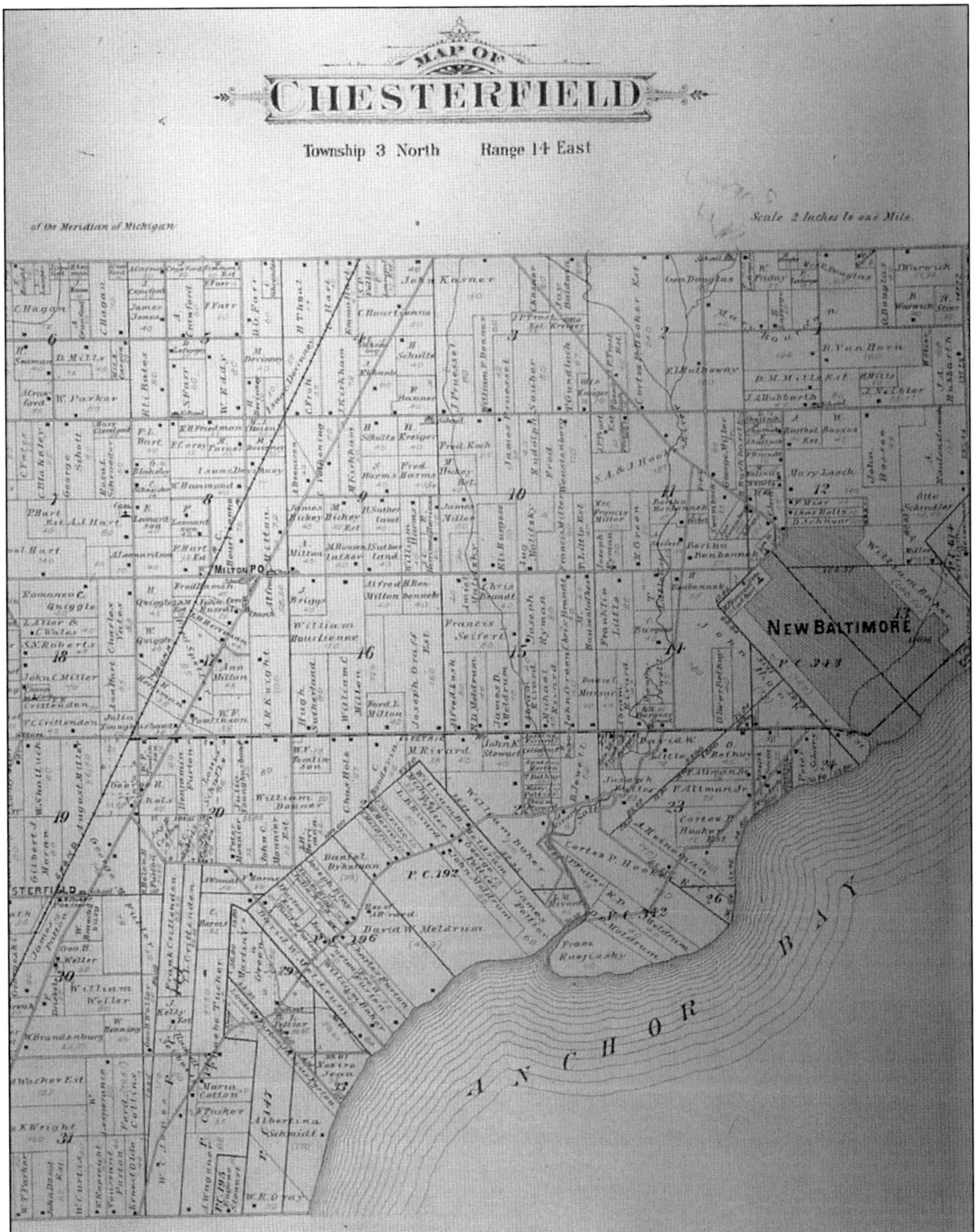

The French built earthen huts and farmed strip farms, which were long, narrow pieces of land with the narrow end near the lake, taking maximum advantage of the available natural waterways. This early map of the New Baltimore and Chesterfield Township area shows the narrow lots connecting to the waterways. The chief commerce of the French settlers was buying, selling, and trading animal furs and pelts.

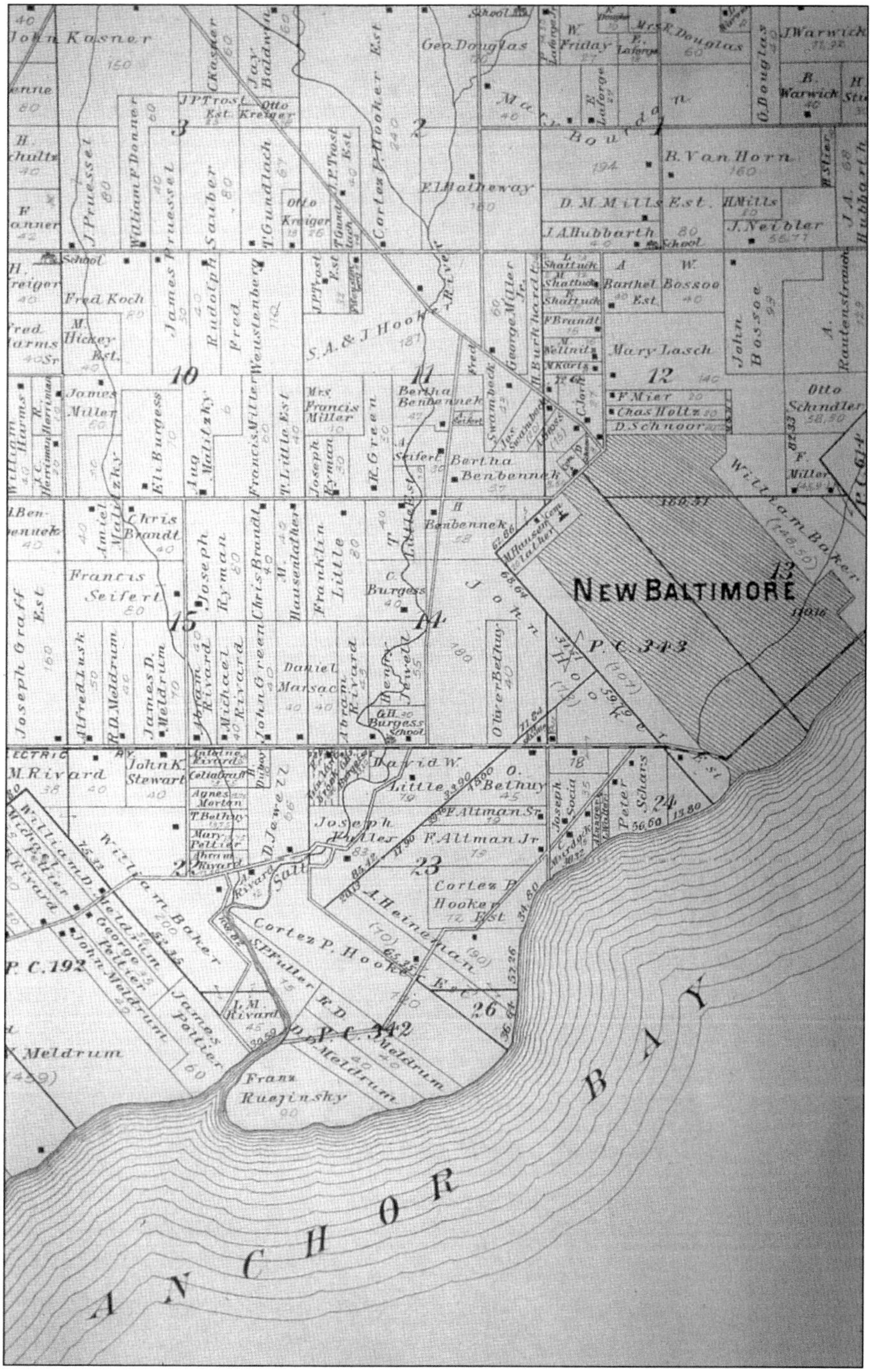

After the French and Indian War ended in 1763, the English controlled the land, although little change actually occurred. The English maintained the salt and fur industries, and most of the French settlers stayed to protect their interests. The British stayed in the area until about 1815, after the treaty ending the War of 1812 gave the American colonies control of the area. Fort Gratiot Turnpike was laid out, leading from Fort Gratiot, near present-day Port Huron, to Detroit. The turnpike was the major road connecting New Baltimore with outlying areas.

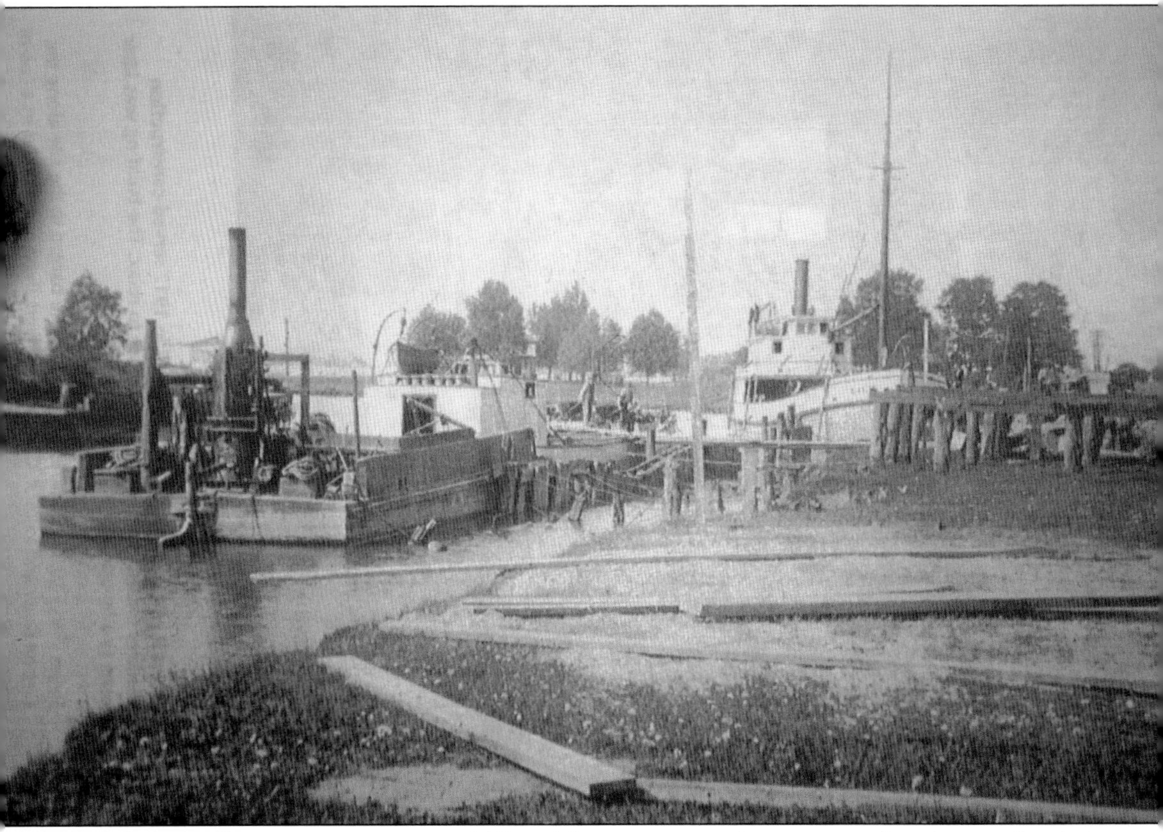

Michigan became a territory in 1805, and larger groups of immigrants began to make their homes in the area. In 1818, Chesterfield Township, including the village of New Baltimore, was surveyed by William Wampler. New farmers had their land recorded, and the first French land claims were re-recorded. During this era, side roads off of Gratiot Turnpike were constructed. New Baltimore's location on Anchor Bay, with easy shipping throughout the area, was a major reason for its settlement and subsequent prosperity.

Two

Alfred Ashley Plats a Village

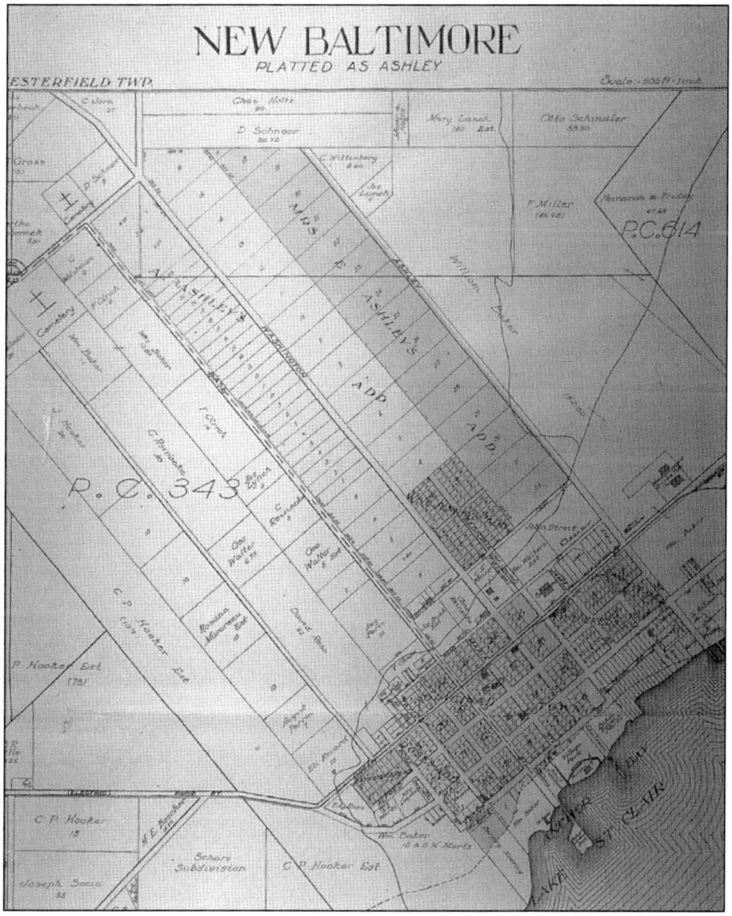

In 1845, Alfred Ashley came from Mt. Clemens and built a dock and a sawmill. In 1851, he platted the village, which was first named Ashley, for its founder. When the village was given its first post office, with Alfred Ashley as the first postmaster, it was called Ashleyville to avoid confusion with other Ashley governmental units in Michigan. After the village still got its mail confused with other towns, the village decided to rename itself New Baltimore upon its incorporation, on March 7, 1855. By some accounts, it was so named because people figured it would soon be as successful as Baltimore, Maryland.

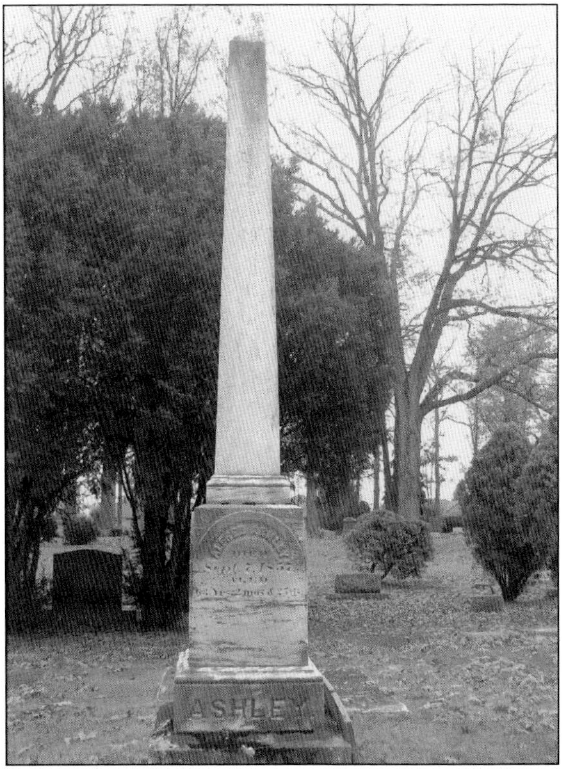

Alfred Ashley served in state and local government, and, in 1846, started the first hotel in the village: the Old Hotel, on Front Street, near the present-day water building. He was the son of Thomas Ashley of Mt. Clemens and had successful progeny, as Alfred Ashley III went on to become the police chief and village president. The plaque below, at Alfred Ashley's grave in New Baltimore's Oakwood Cemetery, reads, "The Founder of Ashley Village in 1845."

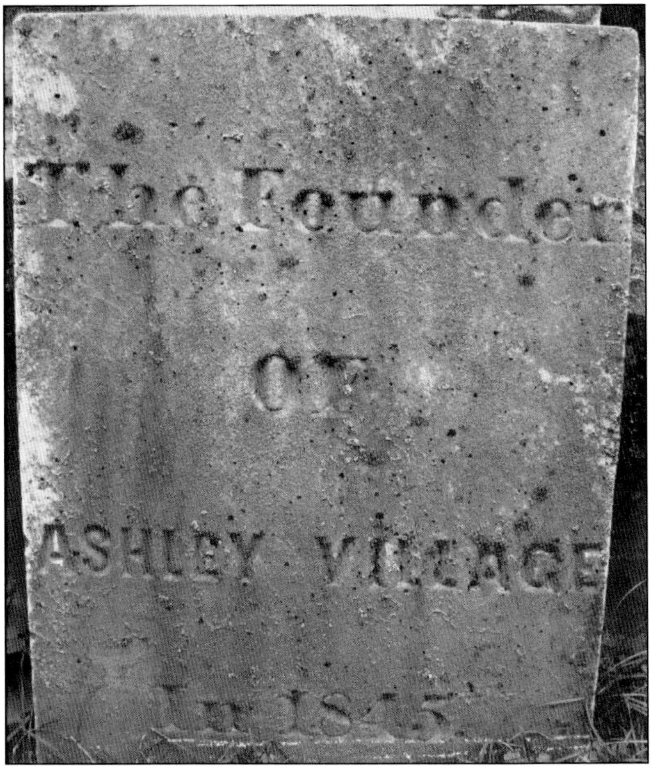

Using wood cut and planed in his sawmill, Alfred Ashley built a wooden road, the Ashley/Romeo Plank Road, which led to the village of Romeo, another major Macomb County settlement. There was a tollbooth located at the intersection of Ridge and Washington Roads, near 24 Mile Road (now Cemetery Road). Alfred Ashley also provided the wood and donated the land for the First Congregational Church in New Baltimore (right) in 1856. The first meeting of the church took place at the Union schoolhouse on April 29, 1856. For a short while, they met at the Red Ribbon Hall on Maria Street at Main Street. The Red Ribbon Hall (below) also hosted plays, shows, dances, and parties for townspeople to enjoy. Local Masonic groups also met there. It was later converted into a dwelling and then demolished in 1857. Kleehammer's Saloon was then built on the site; the establishment was eventually converted by Frank Christie into Christie's Funeral Home.

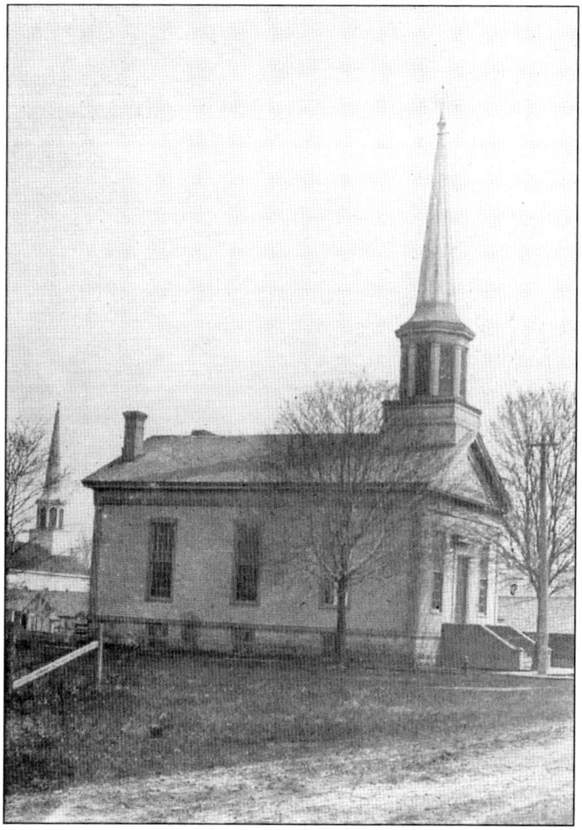

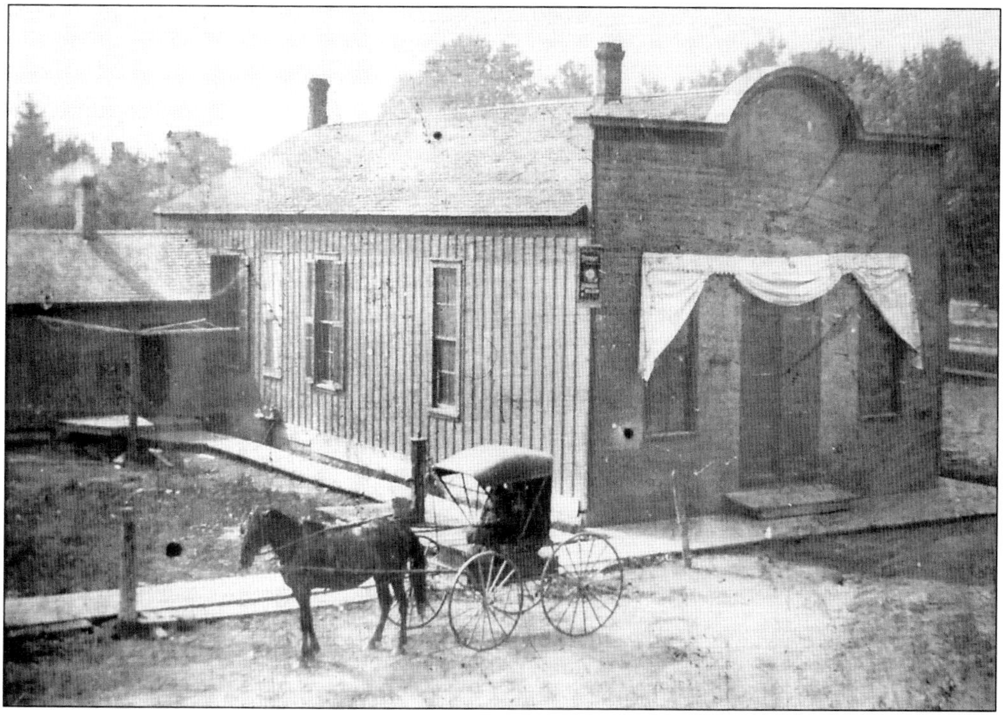

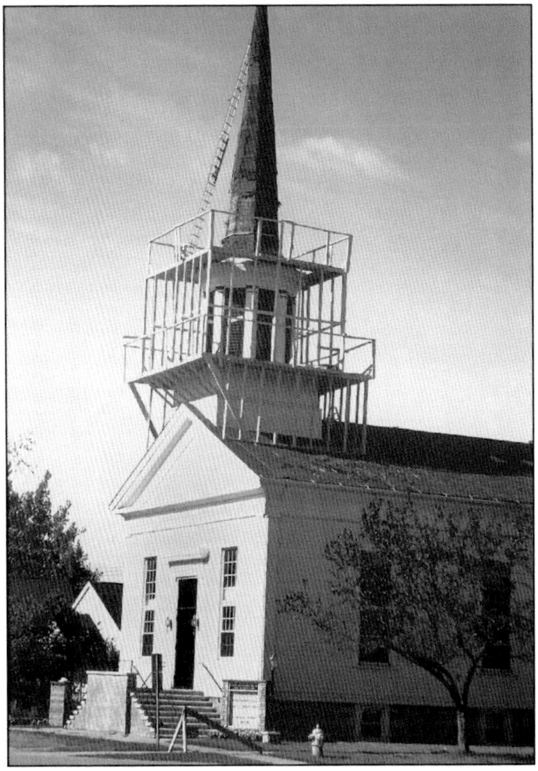

After meeting in various places for a few years, the congregation built their own structure in the Greek Revival style on Base Street facing Alfred Street. The chief architect and builder was Capt. Abel Davis. Many of the rocks in the foundation were originally ship ballast stones, which ships would dispose of when loading cargo. The new church was dedicated on June 20, 1861. Recognized as one of the oldest churches in the area, it has survived two major fires, the first of which, in 1926, destroyed a major part of the rear of the church. This damage was repaired, only to have more damage occur in another fire in 1938, which started in the furnace area. To prevent another occurrence, the furnace room was then enlarged and a new chimney was erected. During rededication services in 1938, the firemen were special guests.

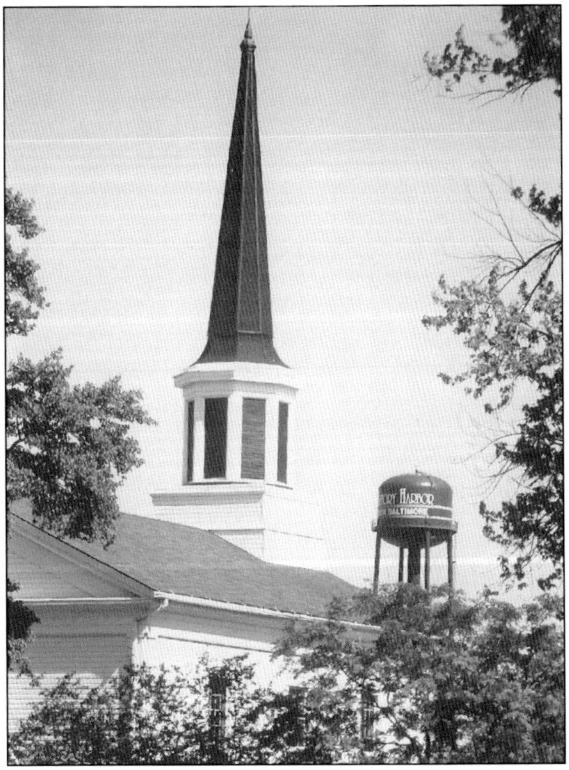

Three

The Manufacturing Days

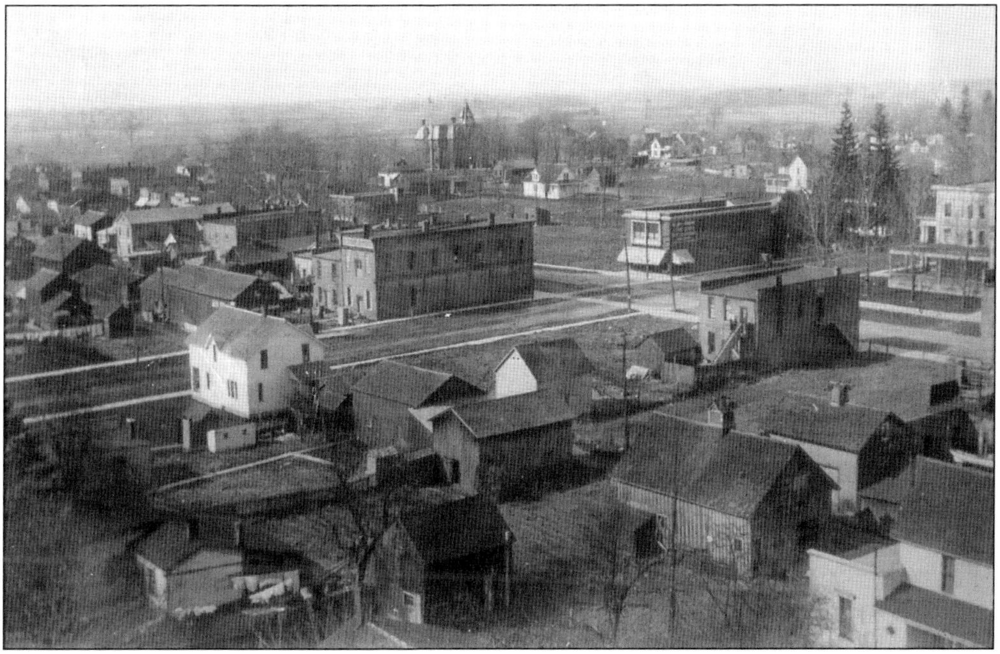

In the early 1900s, many of the major surviving buildings in New Baltimore were on Washington Street. One of these was the Koenig Dry Goods building, later occupied by Bates/Striber's/Anchor Bay Pharmacy. Another was the Baker Building. These buildings still face each other on Washington Street at the corner of Main Street. Moving towards the bay in this image are the Schlosser Building; the building that held the town's first bank, the Sandel Bank; Art & Mary's Grocery store; and a speakeasy, which, ironically, is now a wine shop. Speaking of alcohol, another house in town, which still stands today near the original site of the Hatheway Institute, held Lou Reidel's first bar, which later became the Town Pump.

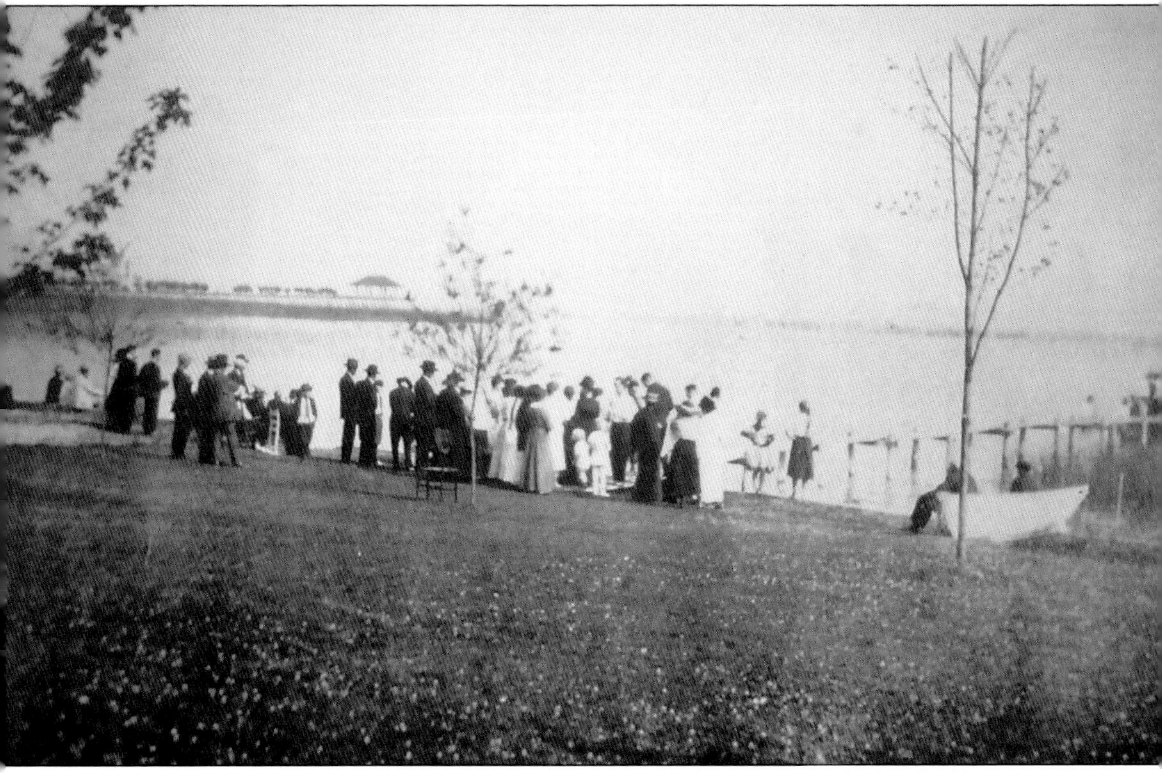

Alfred Ashley built his dock in 1845 at the foot of Atwood Street, where he berthed his steamship, the *Lady of the Lake*. Besides the Atwood dock, there were also the Lozen dock, at the foot of Washington Street; the Perkins dock, at the foot of Base Street, which serviced the stave mill; and the Hatheway dock, between Base and Maria Streets, which handled most of the incoming tourists.

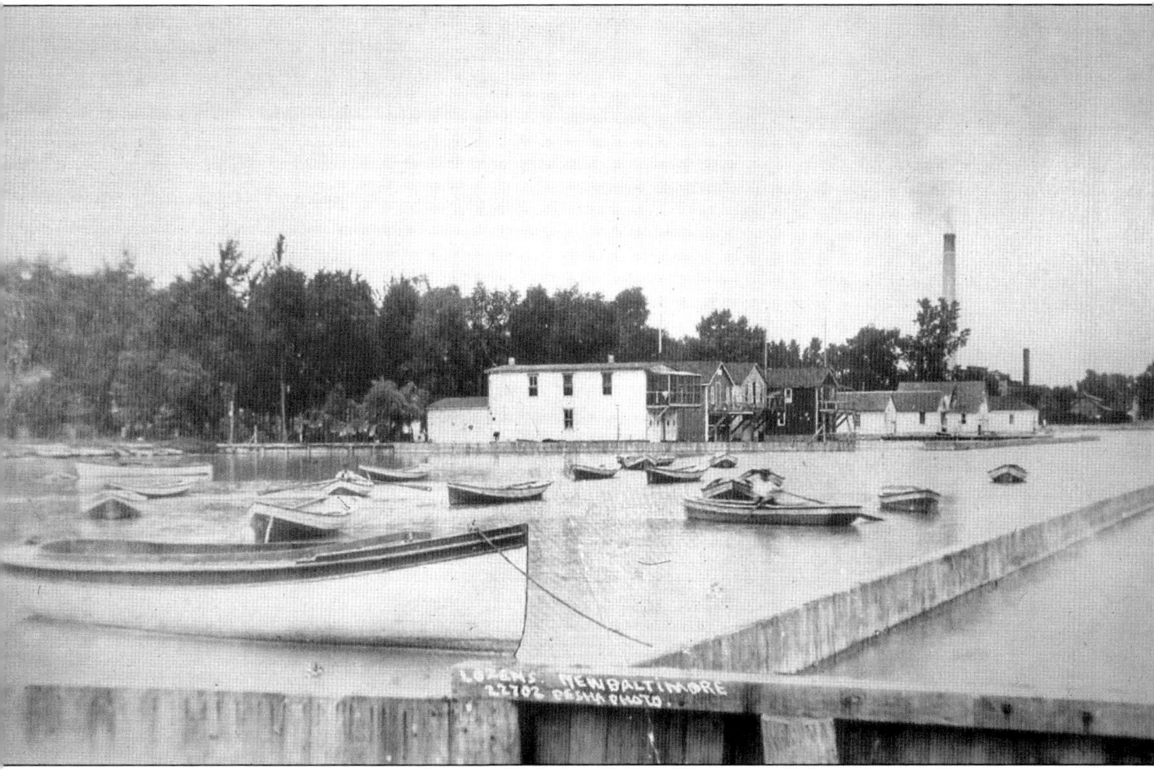

Two of the main steamships at Anchor Bay in the early 1900s were the *Hattie* and the *City of New Baltimore*. The *Hattie* was built in Fair Haven in 1882. The 84-foot steamship carried many types of cargo, including barrel staves, livestock, and human passengers making the trip to Detroit. The 94-foot *City of New Baltimore* carried passengers until about 1912, when it became a tugboat. New Baltimore thrived in the early days; in 1875, it was the third-largest settlement in Macomb County, behind only Mt. Clemens (the county seat), and the village of Romeo.

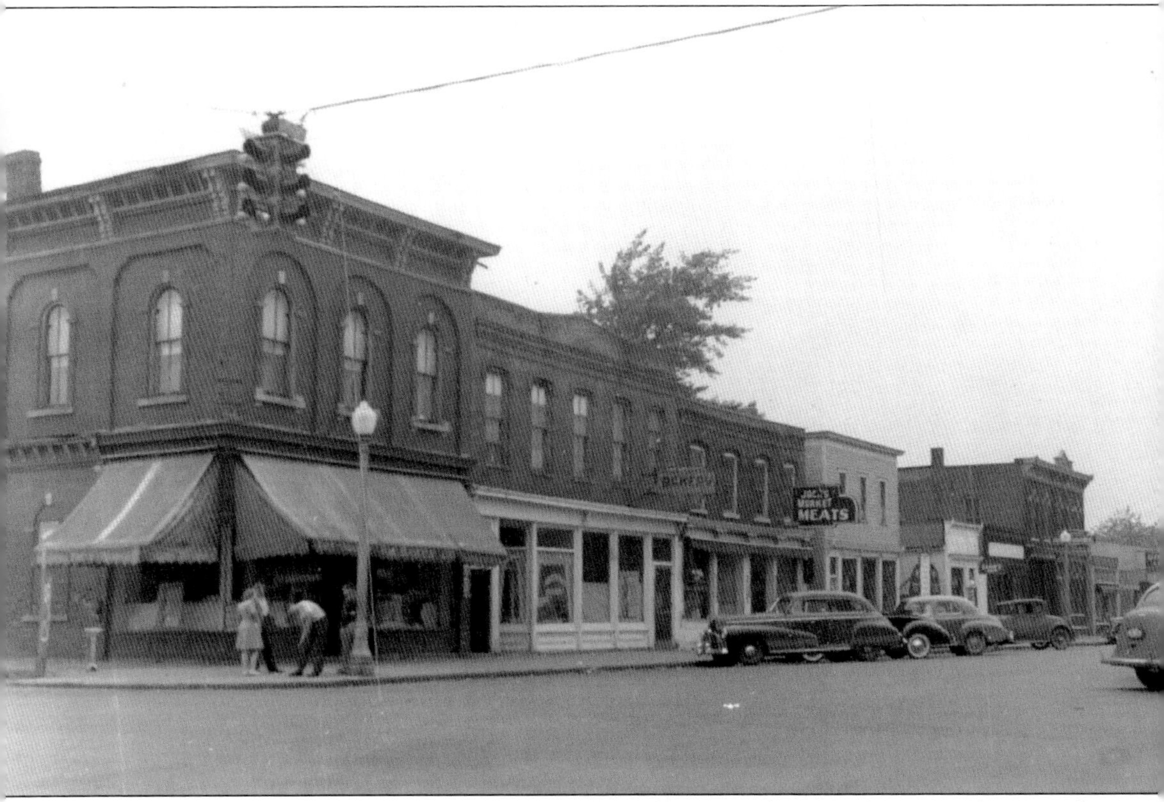

One of the oldest still-standing buildings of the golden age of New Baltimore industry is the Baker Building, built in 1868 on the corner of Main and Washington Streets. Although the whole building is now devoted to one business, Stahl's Famous Original Bakery, it was often subdivided into two businesses.

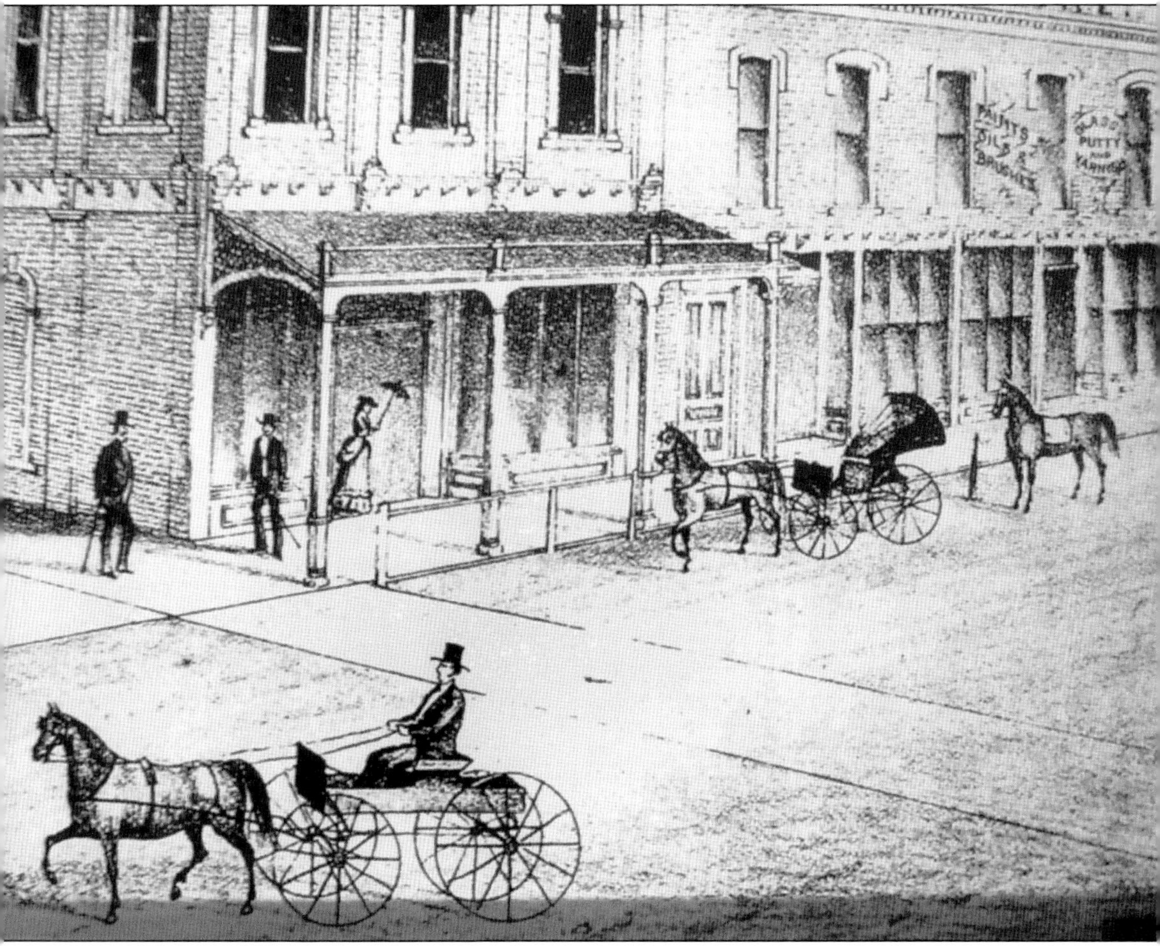

Before the Baker Building was erected, a different building stood in the same location. It was owned by Joshia Robinson, a merchant who sold imported goods. It was sold to Peter Schaars, who tore it down and erected the brick Baker Building.

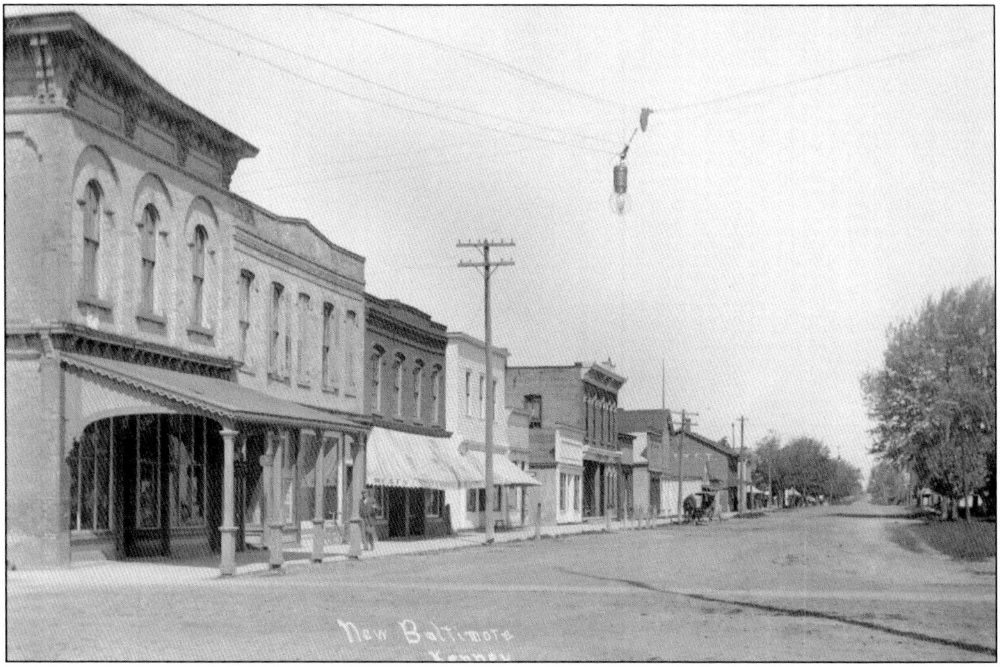

Before the Great Fire of 1870, a previous fire had destroyed many of the wooden buildings. In 1868, the two-story, 8,000-square-foot brick building now known as the Baker Building was erected using bricks from Andrew Streit's brickyard, at the corner of Hathaway and Atwood Streets. Other brickyards included the Joseph Rose brickyard, on the shores of Crappeau Creek on Main Street in the mid-1850s; a brickyard on Green Street, midway between Ashley Street and County Line Road operated by Paul Howcroft in 1912; the Joseph Engelman brickyard at 37079 Green Street, in back of the broom factory, which started in 1916; and William Heineman's brickyard, which operated in the 1890s east of County Line Road and north of Main Street.

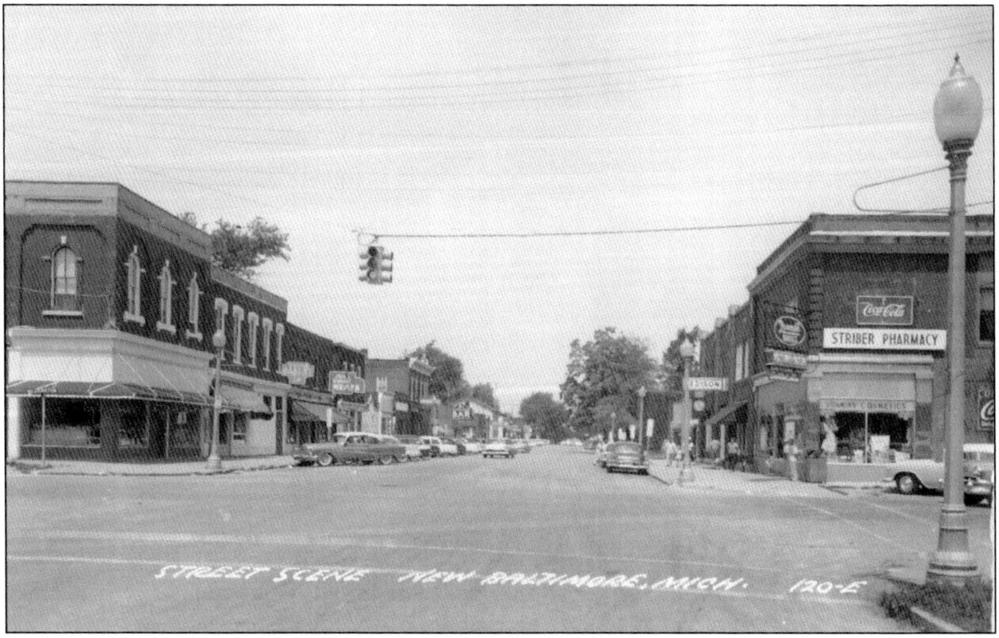

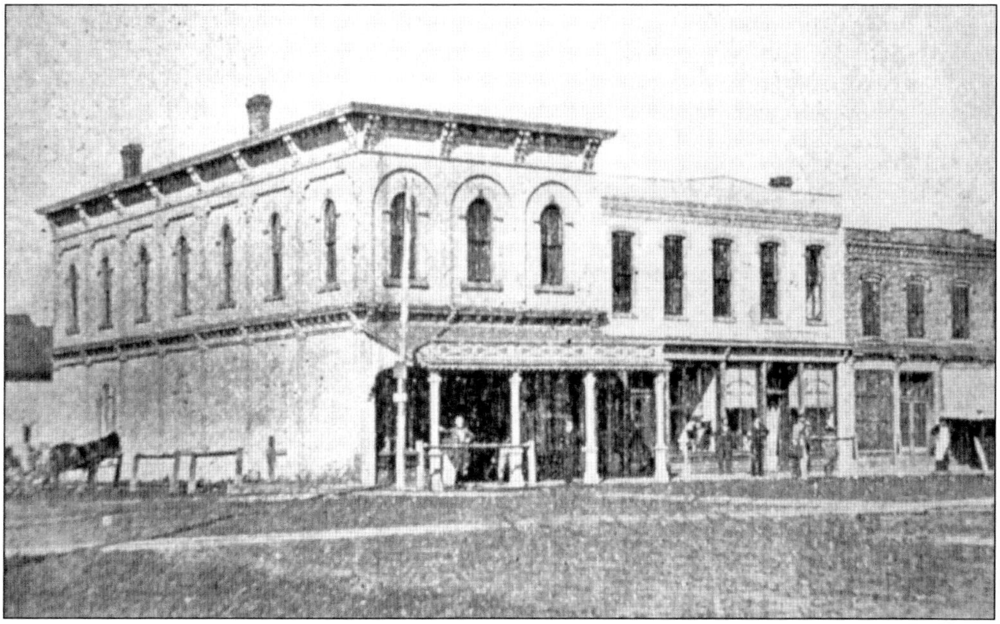

Joshia Robinson sold the original building to Peter Schaars, a former boardinghouse and saloon owner. Schaars erected the brick building in 1868 and sold dry goods, shoes, boots, hats, medicine, and groceries at the store. He also served as postmaster from 1867 to 1870. In 1870, Peter Schaars sold what had become a prime piece of New Baltimore real estate to William Baker Sr. for $4,000. The building was thereafter known as the Baker Building, and his family's businesses used the building for over 100 years, selling everything from petticoats to potatoes.

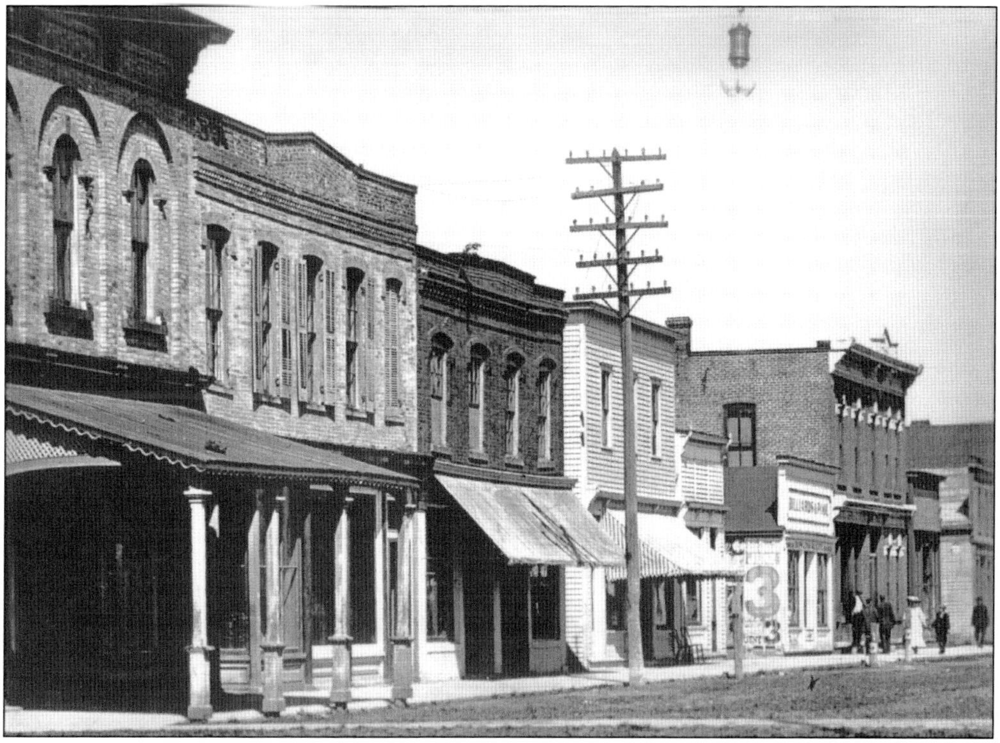

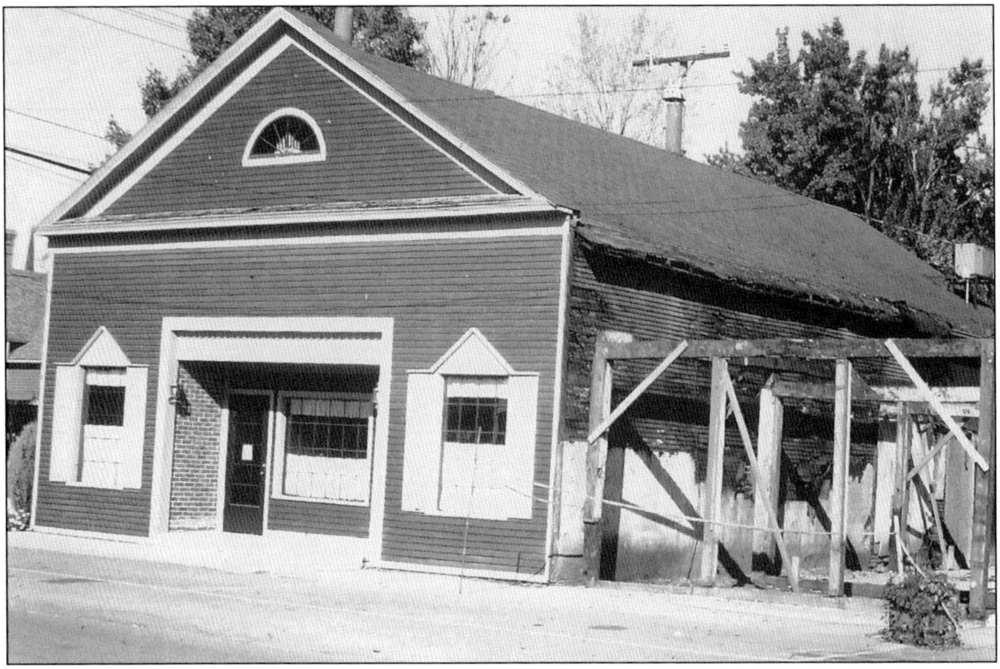

Behind the Baker family business was a barn where William Baker Sr. kept his delivery wagon and horses. This barn survived for many years and was later converted into the Anchor Bay Restaurant, the Cherokee Bar, and, as pictured below, the Stuart Brown printing business. Also, the second film house in New Baltimore was in the former garage. When the theater was renovated in modern times, many old movie posters from the 1930s and 1940s were found. Baker also owned the Baker Lime Kiln, whose product was in high demand across the country due to its high quality. Lime was used to whitewash fences and walls, among other uses. The kiln was 100 feet back from Bedford Street, between Main Street and the lake.

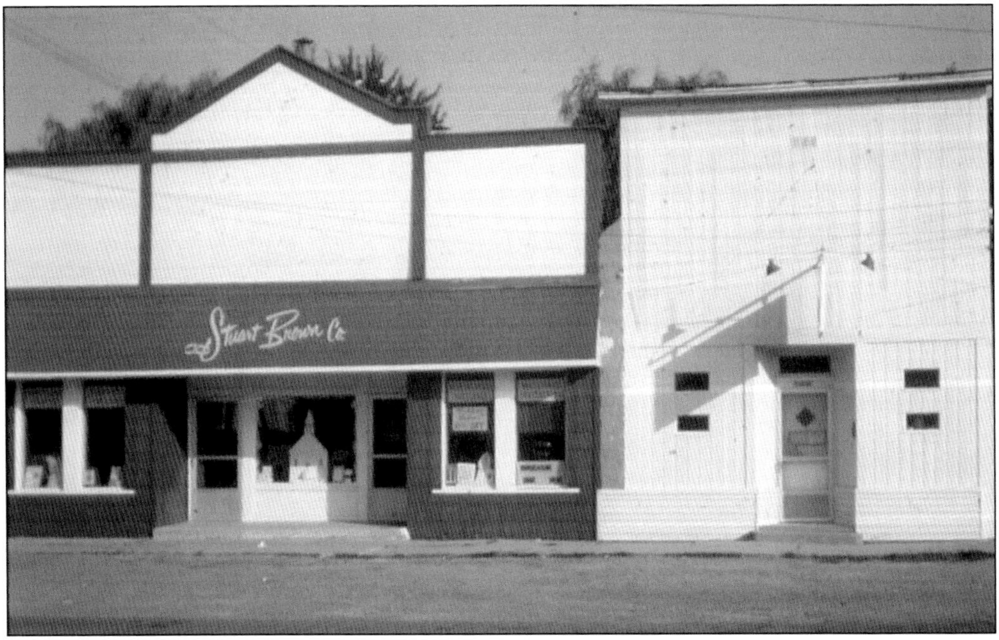

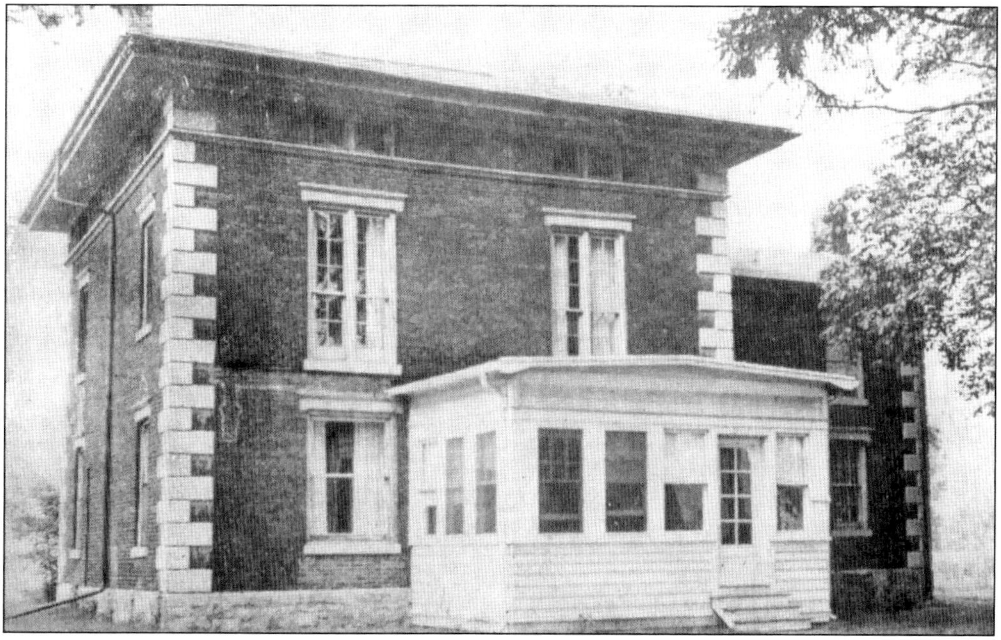

The Baker family had a large house and farm at Alfred and Ashley Streets, which was built by Frederick Kern in 1859. The house survived until the end of the 20th century. On the farm, they grew vegetables and other products that were then sold in the store. William Baker Jr. was the city water commissioner and served for many years on the village council. Later, an order of Roman Catholic nuns inhabited the home.

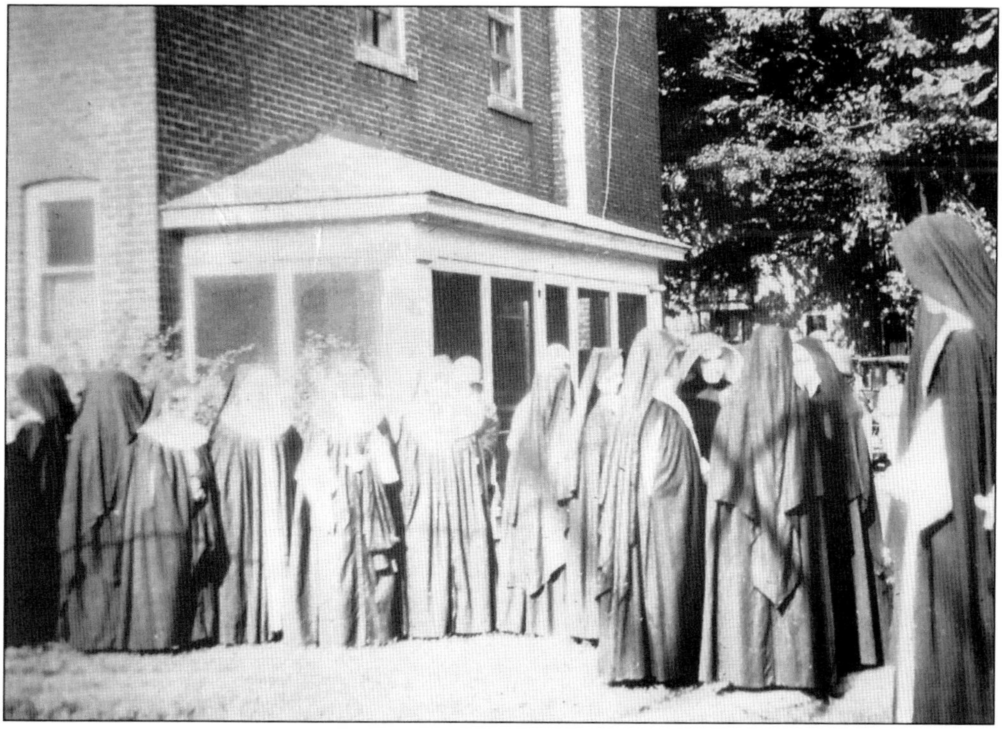

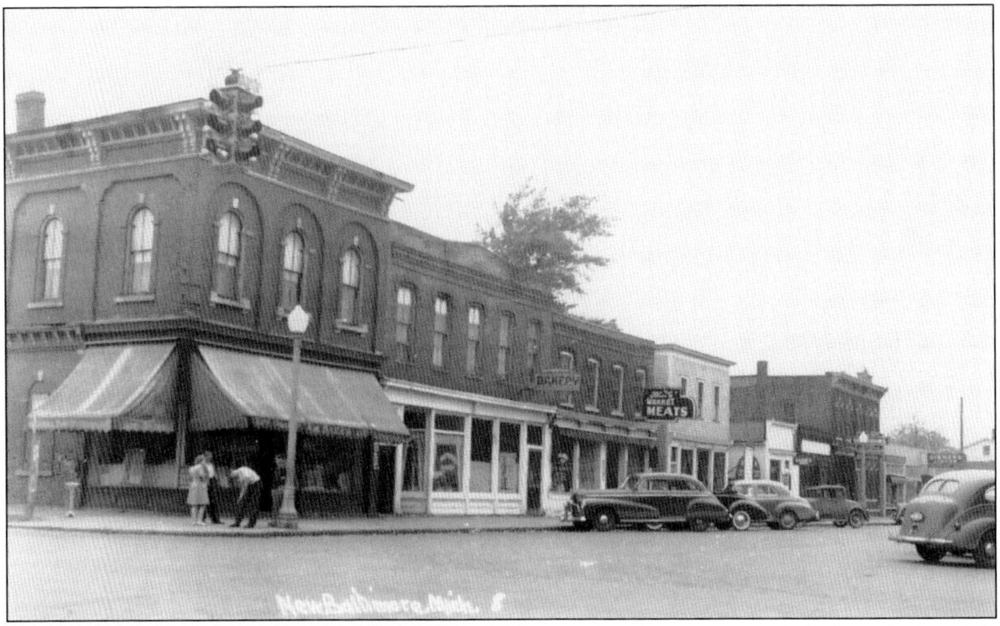

The Baker Building stayed in the family until 1979 under the auspices of William Baker Sr.'s granddaughter Dorothy Schnoor, who ran a women's and children's clothing store there. After her death in 1976, Baker Sr.'s great-granddaughter Dottie Melkert and her husband, Herb, ran the store until the building was sold in 1979.

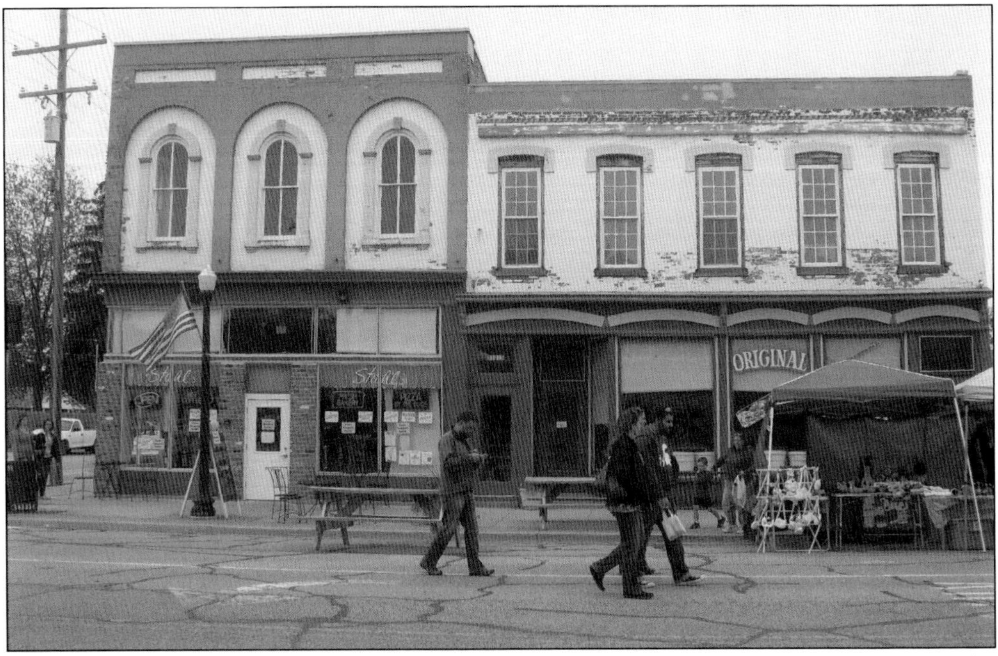

The Baker Building was partitioned in 1920, and many other businesses occupied it over the years, including a drugstore owned by Orvy Bates, who moved to the building directly across the street in 1935. The drugstore building was known over the years as Koenig Dry Goods, Gibbons General Store, Bates Pharmacy, Striber's Pharmacy, and Anchor Bay Pharmacy. It also housed an undertaking business.

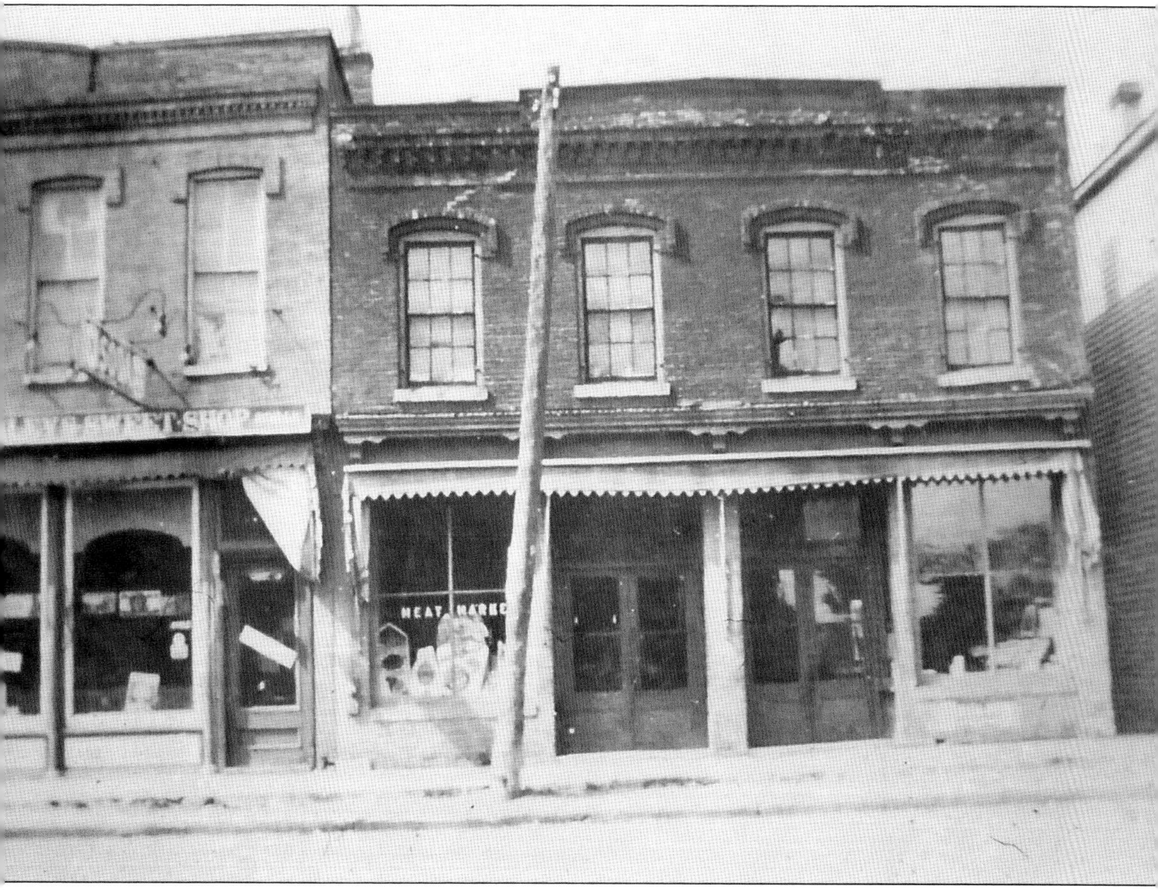

The Central Store also occupied the Baker Building, and sold oils, paints, varnish, and glass. In the mid-1920s, the building was home to Ashley's Sweet Shop, a candy store owned by Alfred Ashley III, the grandson of New Baltimore's founder. The Ashley Sweet Shop was a popular meeting spot for old and young. It did not hurt that the shop also had a soda fountain and a popcorn machine, or that the municipal bandstand was right across the street. Ashley III, a horn player for the city band, was the village president and went on to be the chief of police for 15 years. Mayor E.E. Straffon was a high school science teacher and the conductor of the city band. He hooked up New Baltimore's first pubic address system to help broadcast the free band concerts. New radio stations WBL, owned by the *Detroit News*, and WCX, owned by the *Detroit Free Press*, would broadcast from the area on band nights. Another renowned business in the Baker Building was the American Bakery, also known as Hensel's Bakery. Ewald Hensel came from Hanover, in West Germany, with his wife and bookkeeper, Edith, his two daughters, Ingrid and Renate, and his son Gary, all of whom helped out with the business. They operated the bakery from 1957 to 1975.

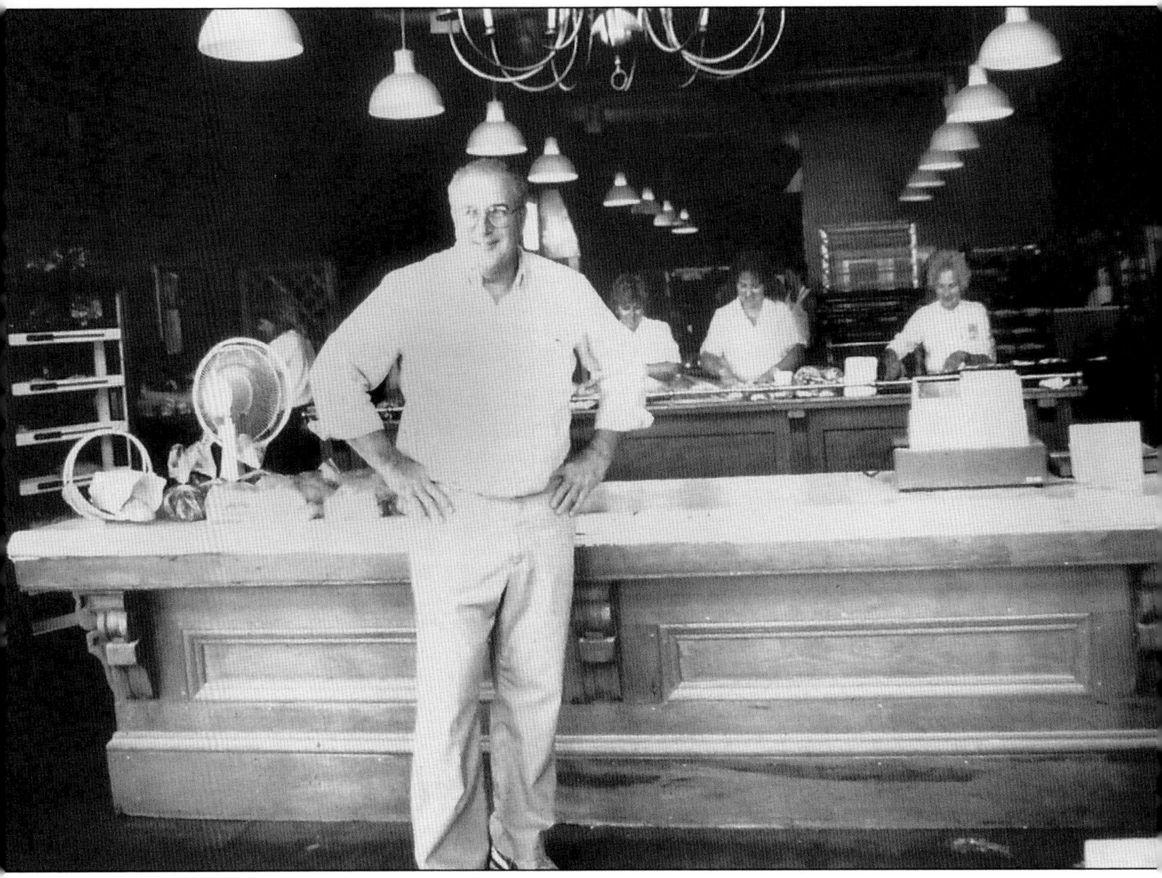

Carrying on the bakery tradition, Max Plante established Stahl's Famous Original Bakery in 1979, and used Hensel's old German recipes. Hensel assisted Plante until he was well into his 90s. One of the first things Max Plante did was expand the bakery operation to once again include the entire first floor of the Baker Building. The bakery, which has survived to this day as a venerable New Baltimore landmark, is one of the few modern bakeries that does not use any machinery, as Plante felt it changed the taste of the bread.

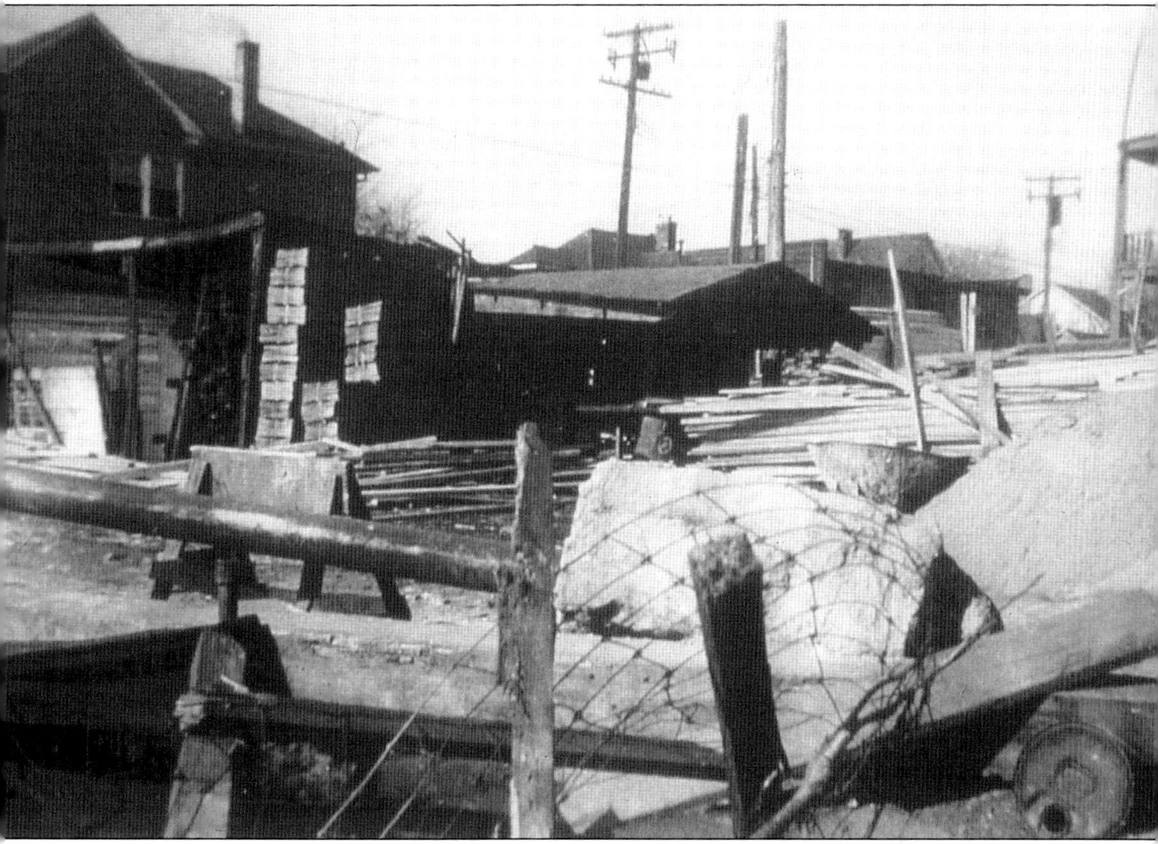

The village's three stave mills dominated the New Baltimore economy from the mid-1800s until around 1900. The largest of these was the Perkins mill, originally called the Stave & Heading Factory. It was erected by William Jenny in 1852 and sold to Bart Perkins in 1855. Located on Front Street, between Base and Taylor Streets down to the bay, the mill employed more than 250 men and shipped its products from its own pier on Anchor Bay.

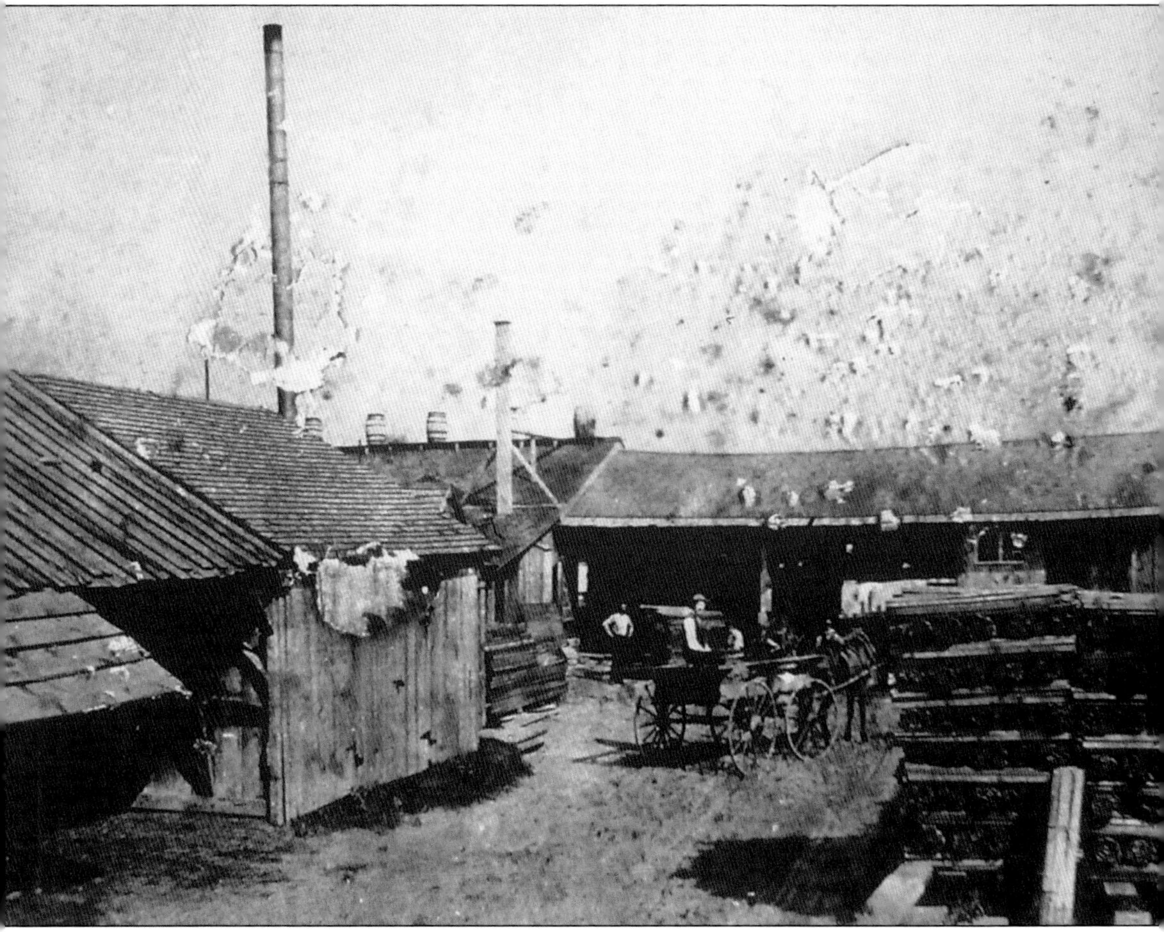

Also shipped from the Perkins dock were brooms, shovel handles, barrelheads, and other items made in New Baltimore factories. These went out on various ships, including the *Garibaldi* and the *Capitolia*. The dock at the foot of Base Street was lined with warehouses. The other two piers belonged to town founder Alfred Ashley, who owned Ashley mill, and David Hatheway, who owned and operated his mill on Atwood Street. The Hatheway stave mill was later operated by his son Gilbert, who donated the money to build the Hathaway Institute in New Baltimore and loaned the city enough to rebuild after the Great Fire of 1870.

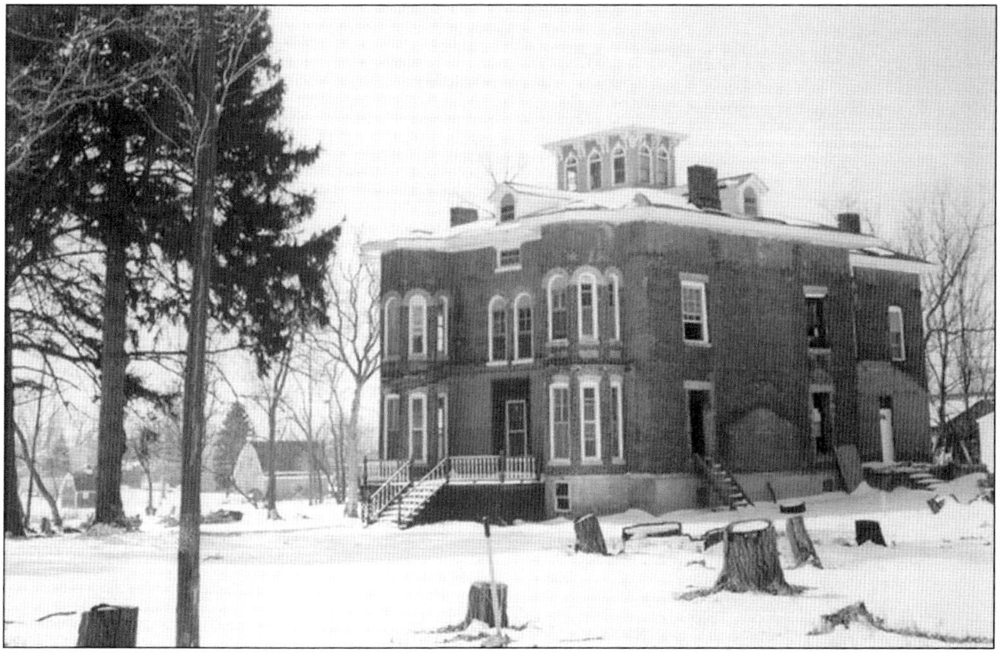

The Hatheway Mansion, on Cemetery Street (24 Mile Road), survived until early 2000, when it was razed after unsuccessful renovation attempts. After Gilbert Hatheway died, his son James inherited the house. When the house left the Hatheway family, it was first intended to be a mental institution. But when proper state licensing could not be obtained, it became a bed and breakfast called The Firs in the early 1900s, under the management of Abby Tilitson. The west portion of the mansion was later used as a hospital, under the auspices of Dr. Virginia French. After Tilitson sold the home, it changed hands many times. The mansion was infamous for its many reports of paranormal activity over the years.

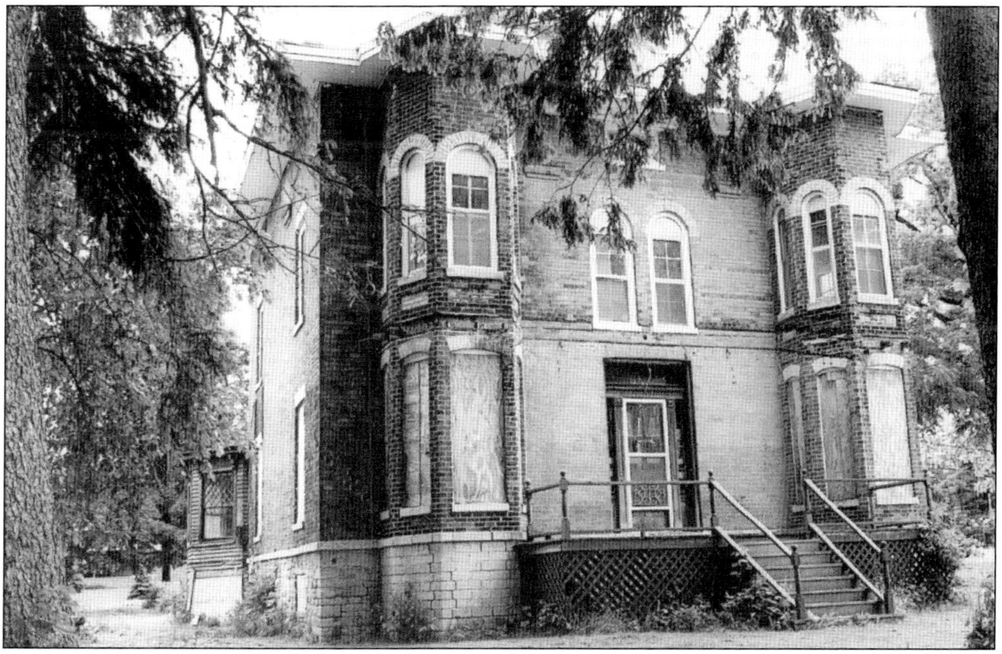

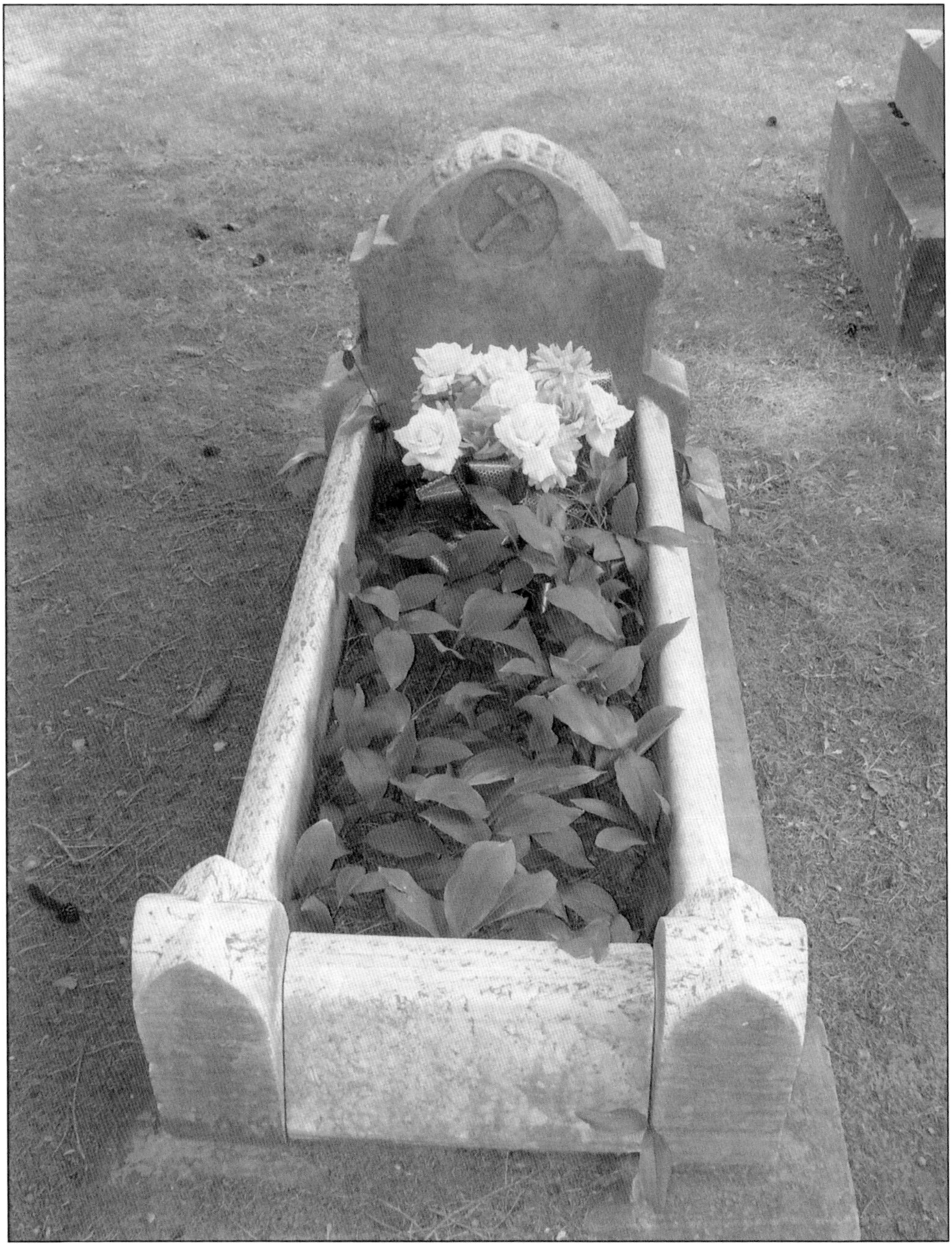

The Hatheway Mansion is in the same area as two cemeteries and is said to be located on the site of an ancient Native American village known as Sippican (later Marion). A lot of the paranormal incidents reported there seem to center on the daughter of James Hatheway and granddaughter of Gilbert Hatheway, Mabel, who is buried in nearby Oakwood Cemetery in a glass coffin. Elaborate marble surrounds her gravesite. She was only 20 years old when she died, only three months after marrying Oren Dunham of Paw Paw, Michigan. Her grandparents Gilbert and Abigail Hatheway were originally buried here also, but were exhumed by their daughter and reburied in a different Oakwood Cemetery, in Adrian, Michigan.

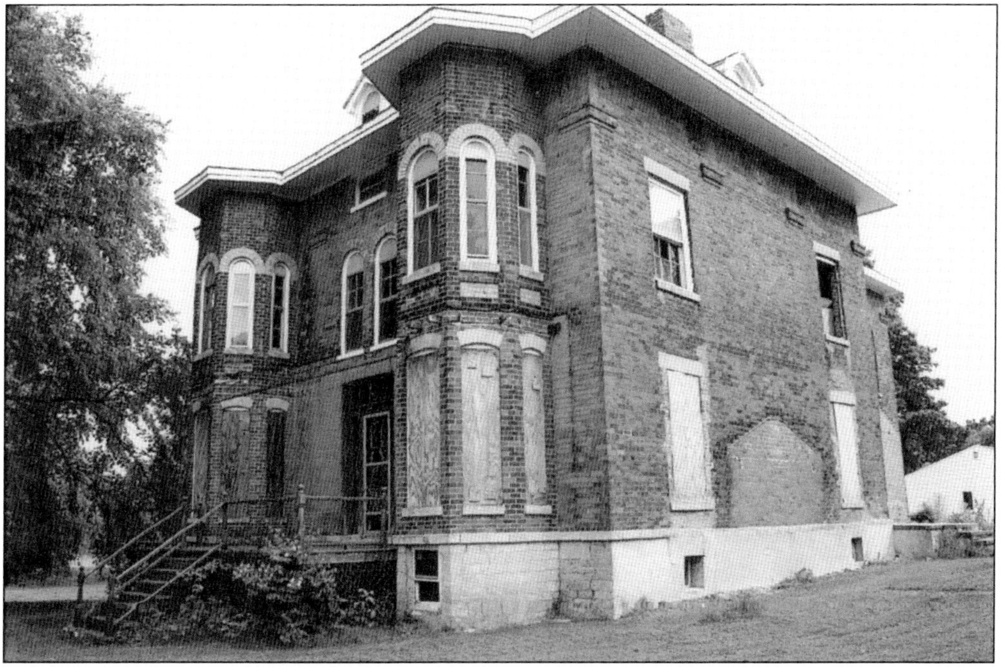

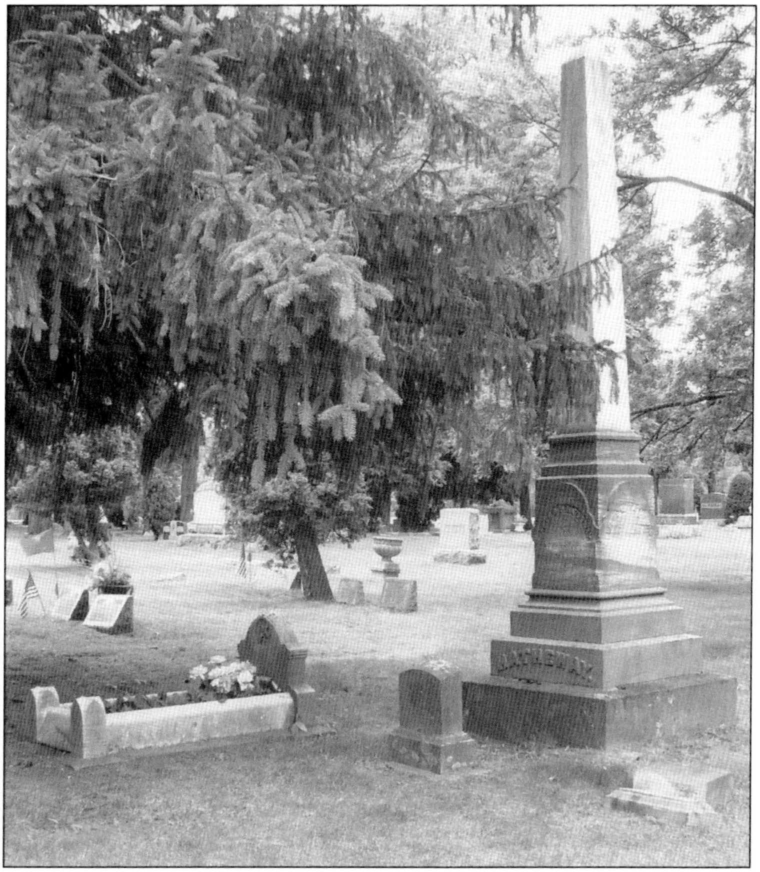

Gilbert Hatheway donated the land and $100 for the German Lutheran Church. Now called St. John's Lutheran Church, it once served the many German immigrants in the area. They started coming to the area in 1853, first settling on land they cleared by the Salt River. The first meeting place for their Lutheran church was in a chapel on the corner of Washington and Green Streets, which was rented from a Baptist congregation from 1868 to 1870.

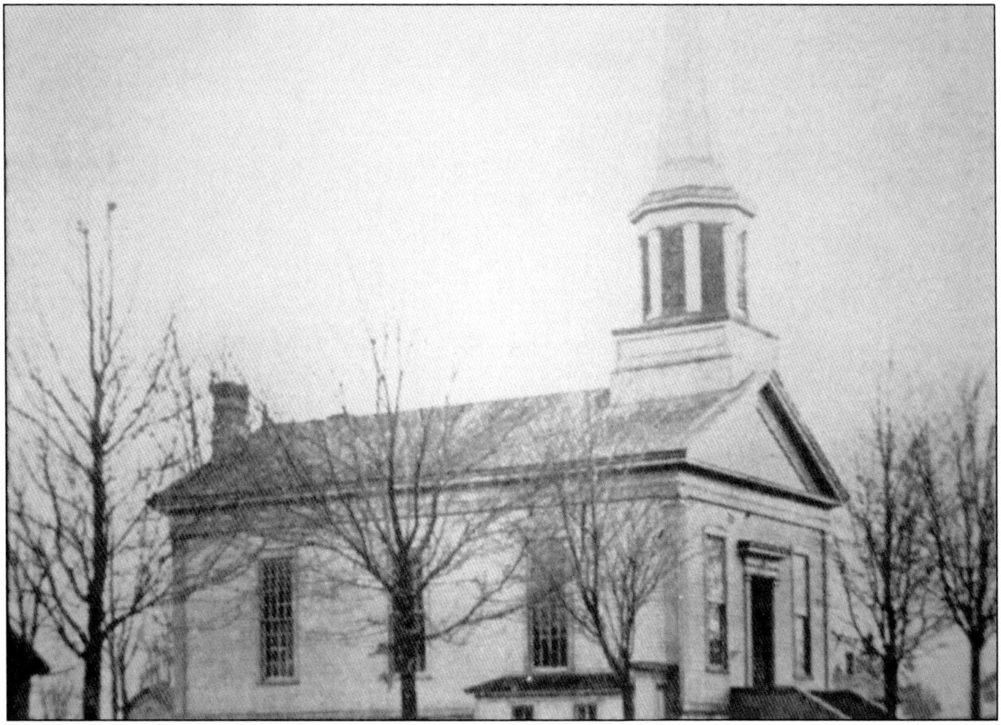

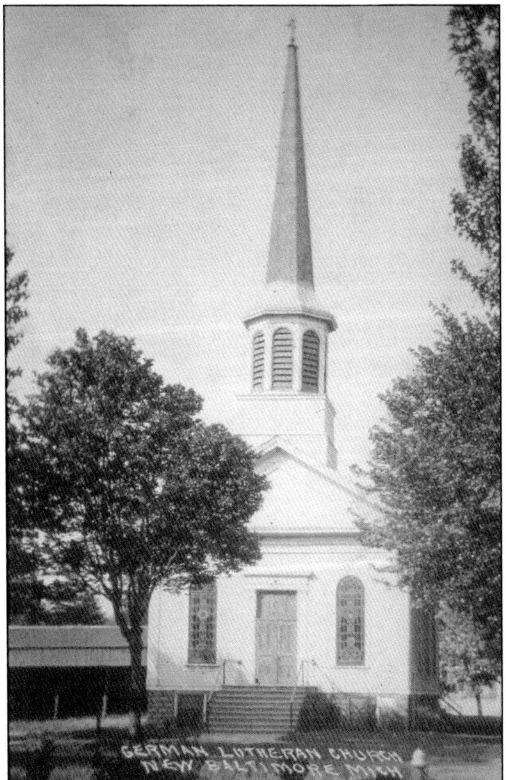

After Gilbert Hatheway donated the land in January 1869, the German Lutheran Church was completed in 1870. The church had services in German until 1916, when it phased in English, having one service every month in English. By 1934, it no longer offered services in German.

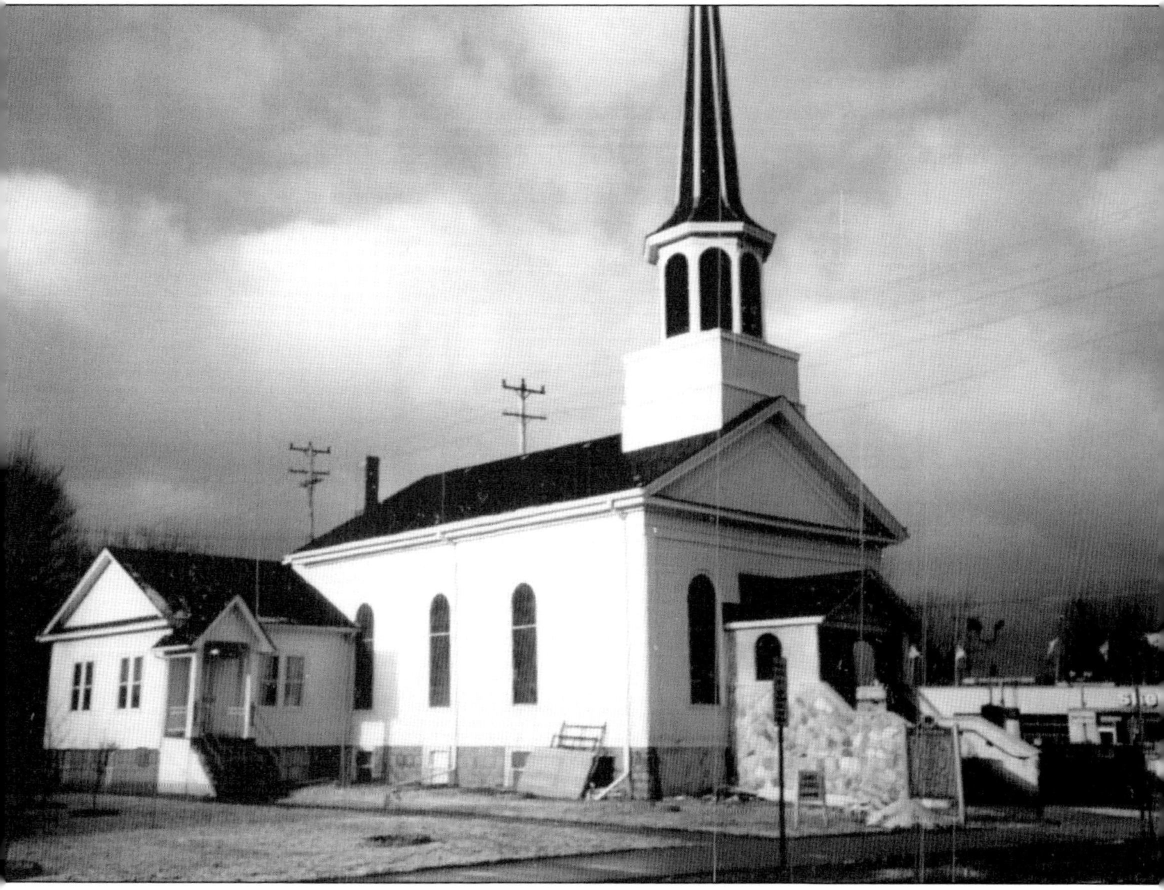

In May 1916, an ambitious and successful renovation of the German Lutheran Church was undertaken. The church was raised several feet, a basement was dug, an altar niche with a new pulpit and altar was added, and a furnace room and kitchen were built. New oak pews, carpeting, and electric lights were also part of the renovation.

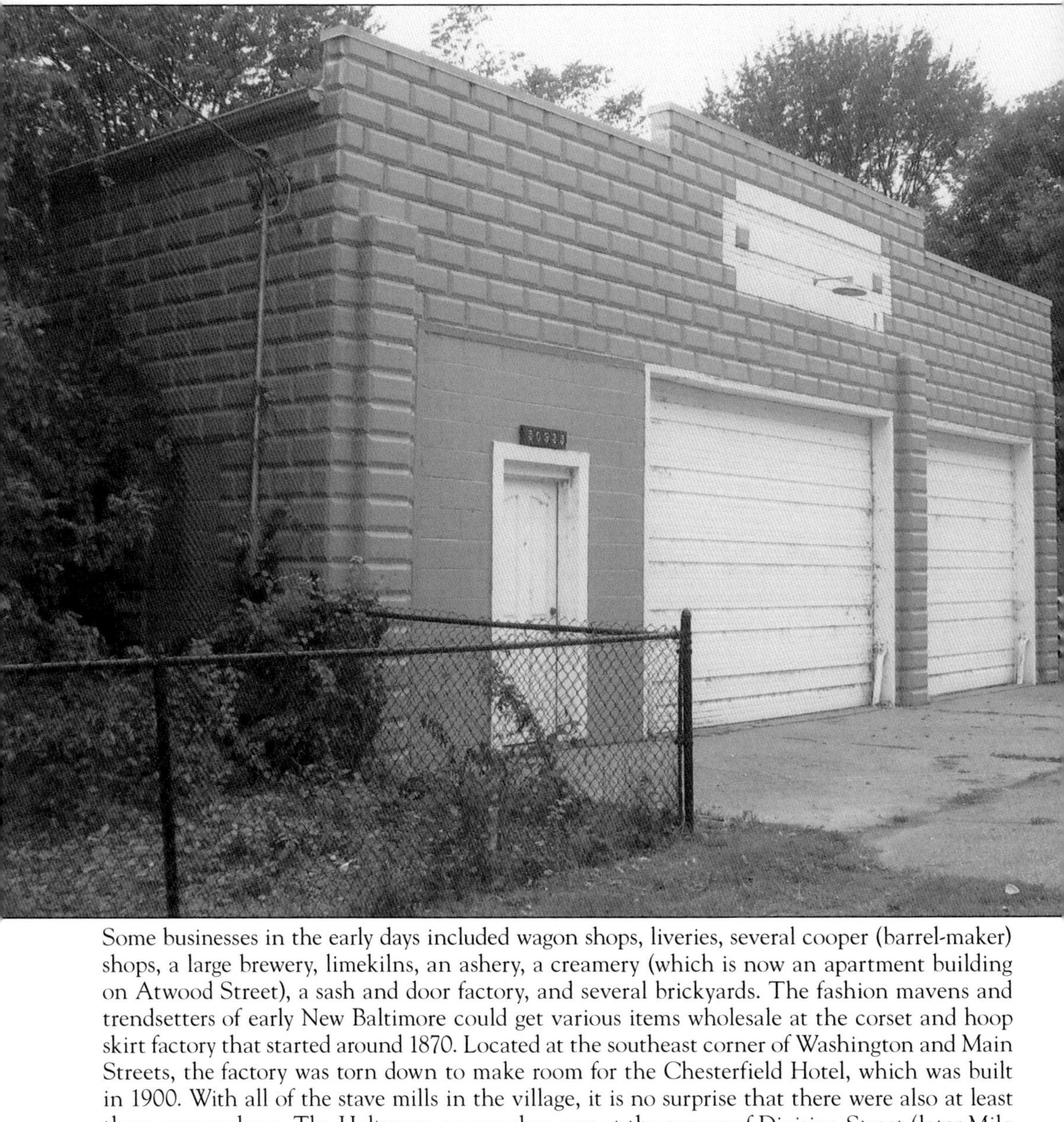

Some businesses in the early days included wagon shops, liveries, several cooper (barrel-maker) shops, a large brewery, limekilns, an ashery, a creamery (which is now an apartment building on Atwood Street), a sash and door factory, and several brickyards. The fashion mavens and trendsetters of early New Baltimore could get various items wholesale at the corset and hoop skirt factory that started around 1870. Located at the southeast corner of Washington and Main Streets, the factory was torn down to make room for the Chesterfield Hotel, which was built in 1900. With all of the stave mills in the village, it is no surprise that there were also at least three cooper shops. The Hultgreen cooper shop was at the corner of Division Street (later Milo Street). Dink's cooper shop was behind the German Lutheran Church on Maria Street. In 1864, Alexander Rivard was a wood dealer with the Perkins mill and also operated the Rivard cooper shop at 51718 Washington Avenue. The New Baltimore Creamery Company was a major area business. Its former storage area is now used by the Bay-Rama committee to store items for the city festival.

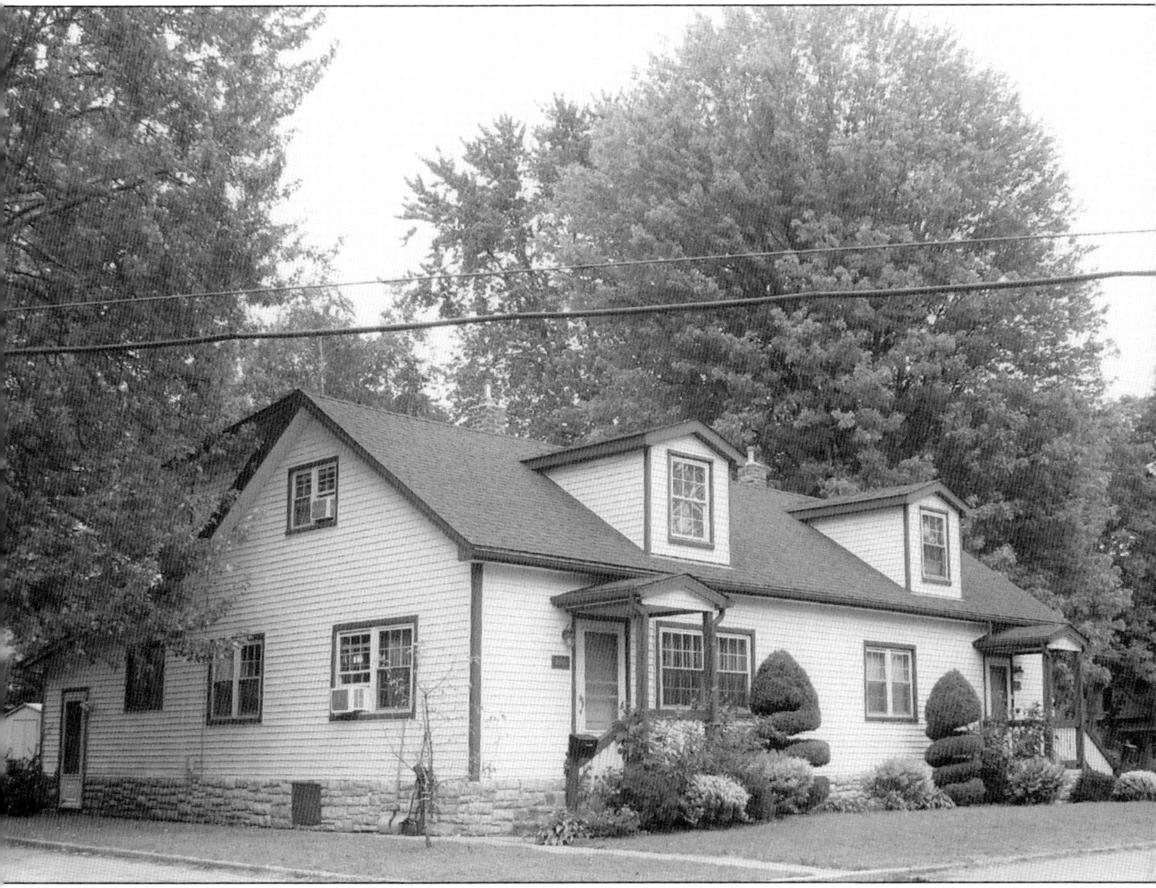

The creamery was located on Atwood Street near Main Street. The icehouse in the back burned down, and the creamery was eventually transformed into a duplex apartment building. A creamery was where cream was separated from whole milk and pasteurization was completed. Butter, buttermilk, ice cream, and other dairy products were also processed there.

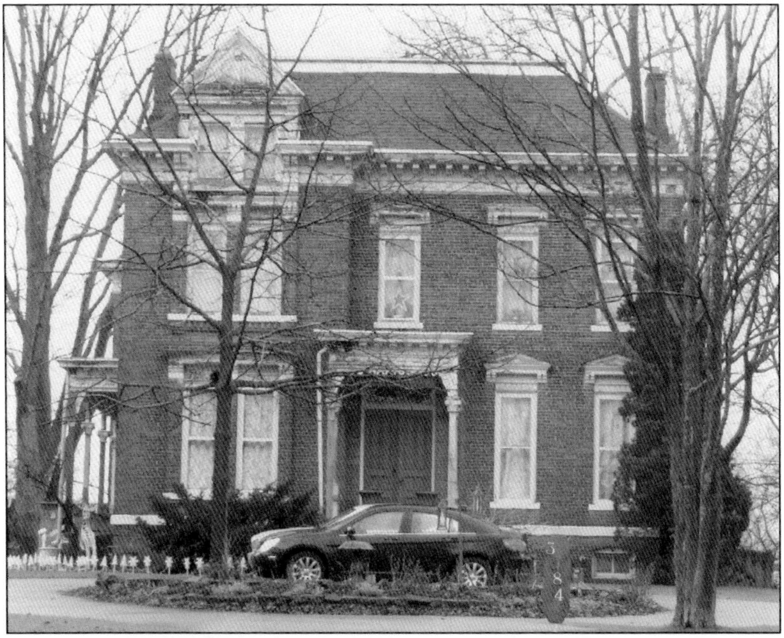

Besides the Baker Building, two other notable historic buildings still stand today, both of which were constructed with locally manufactured bricks. One is the Schnoor Mansion and its carriage house on Main Street near Ashley Street. It is one of the best-preserved older residences in the area.

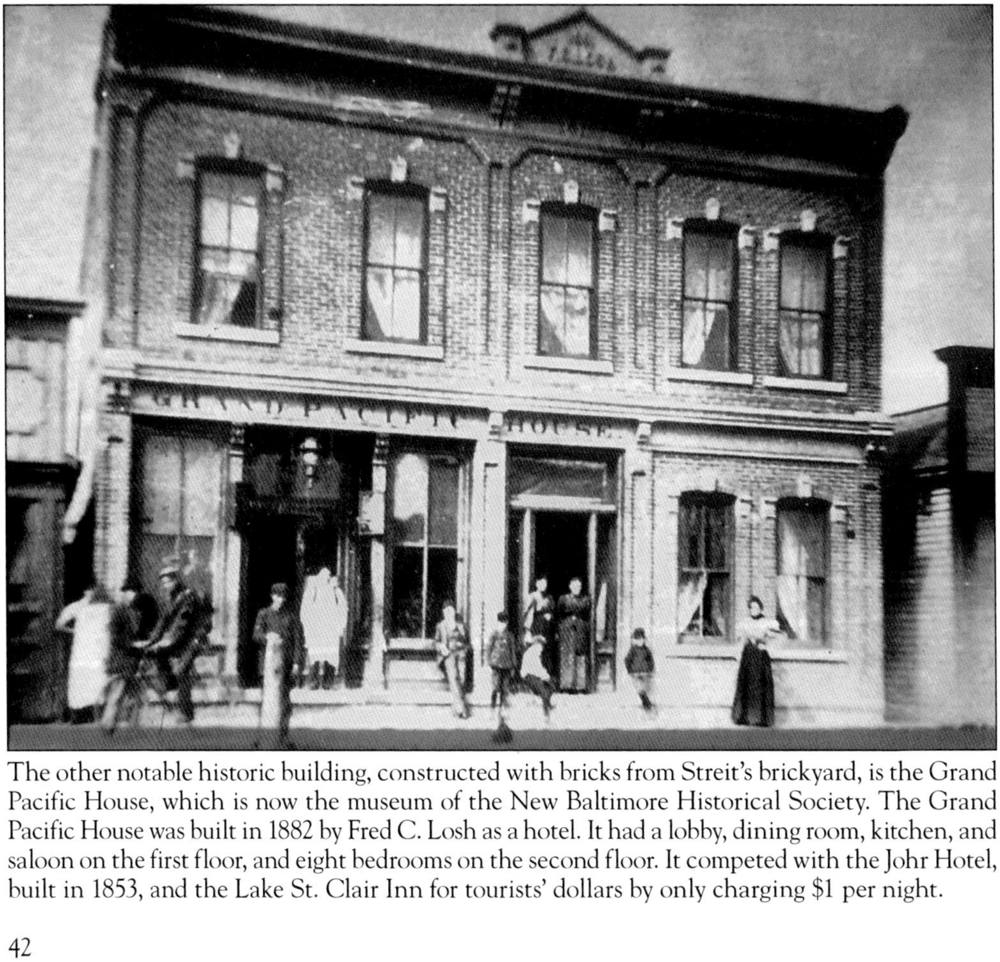

The other notable historic building, constructed with bricks from Streit's brickyard, is the Grand Pacific House, which is now the museum of the New Baltimore Historical Society. The Grand Pacific House was built in 1882 by Fred C. Losh as a hotel. It had a lobby, dining room, kitchen, and saloon on the first floor, and eight bedrooms on the second floor. It competed with the Johr Hotel, built in 1853, and the Lake St. Clair Inn for tourists' dollars by only charging $1 per night.

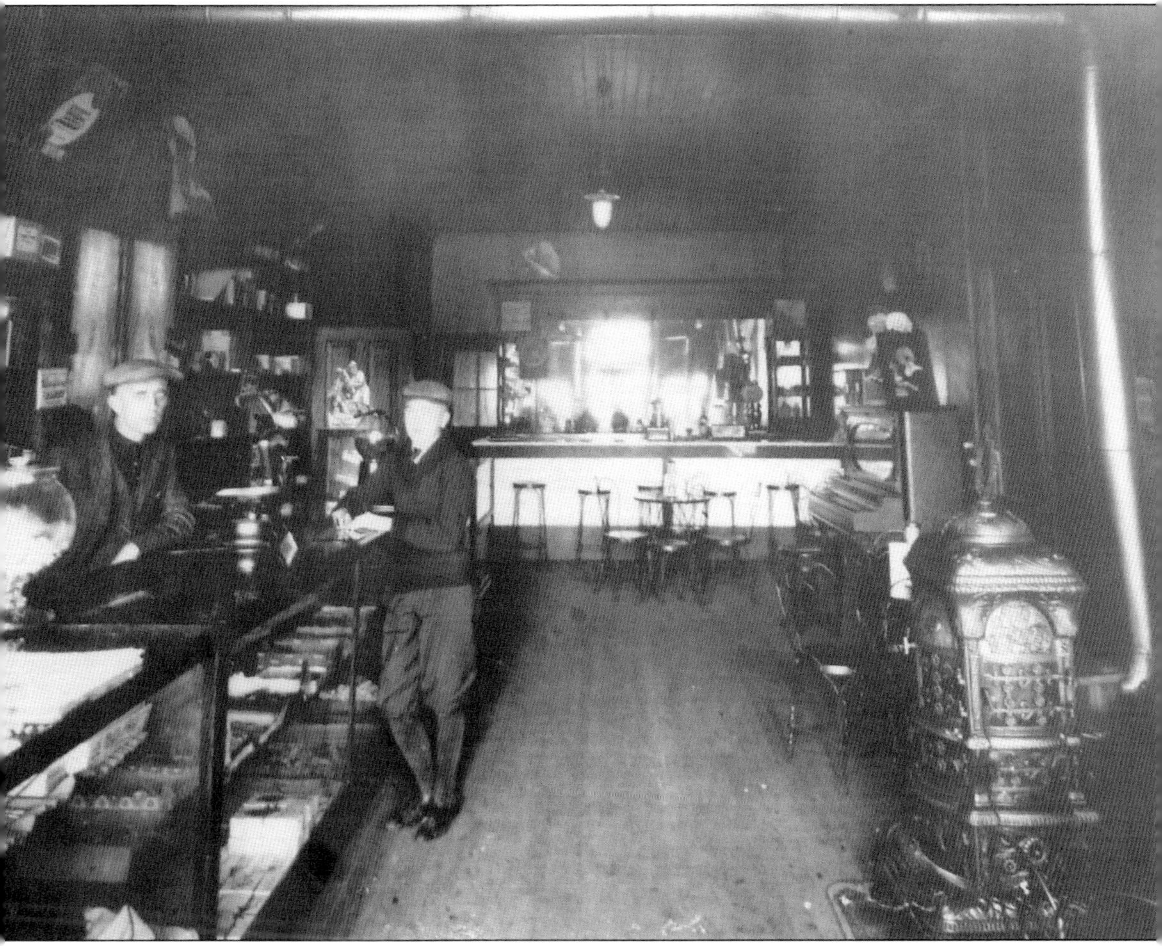

For entertainment, guests at the Grand Pacific House needed only to go downstairs to the saloon, seen here, where a combo from Fair Haven performed and beers were a nickel. The Losh family used one of the bedrooms facing Washington Street as their own quarters. Fred Losh died of typhoid in the room in 1890, probably because the hotel's water supply was too close to the outhouse. After Losh died, the hotel became a boardinghouse. Later, a relative of his, Herbert Losh, ran a candy store with a soda fountain on the site. The whole building then became Maliskey Hardware Store for many years after. In 1987, the building was purchased by the New Baltimore Historical Society. After a beautiful and meticulous restoration, the hotel, after turns as a candy store, a boardinghouse, and a hardware store, became the Grand Pacific House Museum.

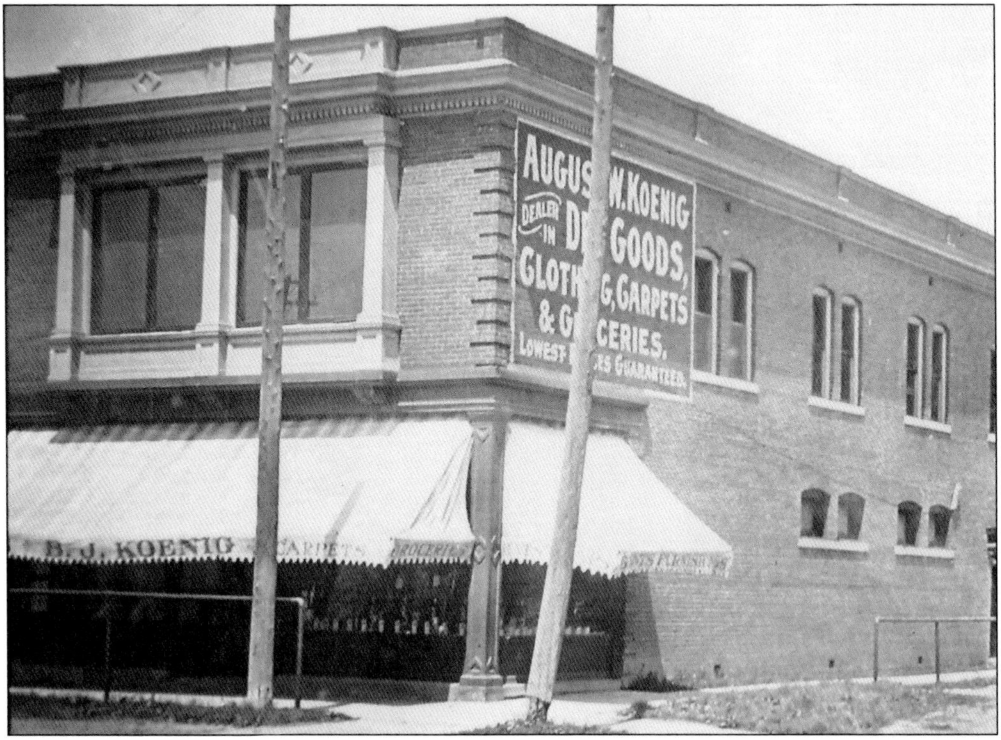

The Koenig Block, at Main and Washington Streets, was one of many buildings constructed between 1896 and 1906. It was first a dry goods store, and later became a drugstore under many different names, the most recent being Dennis Halstead's Anchor Bay Pharmacy. Also built in this era was the Fink Block, at Alfred and Washington Streets, where the Chase barbershop was and where Red's Barber Shop is today.

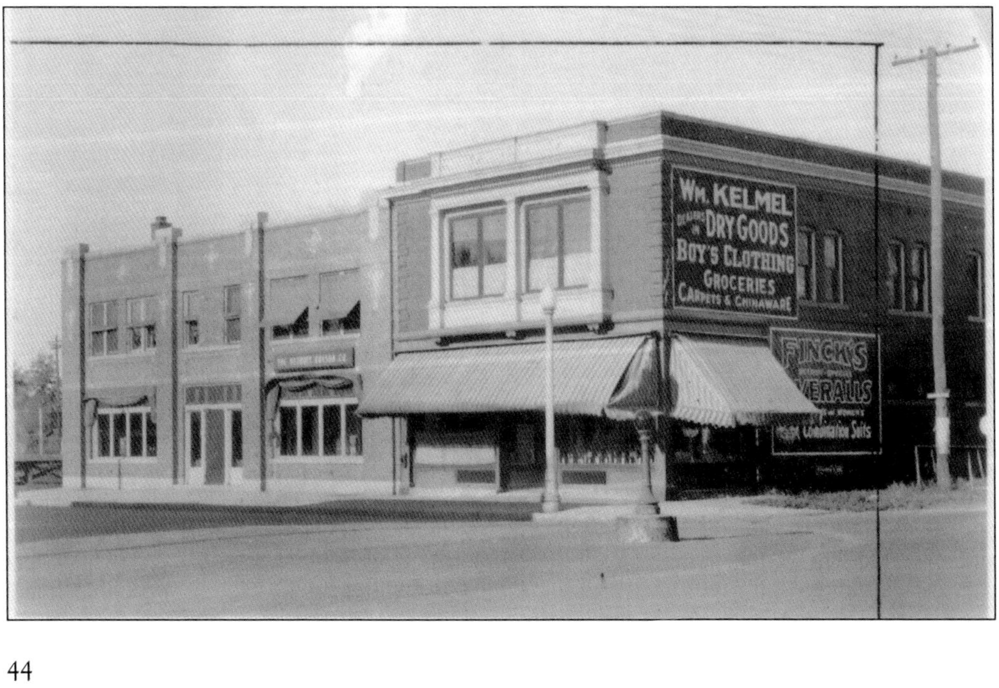

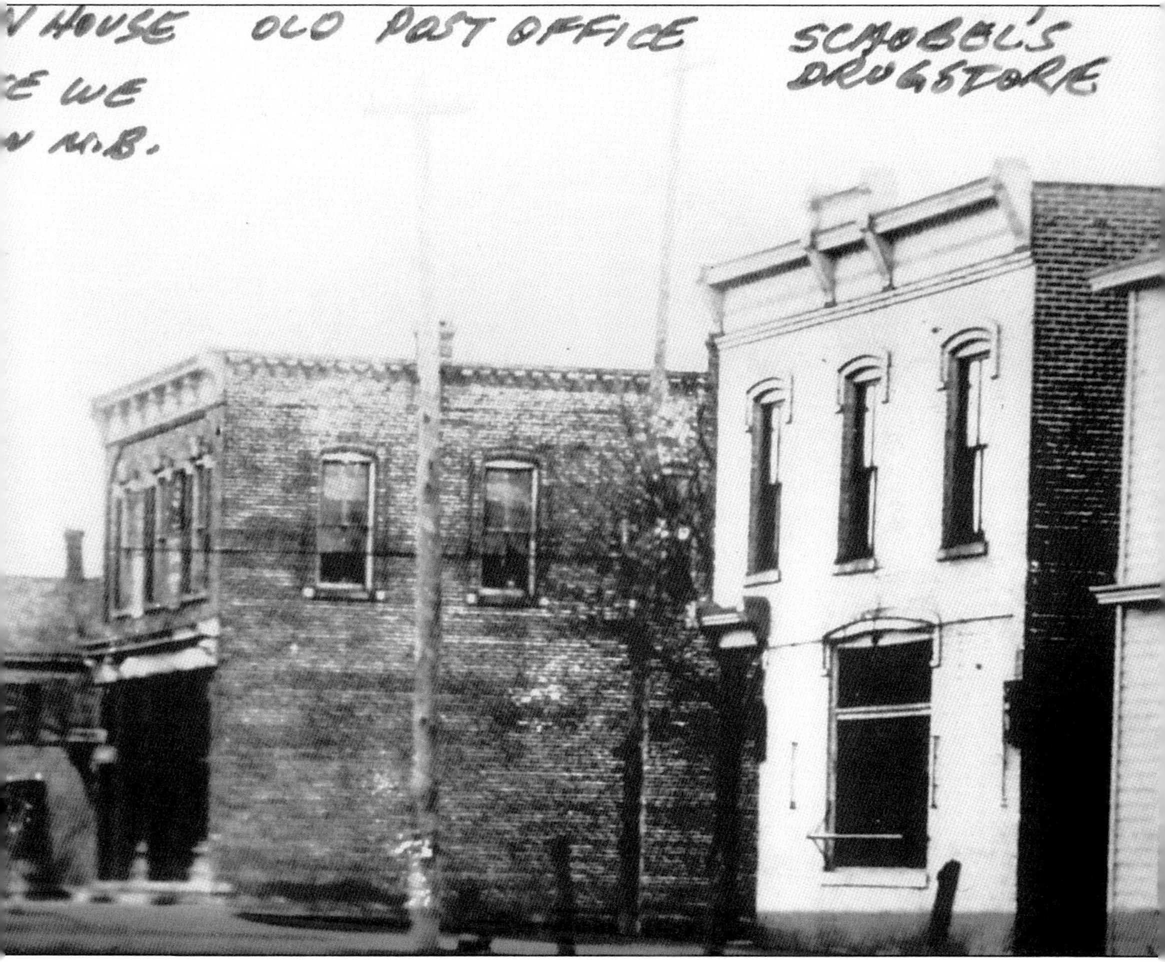

David H. Heath was a major businessman in New Baltimore. After coming to the area in 1853, he opened the community's first shoe and harness store, and ran the post office from 1870 to 1885. In 1898, the building that held his former business became New Baltimore's first train station. Heath's son D. Milo Heath had a harness and shoe store built at the southwest corner of Green and Washington Streets in the late 1800s, across the street from what was later Schoebel's Drug Store. Milo Heath also ran the local post office out of the two-story brick building from 1889 to 1893.

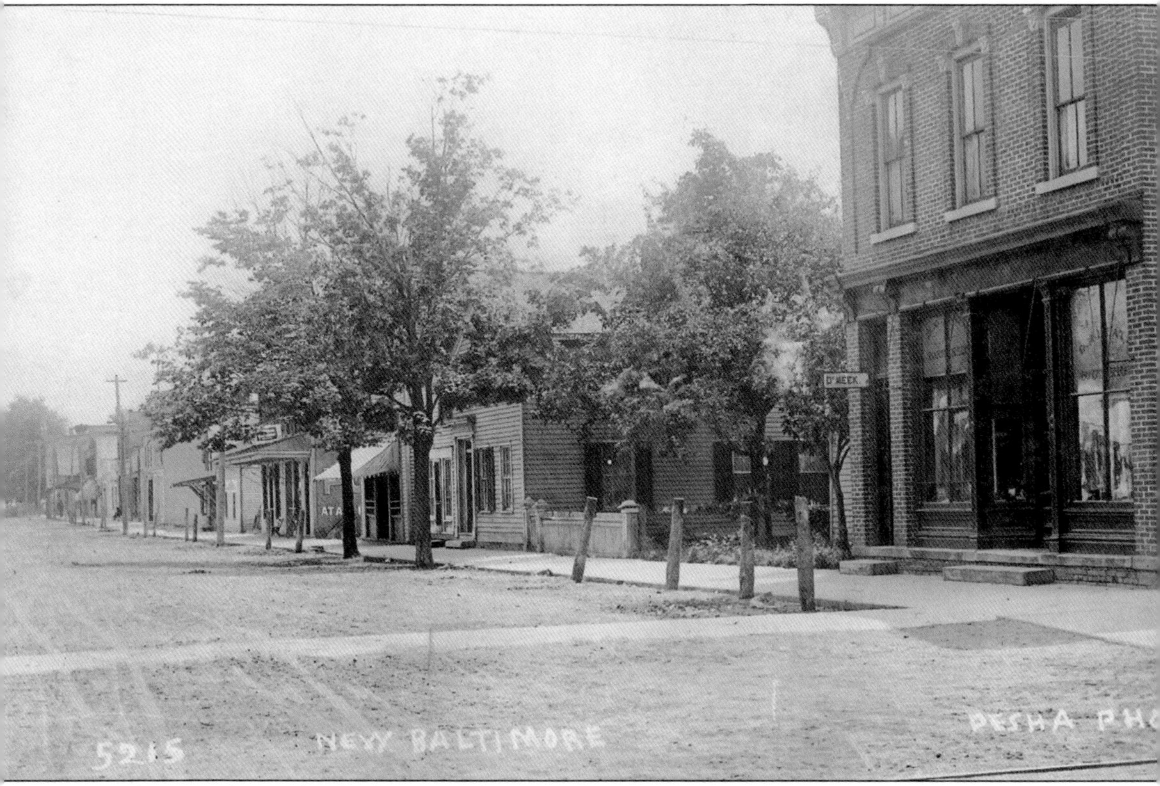

After D. Milo Heath's death in 1895, his son Robert A. Heath took over his store. Besides shoes and harnesses, the store sold trunks, lap robes, whips, carriages and buggies, and more. Carrying on the family tradition, he was also postmaster from 1898 to 1914. Robert Heath lived on the second floor of his building. When he heard the post office being robbed one night, he thwarted the would-be thieves by shooting a shotgun through a hole in the floor, severely injuring one of the two. The robbers were captured while attempting to make their escape on a stolen Shetland pony.

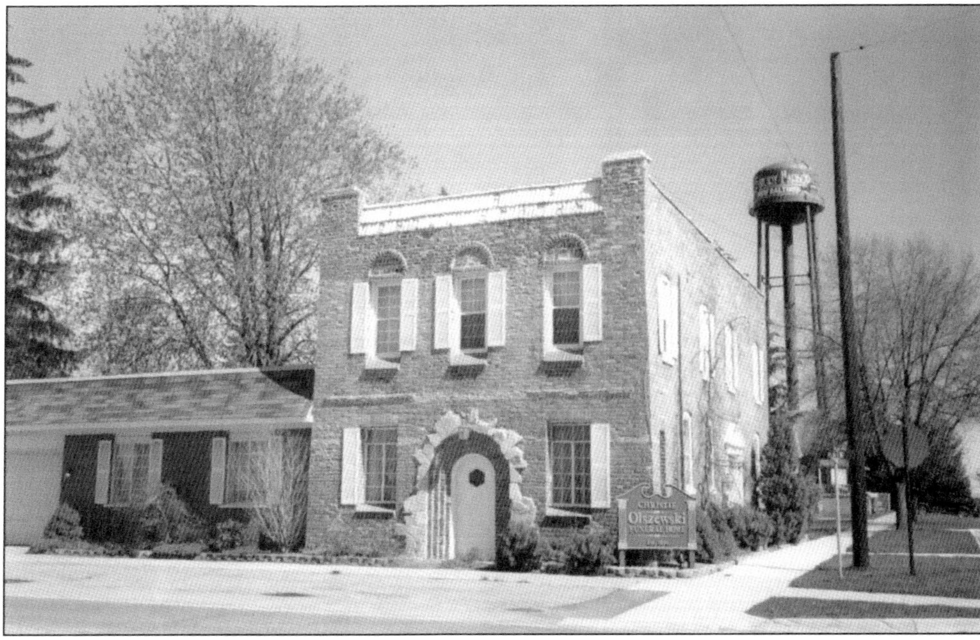

Other important businesses around 1900 were Kleehammer's Saloon, at Main and Maria Streets, which was run by John Kleehammer and later became the Christie Olszewski Funeral Home, and the opera house, at the corner of Main and Base Streets. The opera house, which later became the Bethel Temple Evangelistic Center, was built by the Order of the Maccabees.

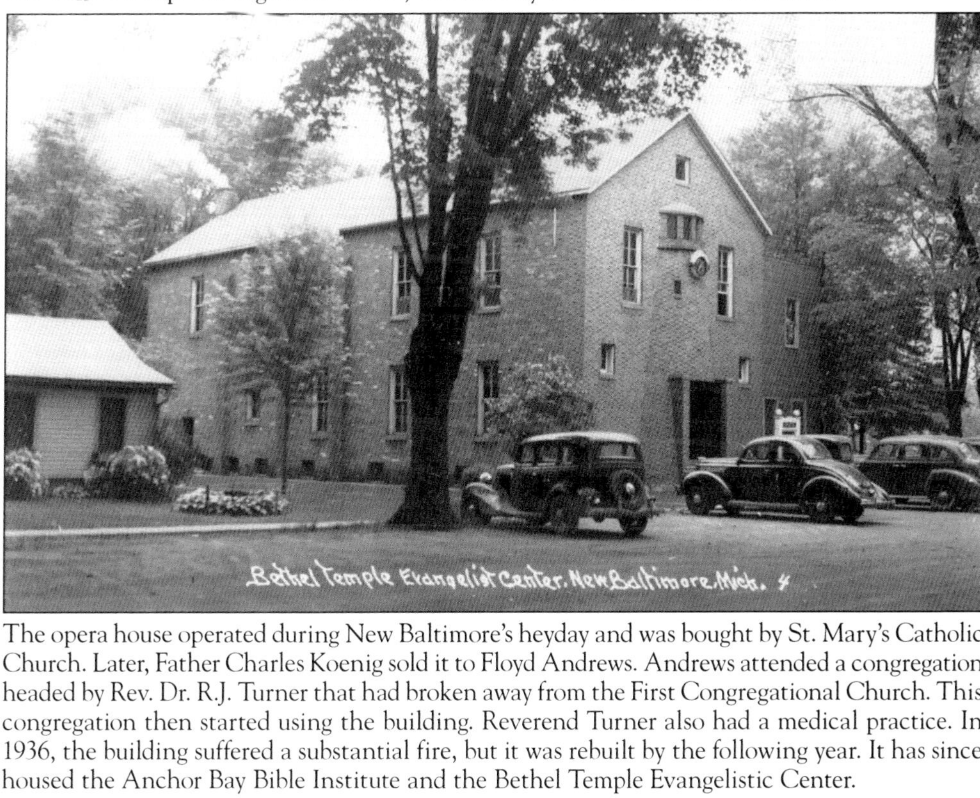

The opera house operated during New Baltimore's heyday and was bought by St. Mary's Catholic Church. Later, Father Charles Koenig sold it to Floyd Andrews. Andrews attended a congregation headed by Rev. Dr. R.J. Turner that had broken away from the First Congregational Church. This congregation then started using the building. Reverend Turner also had a medical practice. In 1936, the building suffered a substantial fire, but it was rebuilt by the following year. It has since housed the Anchor Bay Bible Institute and the Bethel Temple Evangelistic Center.

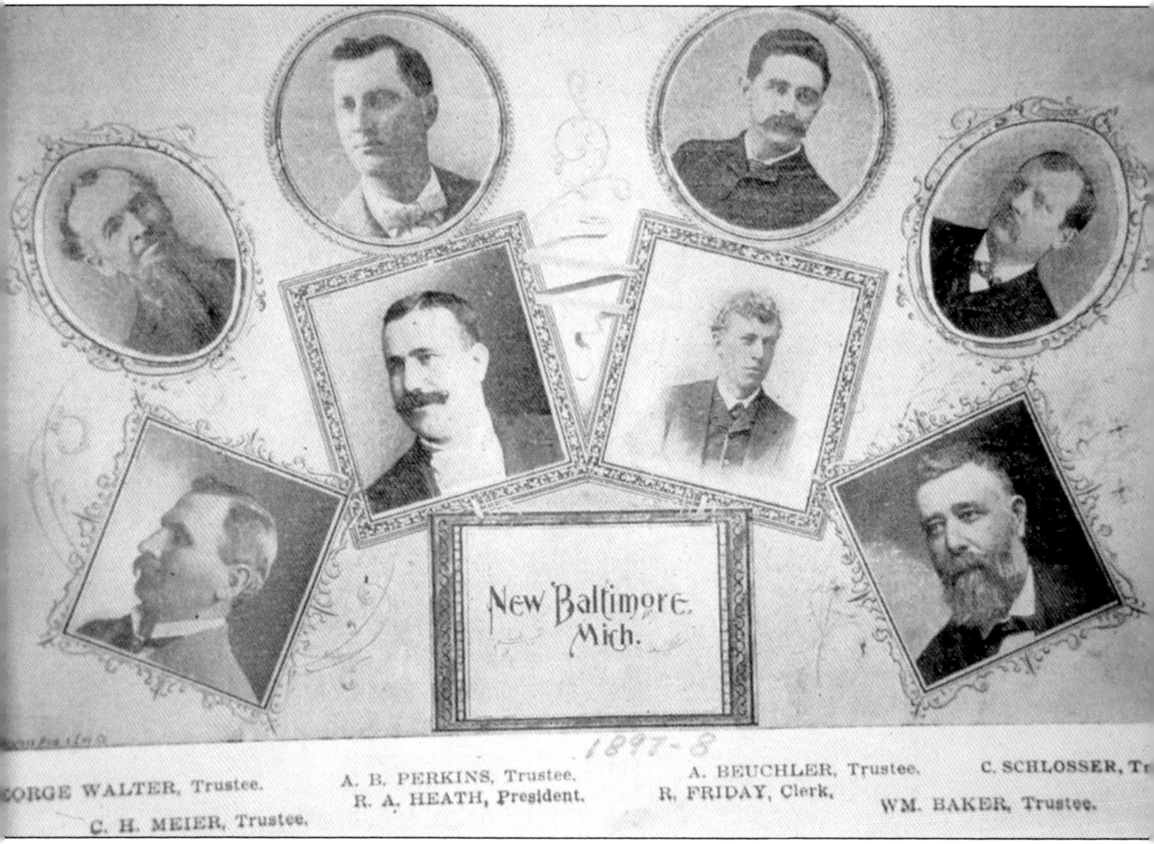

C.H. Meier operated a livery on Washington Street near Crappeau Creek in the 1880s, which housed the New Baltimore stagecoach. He also operated an ashery at the corner of Washington and Milo Streets. A two-story structure, the ashery manufactured soap and potash. Unfortunately, the sometimes dangerous business claimed the lives of two employees. The buildings were leveled in the 1930s. Both Meier and Robert A. Heath, along with other notables in New Baltimore history, were featured in this early issue of the *New Baltimore Star*.

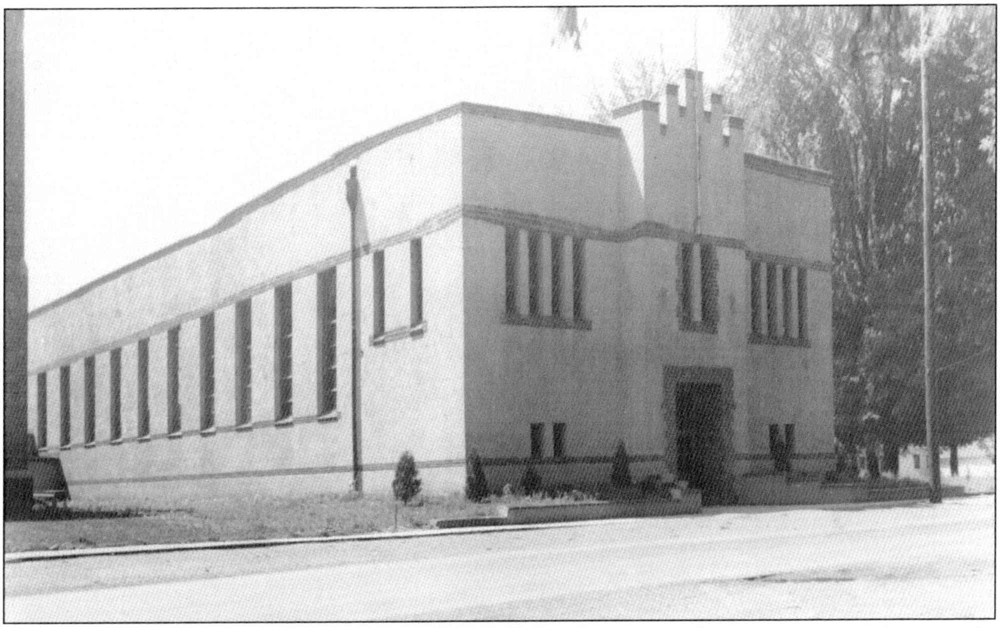

Many of the notable buildings in New Baltimore served time as saloons or taverns. It certainly did not hurt business to have a brewery nearby. One of the big breweries in town was Heiser Brewery, which took up the entire block of Main Street between Maria and Base Streets. Today, St. Mary's School is in that location. When the school began construction in August of 1926, more than 50 years since the brewery had operated, a skeleton with a crushed skull was found in the basement of the old brewery. It had often been said that the best place to hide a body would be in the immense basement of the brewery. Whoever proved that true and smashed in the unfortunate skeleton's head was never found. Forensic science judged the bones to be that of a male aged about 40, a description that would match Charles Wauke, who had disappeared about 50 years earlier. The brewery's brick office building is now used as the St. Mary's Church convent and other church buildings occupy the block.

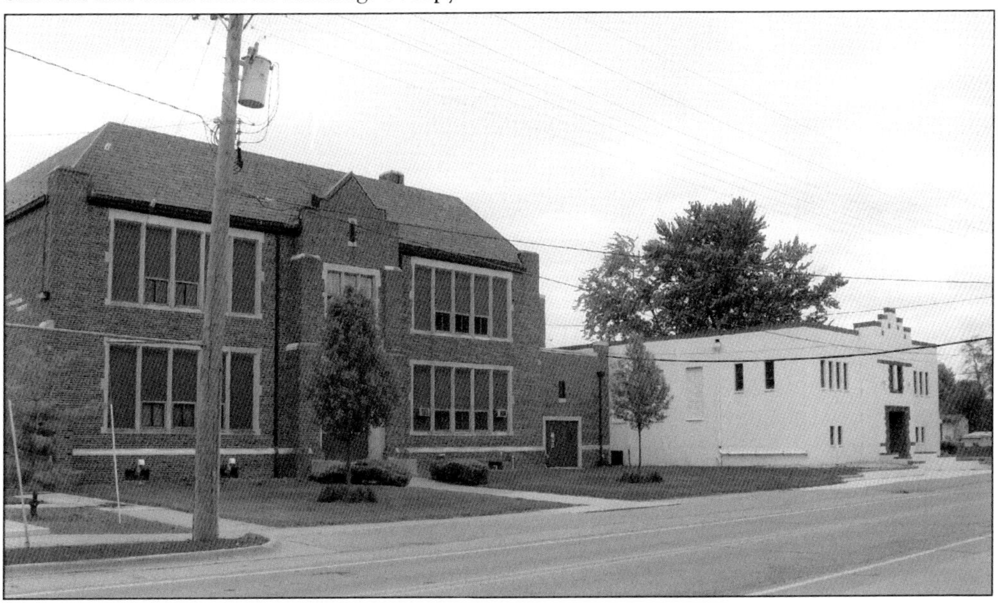

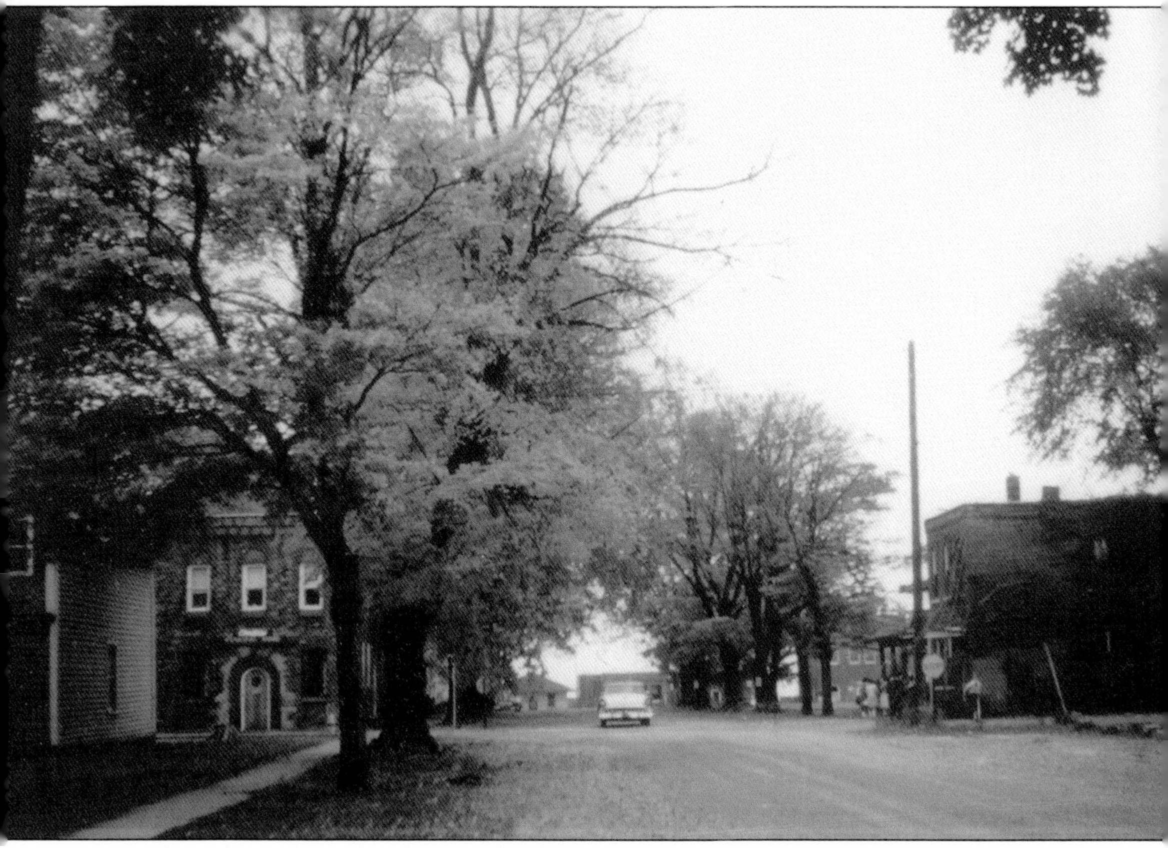

On the right in this 1950s photograph of Maria Street is St. Mary's Rectory. Behind it was the Heiser Brewery.

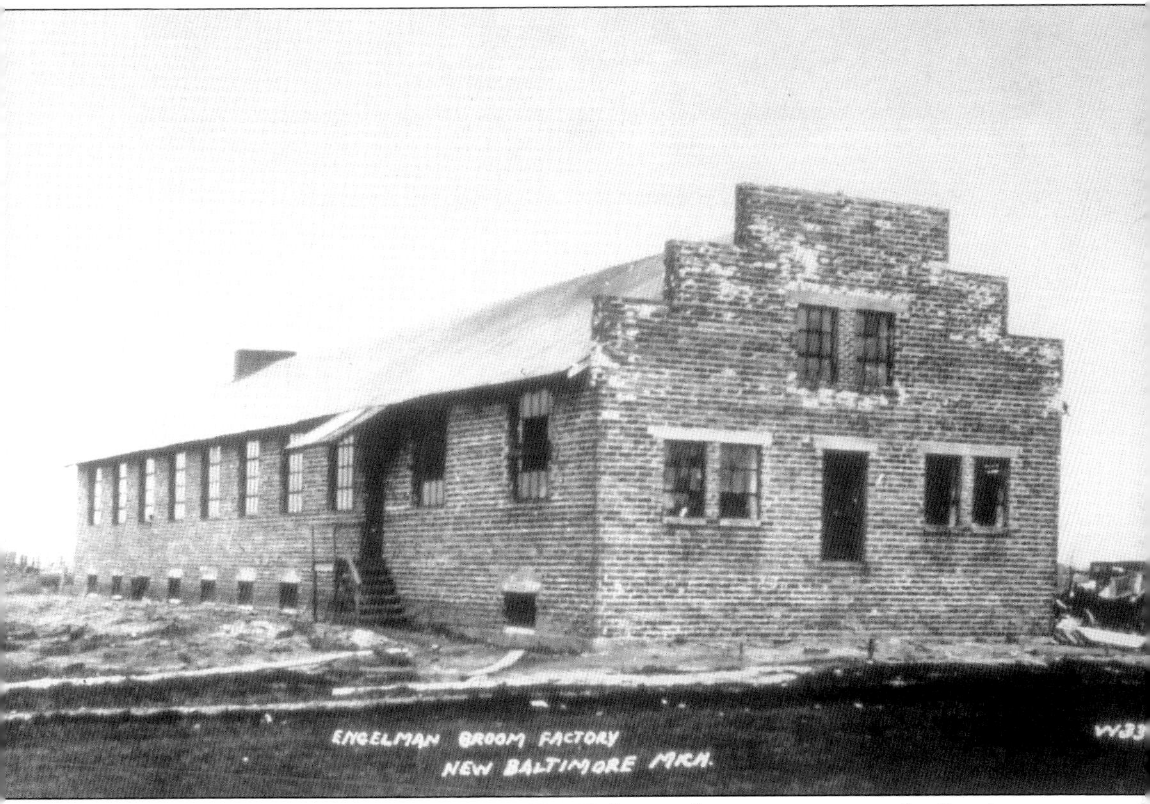

One business that was a sweeping success in New Baltimore for many years was the Engelman Broom Factory. Joseph Engelman was born in Austria in 1879. At an early age, he moved with his parents to Buffalo, New York, and then on to Detroit. At the age of 15, he and his mother opened a small broom factory at the corner of St. Aubin and Scott Roads in Detroit. At first, the operation was small; Joseph Engelman would acquire just one bale of broomcorn and he and his mother would assemble brooms using wire from the Detroit city dump. He would then sell the brooms door-to-door. After a fire destroyed his original factory barn, he built a two-story brick building in Hamtramck, at the corner of Clay and Jos Campau Streets.

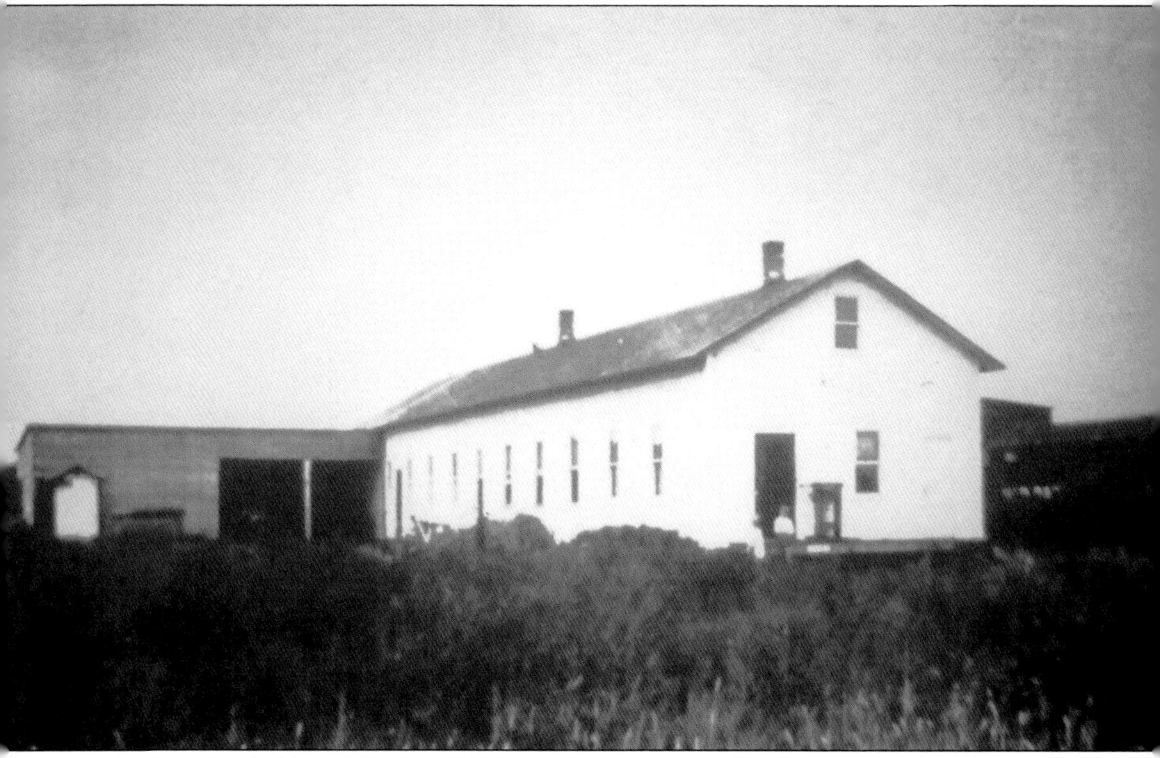

At the tail end of World War I, in 1918, Joseph Engelman moved his broom factory from Hamtramck to New Baltimore, a community he saw as "a thriving and progressive community." He first used a wood frame building on the north side of Green Street just west of County Line Road. He then erected a new brick building for the factory with bricks from his own brick and tile factory, which was behind the new broom factory.

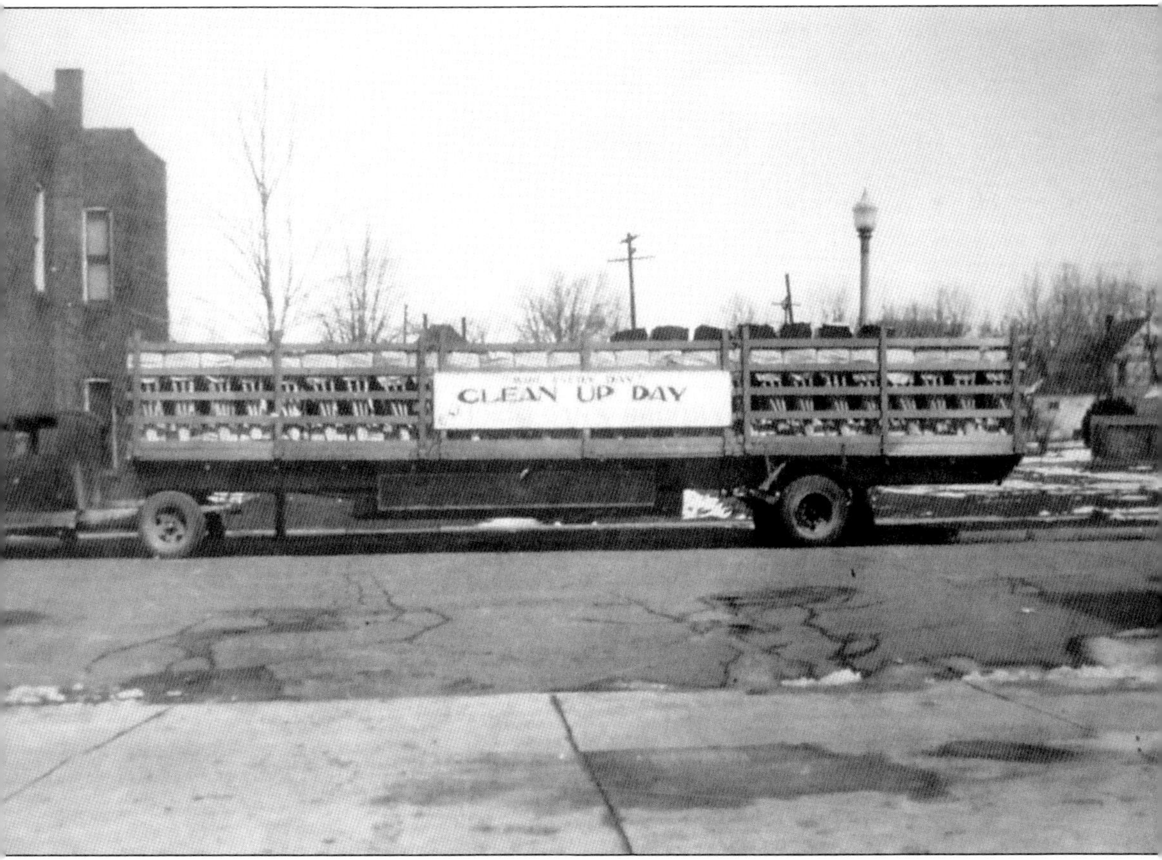

At its peak, the Engelman Broom Factory had more than 30 employees and produced a minimum of 1,800 brooms a day. As a result, New Baltimore was long one of the top producers of brooms in the United States. Their top-of-the-line broom was called the New Yorker, while the Daisy was their standard kitchen model. They also produced large factory brooms, barber brooms, whisk brooms, and more. Some of their major customers were Sears and Kroger.

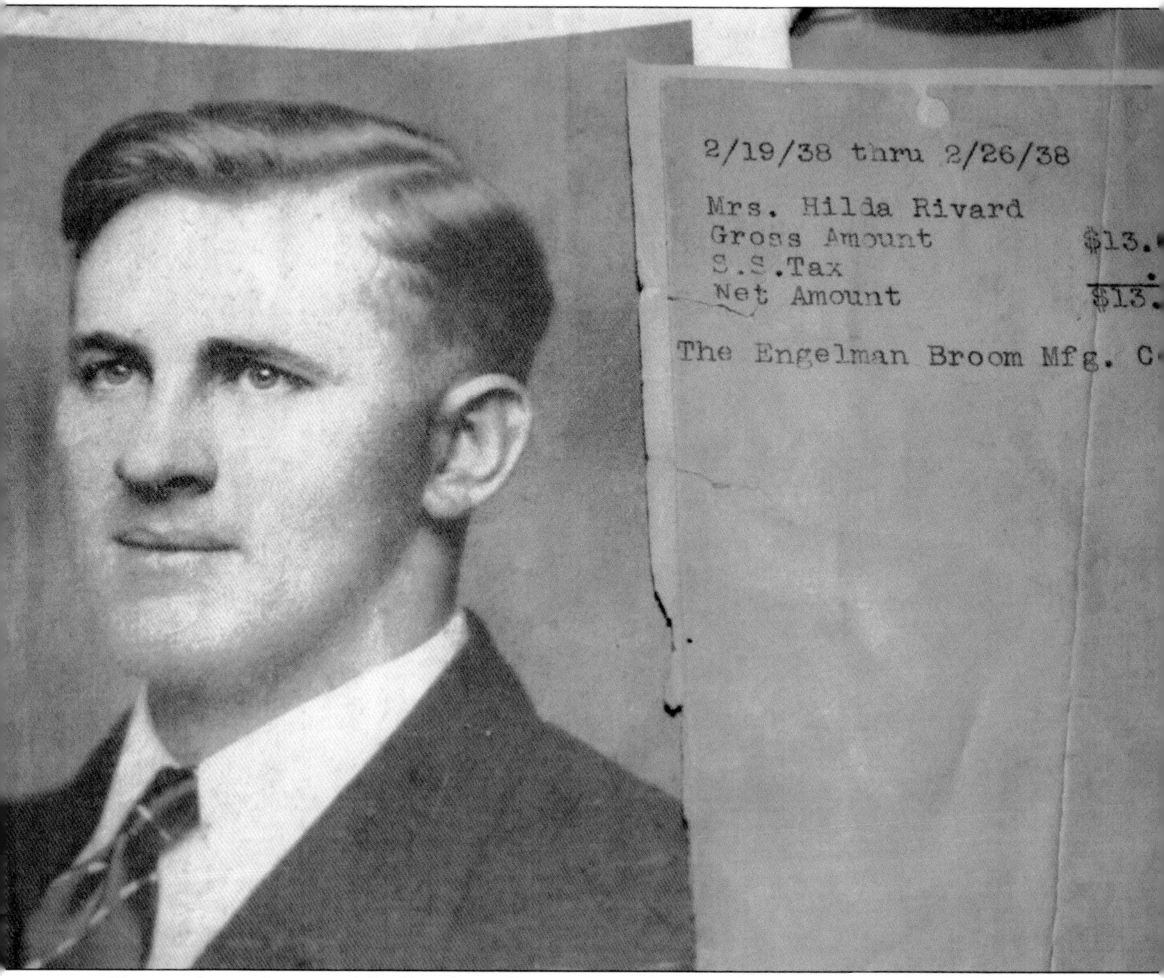

During the peak years of the Engelman Broom Factory, more than 300,000 brooms were produced a year. As the years passed, the factory staff grew to include Joseph's sons Harold and Elmer and his daughters Hilda and Eleonnore.

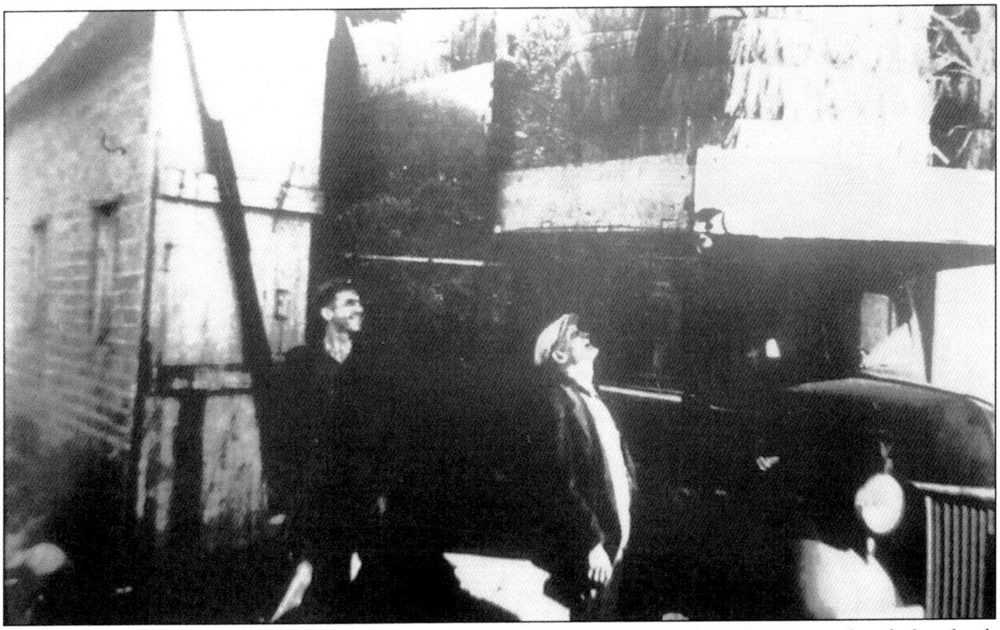

Harold Engelman worked as a buncher, tying broomcorn onto the handle. Just as his father had, Harold served as village president/mayor of New Baltimore. He was mayor when the water filtration plant was built. Eleonnore Engelman was the editor of the town paper, the *New Baltimore-New Haven Star*. The town's first newspaper appeared in 1853, when Thomas M. Perry founded the *Ashleyville Independent*, also known as the *Ashley Independent*. The newspaper was later revived with the same name by Martin V. Ferris, although neither version lasted long. New Baltimore's next regular newspaper, the *New Baltimore Era*, appeared in 1897 and was published weekly by Frank Andrews until 1916. The Engelman Broom Factory survived the Great Depression, providing many needed jobs for residents of New Baltimore. In 1941, the steel used in broom production was reserved for the World War II effort, which forced the stalwart factory to halt production after providing brooms to thousands of people over the years. The building itself, constructed of bricks made from the mud of Crappeau Creek, lasted far longer, until the late 1980s. Harold Engelman was lauded for his work in the community, mainly through St. Mary's Catholic Church. He often paid his crew to do work at the church, including digging a basement for it.

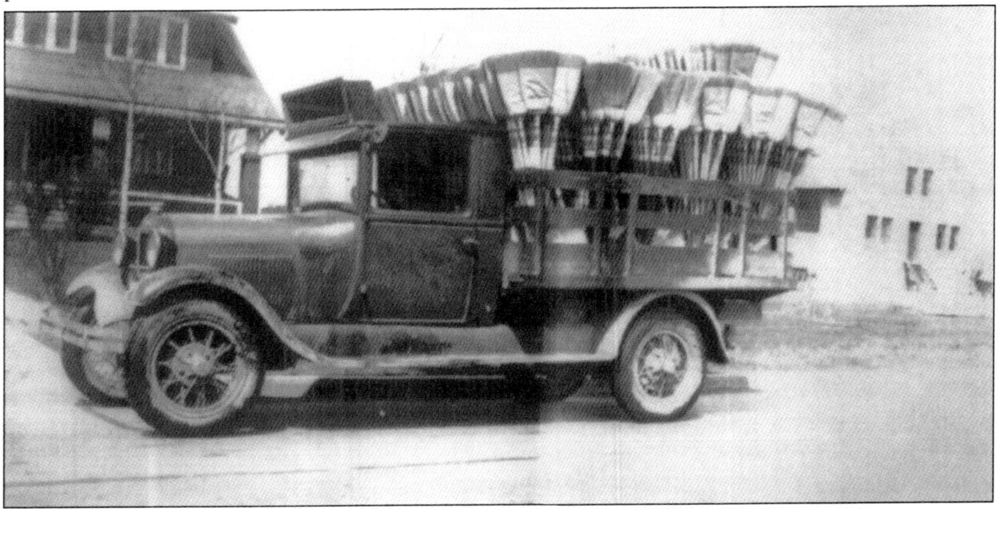

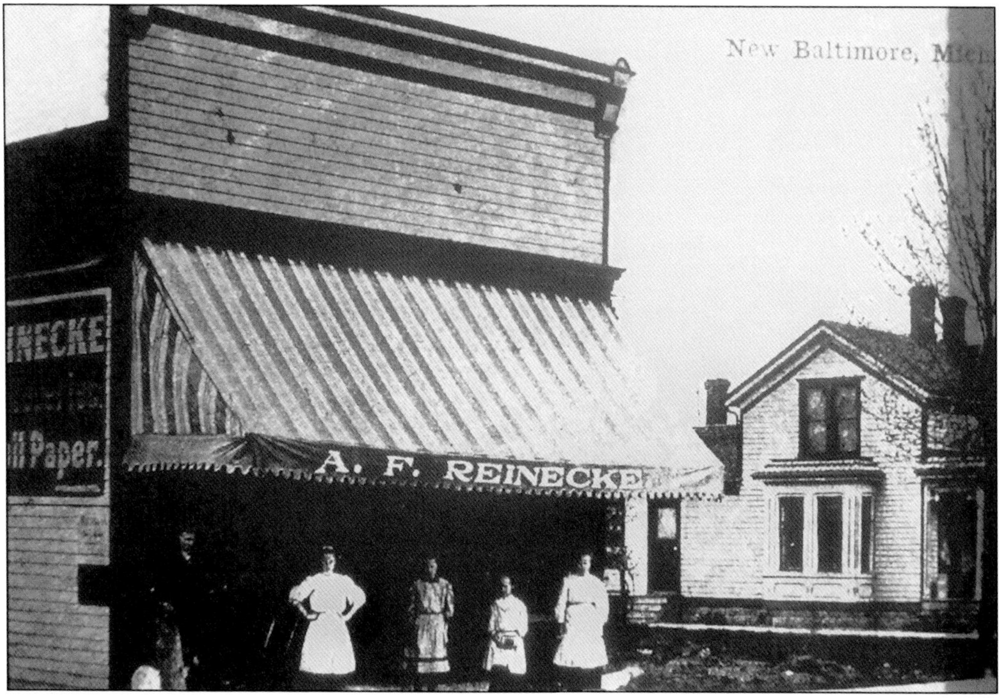

August Reinecke had a dry goods and grocery store and was also the postmaster from 1914 to 1921. He lived in the house to the right of his establishment. In the same vicinity were two different tin shops, Langell's, at the corner of Washington and Hathaway Streets; and Steele's, on the opposite side of the street, midway between Green and Hathaway Streets. Eugene Height's tin shop, at 36355 Main Street, had a photography gallery above it and sold tintypes for a dime a dozen.

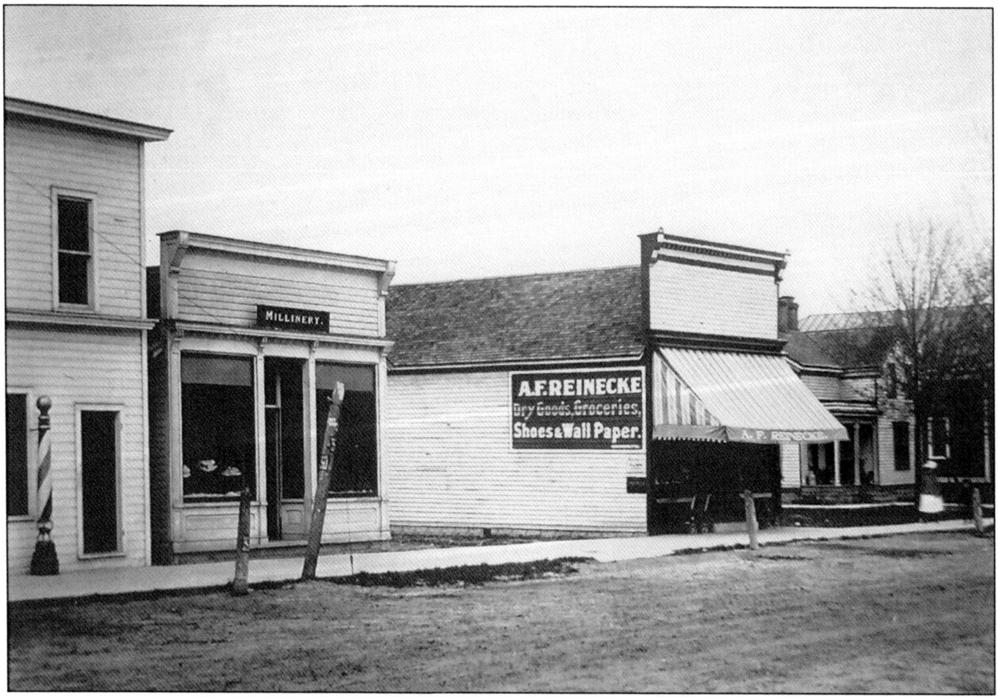

Four

Tourist Days

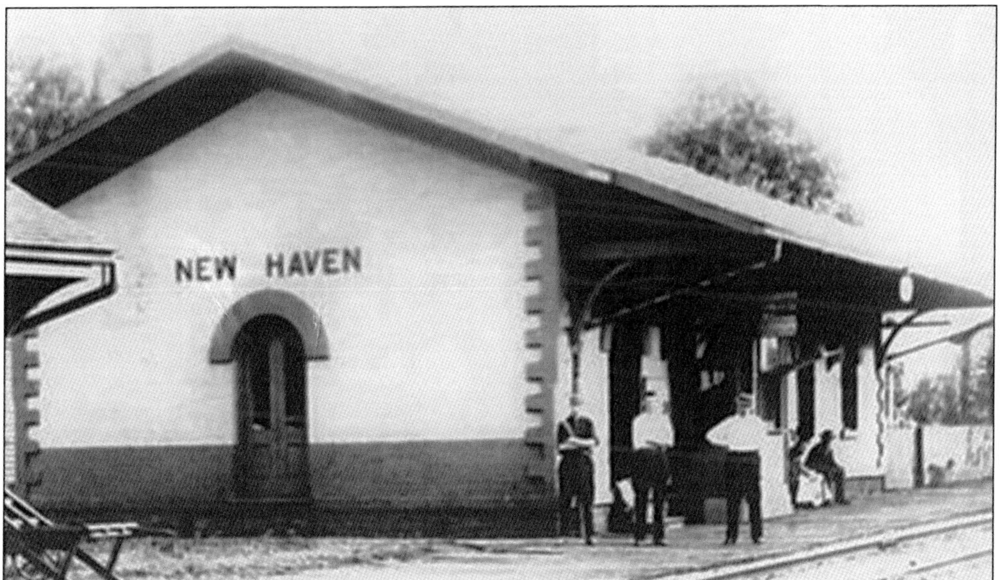

In the late 1860s, New Baltimore began to boom, and a regular stagecoach ran twice a day on the plank road between New Baltimore and the New Baltimore station, the railroad depot that was shortly thereafter renamed the New Haven station. In 1875, the steamship *City of New Baltimore* was built in Marine City. It was 94 feet long and 20 feet wide and ferried passengers and freight to and from New Baltimore. In 1897, the 84-foot-long and 18-foot-wide steamer *Hattie* also began ferrying passengers and freight to New Baltimore and its hotels, providing some competition between the ferry companies.

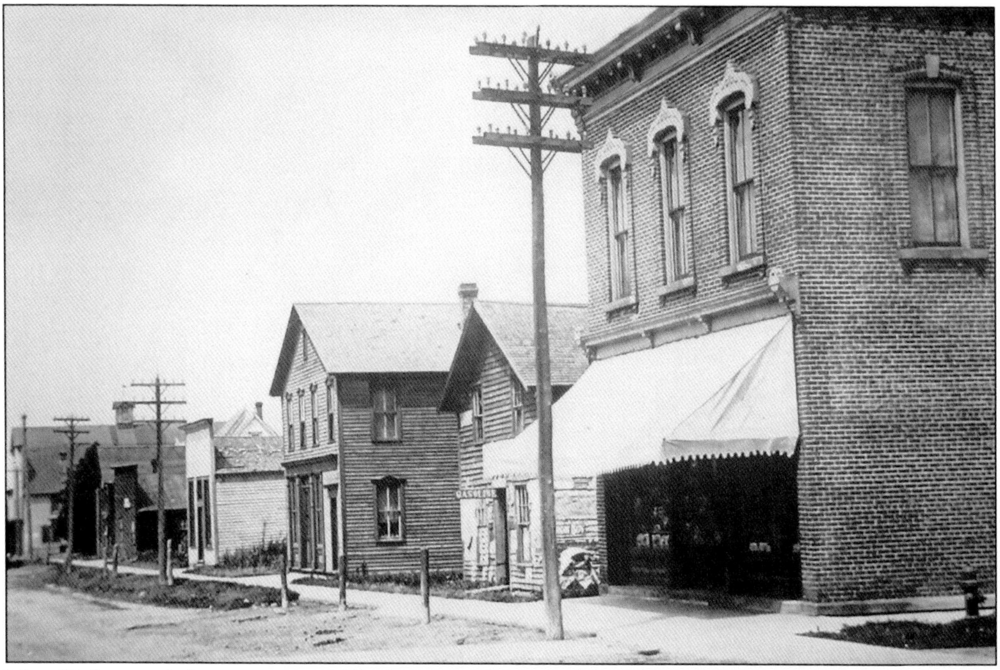

New Baltimore's biggest street, Washington Street, although empty in this photograph, was usually full of tourists and peddlers, who found they could make a good living there. Once, the streets were so crowded with peddlers that legislation was enacted requiring peddlers on foot to pay 50¢ a day for a village license. If the peddler was on a horse, the price was 75¢. There were other regulations for auctioneers, hawkers, and traders, as well as for traveling circuses.

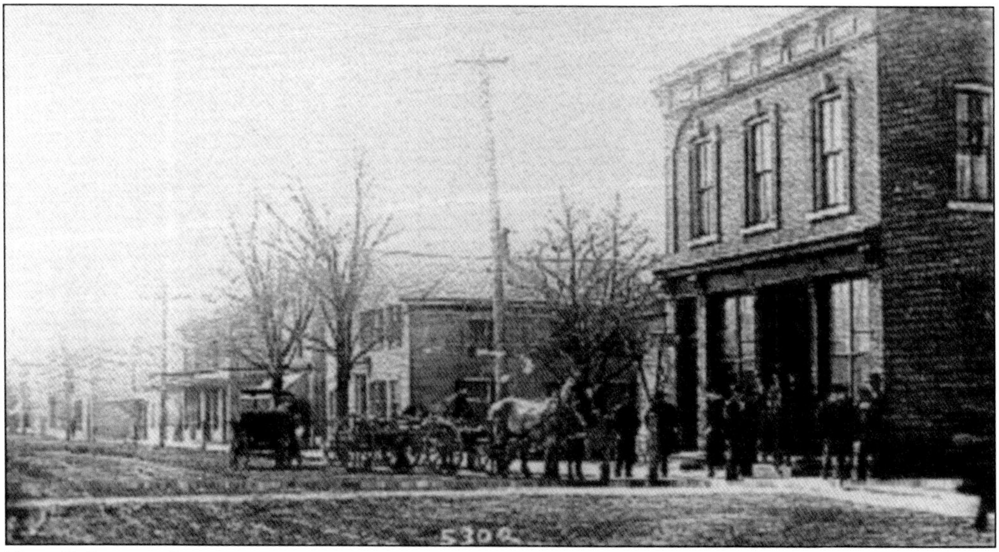

New Baltimore became an important stop along the Detroit United Railway (DUR) when the electric interurban railroad began running from Detroit to Port Huron in 1898. The stops were often listed on the side of the DUR train. Mt. Clemens, New Baltimore, Anchorville, Fair Haven, Pearl Harbor, Algonac, Marine City, St. Clair, and Port Huron were the usual stops for the New Baltimore area. Because of its position in the middle of the route, the powerhouse for the trains was built in New Baltimore.

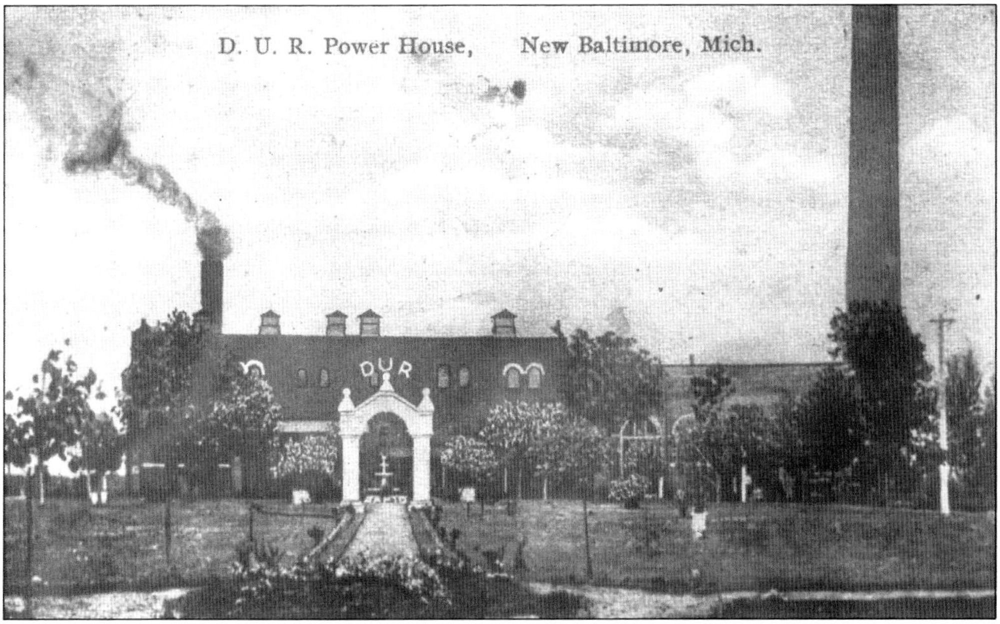

The DUR powerhouse was located on Highview Road near County Line Road and Main Street. At the DUR's peak, there were 14 local trains making seven daily round trips and 30 limited trains making 15 daily round trips from Detroit to Port Huron, thereby providing hourly service.

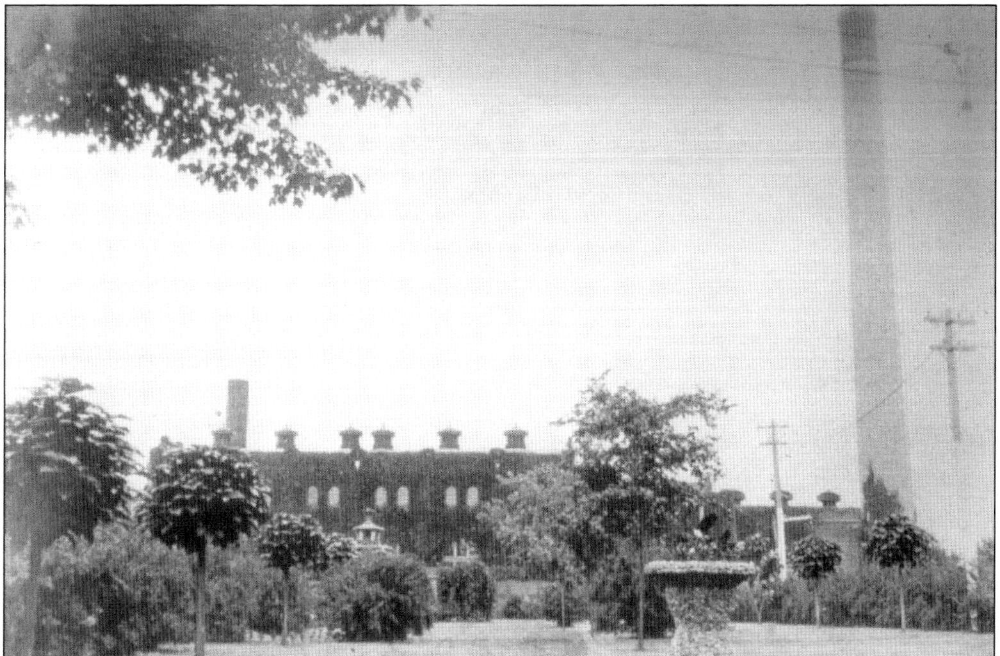

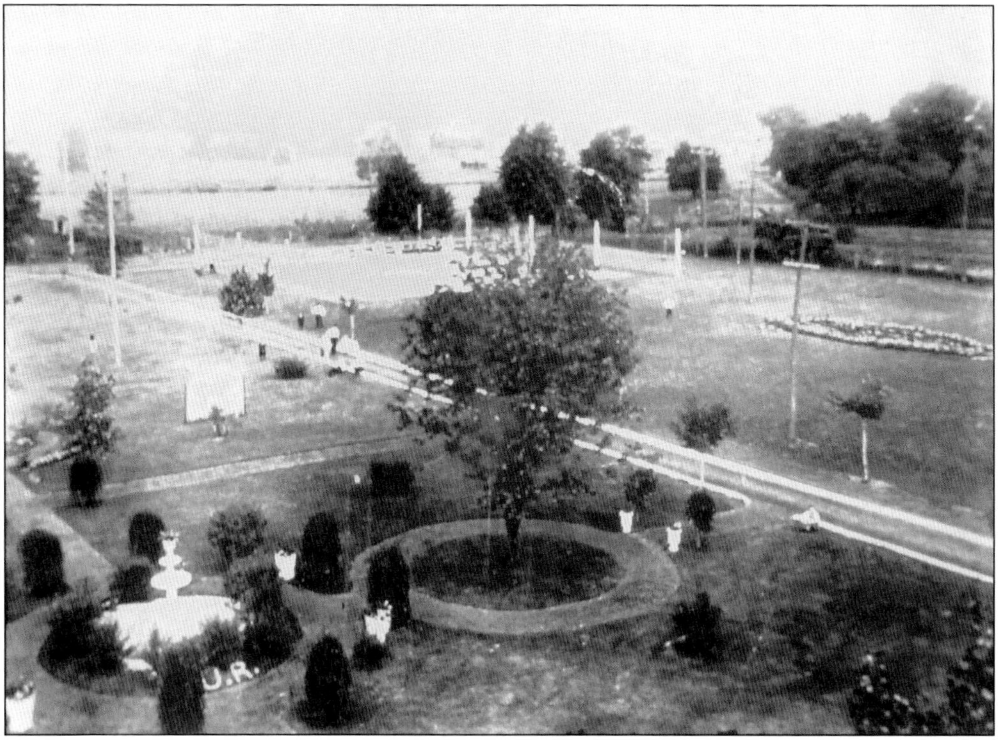

The interurban DUR trains ran along Gratiot Road, down 23 Mile Road into New Baltimore, and out along M-29 to Anchorville and Fair Haven. Below is an inside view of the DUR power plant, where electricity was generated to run the trains.

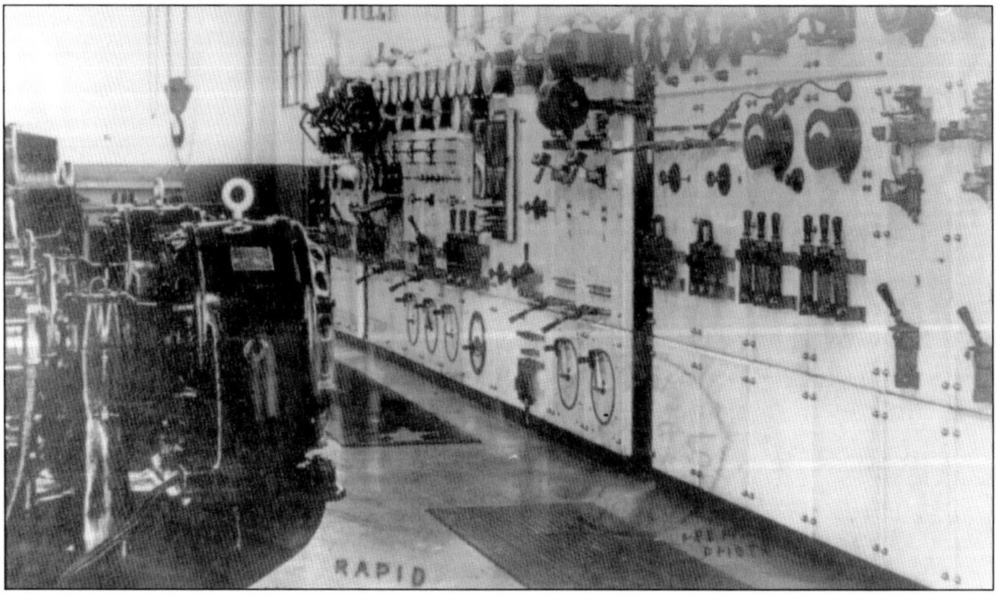

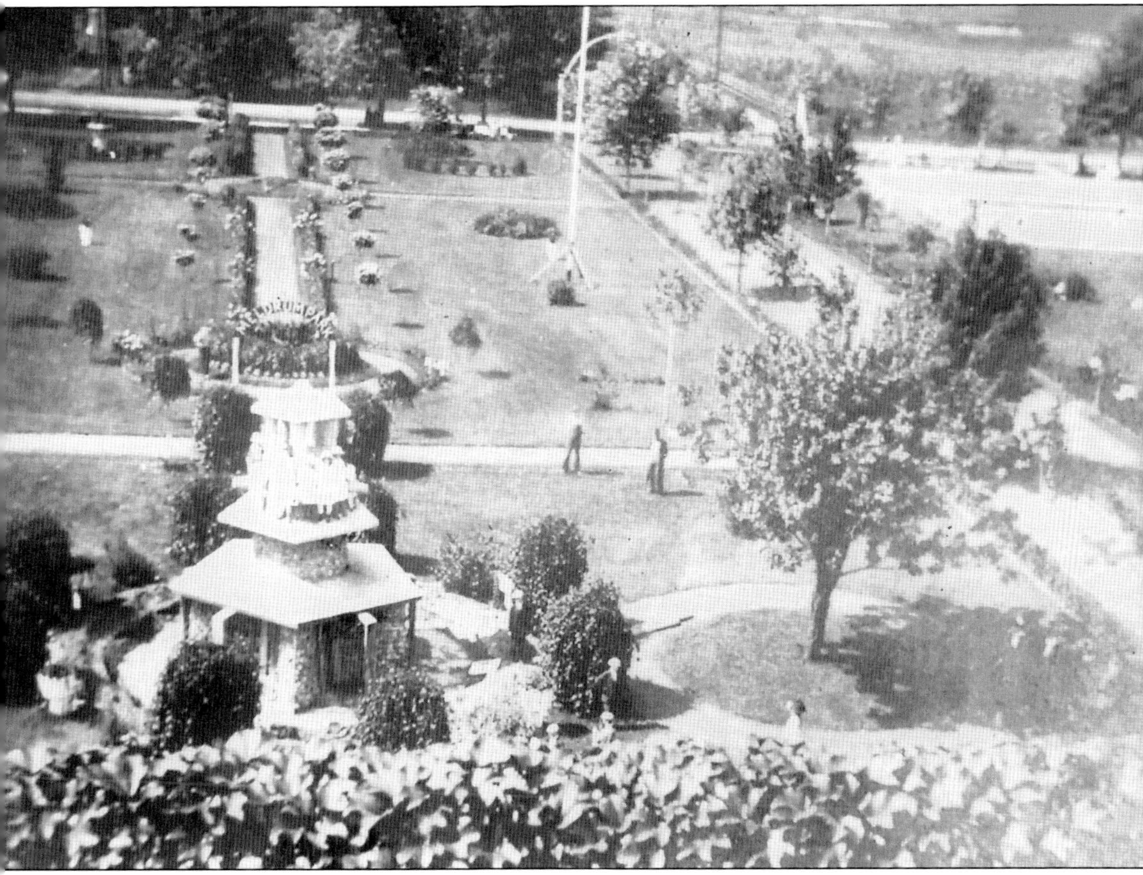

The New Baltimore depot was across the street from where the New Baltimore municipal offices are today. The Hatheway Institute was previously on the site as well. Surrounding the DUR powerhouse was a beautifully landscaped park that was accessible to the public. It was a popular picnic area, with its fountains, majestic trees, and cool lake breezes.

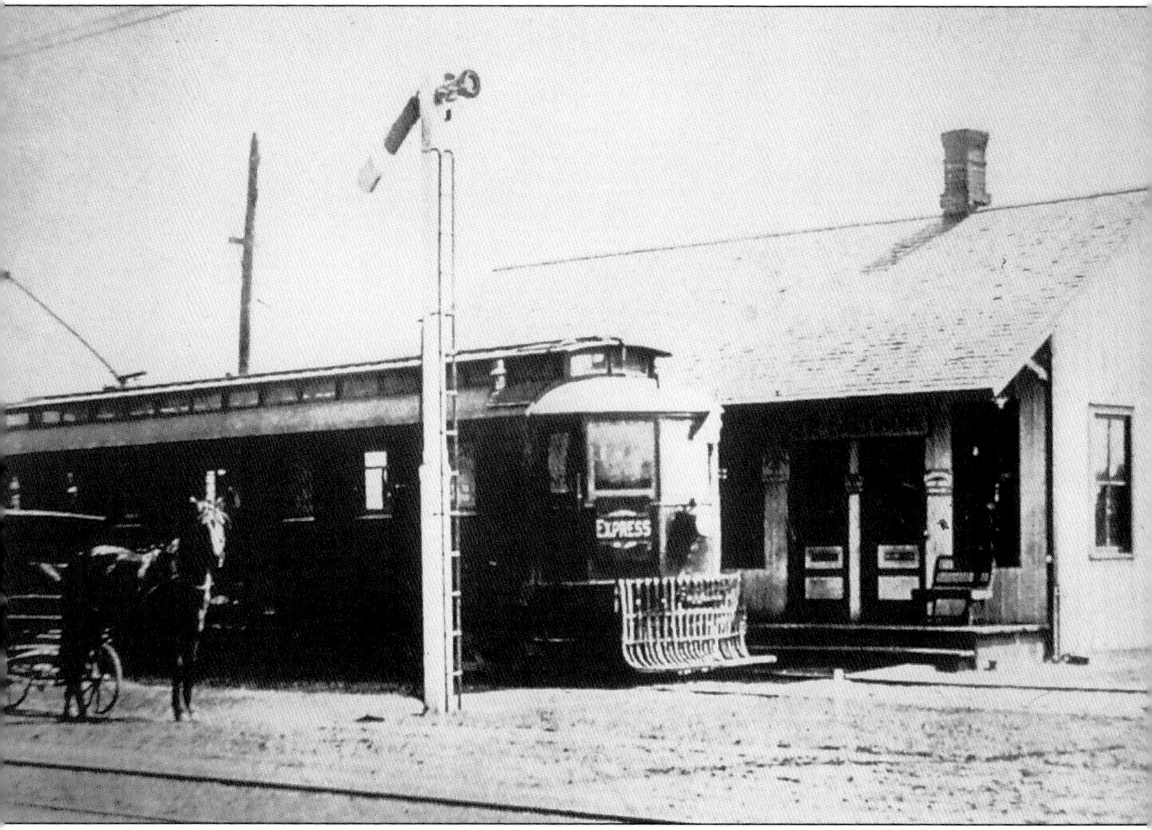

The trains provided an alternative to the horse and buggy, and one that was relatively nonpolluting, inexpensive, and convenient, especially during the seasons when the roads were generally impassable. The railroad kept a roundhouse and storage area at Green Street and County Line Road.

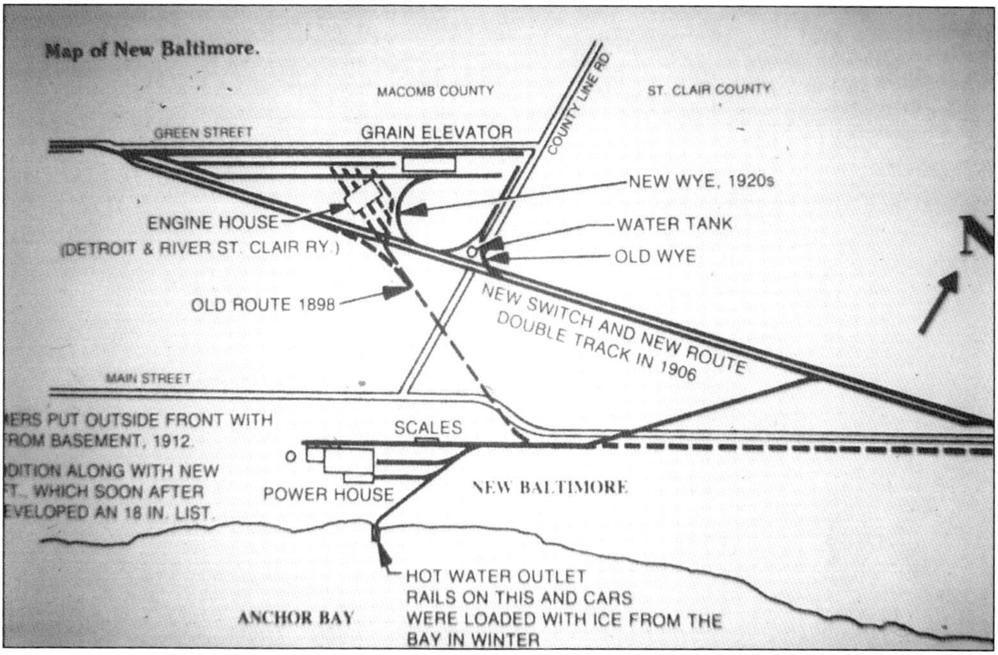

Native Americans, who rode for free on the interurban, would weave baskets on their way to Detroit to sell them. The grasses from their baskets always left a pleasant aroma. Many of the tracks in New Baltimore were just paved over instead of being removed. Sometimes when roads are in disrepair, the tracks can still be seen.

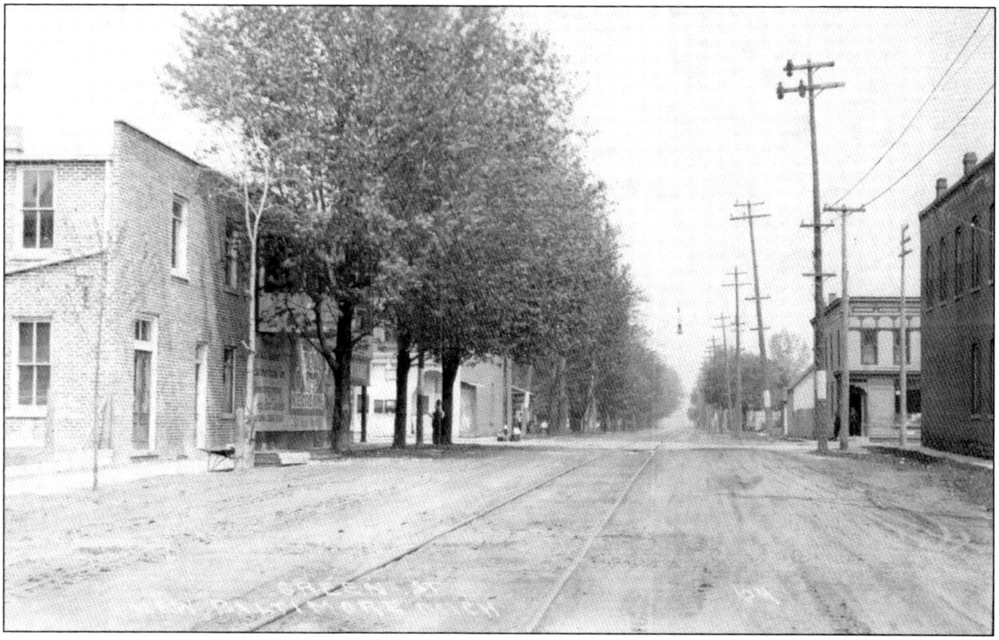

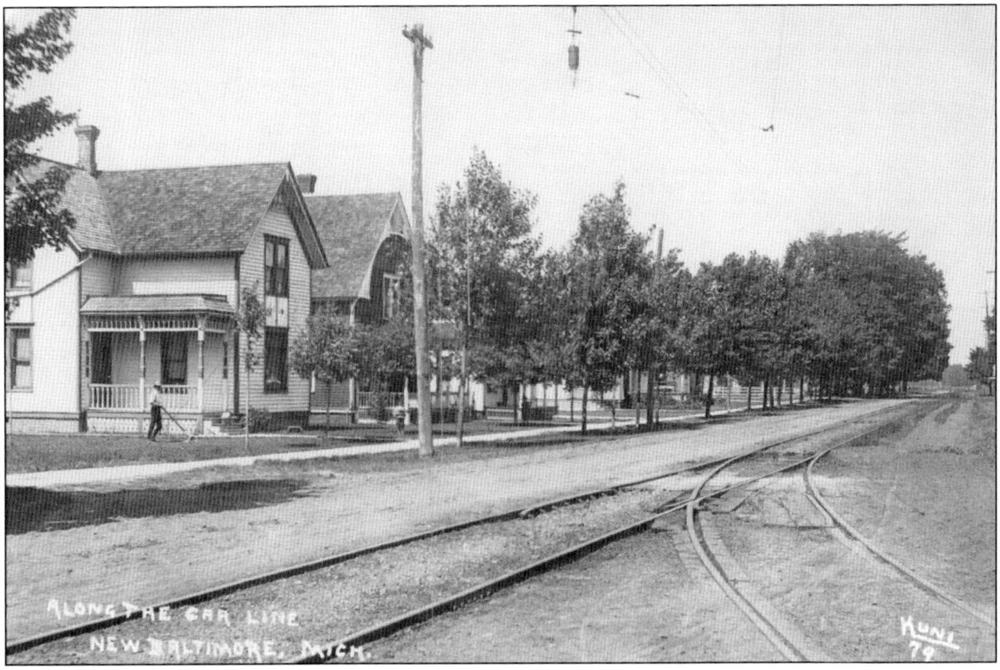

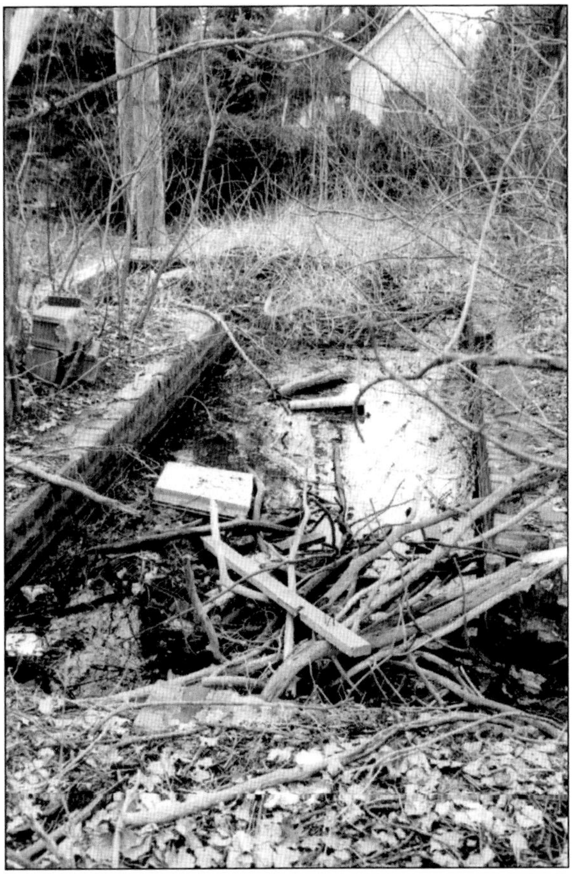

The interurban train was a victim of the rising attractiveness of the motorcar. The once-majestic edifice and the beautifully landscaped grounds of the DUR powerhouse gave way to the Highview subdivision. The ruins of the powerhouse, which was razed not long after the trains stopped running in early 1930, are pictured at left as a mere hole in the ground.

January 10, 1865.] UP TRAINS [No. 42.

LONDON BRANCH—ST: MARY'S TO LONDON:

TORONTO TIME,

Inter. Distance.	Total Distance.	STATIONS.	No. 2. Expr.	No. 4 Mixed.	No. 6 Mail.
			P. M.	A. M.	P. M.
		St. Mary's	4.35	8.00	8.25
12	12	Thorndale	5.05	8.35	8.50
10¼	22¼	London	5.25	9.10	9.20

GALT BRANCH—BERLIN TO DOON.

Inter. Distance.	Total Distance.	STATIONS.	No. 2	No. 4
			A. M.	P. M.
		Berlin	10.20	6.35
7		Doon	10.50	7.05

DETROIT DIVISION—PORT HURON TO DETROIT.

CHICAGO TIME.

Inter. Distance.	Total Distance.	STATIONS,	No. 2 Expr.	No. 4 Expr.	No. 6 Mixed.	No. 8 Buffalo Ex. Fr't
			P. M.	P. M.	A. M.	A. M.
		Port Huron	**9.30**	**3.20**	7.30	**9.30**
10¾	10¾	Smith's Creek	10.00	......	8.12	10.03
18¾	21½	Ridgeway	10.25	4.05	8.55	10.40
5¾	27¼	New Baltimore	......	*4.17	9.17	**11.00**
10¼	37½	Mount Clemens	11.00	4.40	10.00	11.47
5¼	42¾	Utica Plank	......	*4.52	**10.20**	**12.10**
11½	54¼	Milwaukee Junction	P. M.	5.20	11.00	
5	59¼	Detroit Junction	11.45	5.30	**11.15**	**1.15**
3	62¼	**Detroit**	12.00	5.45	11.30	
			A. M.	P. M.		P. M.
		M. C. R. Depart	7.30	5.30	......	1.50

CROSSING STATIONS FOR UP TRAINS—GOING WEST.

No. 2—Express—at Smith's Creek No. 3; failing to arrive at Detroit Junction at 9.30 A.M., keep clear of Nos. 1 and 3.

No. 4—Express—at Port Huron No. 5; failing to arrive at Detroit Junction at 8 P.M., keep clear of Nos. 3 & 1.

No. 6—Mixed—at Utica No. 1; at Detroit Junction No. 5.

No. 8—Express Freight—At Baltimore No. 1; at Utica No. 5.

*Flag Stations.

Although the interurban railroad was phased out as automobiles became the preferred method of travel, traces of the railroads remain today. Many municipalities waited years before removing the tracks. Many depots found renewed life as they were repurposed into other structures. The New Baltimore depot was moved down to Ashley and incorporated into another structure. In many cities, bits and pieces of track can still be seen. Even though the interurban trains went out of business, the Grand Trunk Railroad and its successors still operate today. Pictured here is an 1865 train schedule showing the New Baltimore stop between Ridgeway (present-day Richmond) and Mt. Clemens.

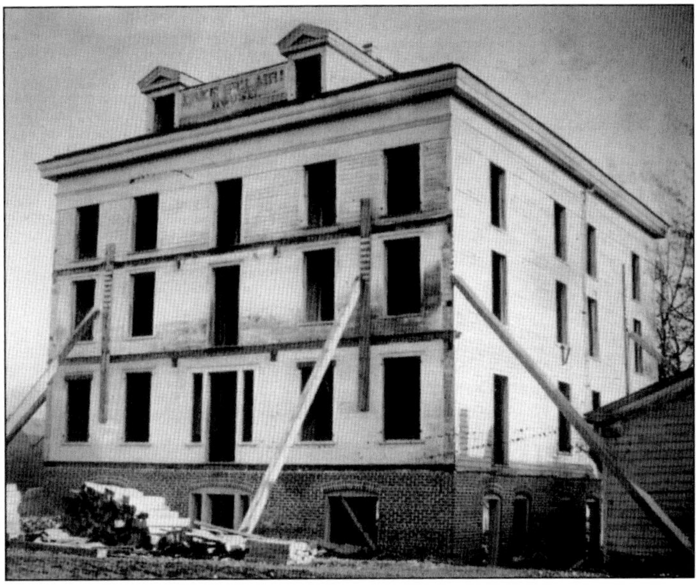

William Randall is credited with starting an early hotel. Called the Randall House and also The Olds, it was located on Front Street, on the lakefront, near the corner of Maria Street. The Lake St. Clair House was one of the major hotels of New Baltimore. It is seen here being lifted up to add a new foundation. Located near the Randall House on Front Street, it was later called the St. Clair House and then the St. Clair Inn and the New Baltimore Inn. It was built in the 1850s by Abel Davis.

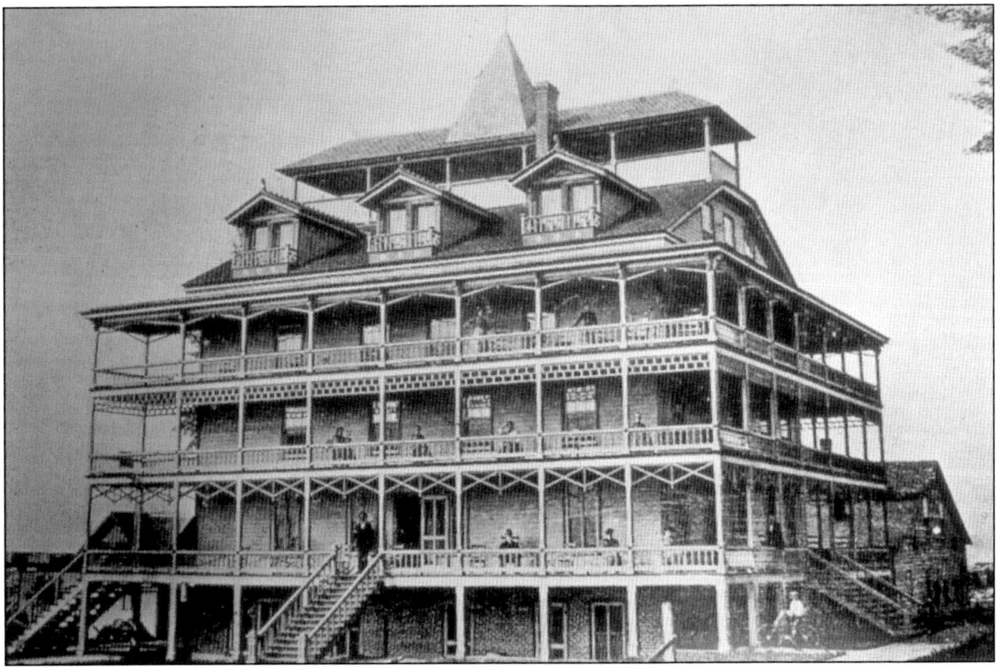

The wooden Lake St. Clair House had five stories, with a dance pavilion on the top. The premier resort hotel advertised "good fishing, rowing, sailing, bathing and bicycling for only two dollars a day." The original Lake St. Clair House sign is now in the Grand Pacific House Museum; it was donated by the son of one of the carpenters, who discovered the sign being used for a workbench among his father's effects. When the building was remodeled, it was elevated and put on a brick foundation. Porches were added on each floor, which could be reached from a stair to each veranda. Towering over the water with the dance floor on the roof, it was famous for its cool lake breezes and beautiful views of Anchor Bay.

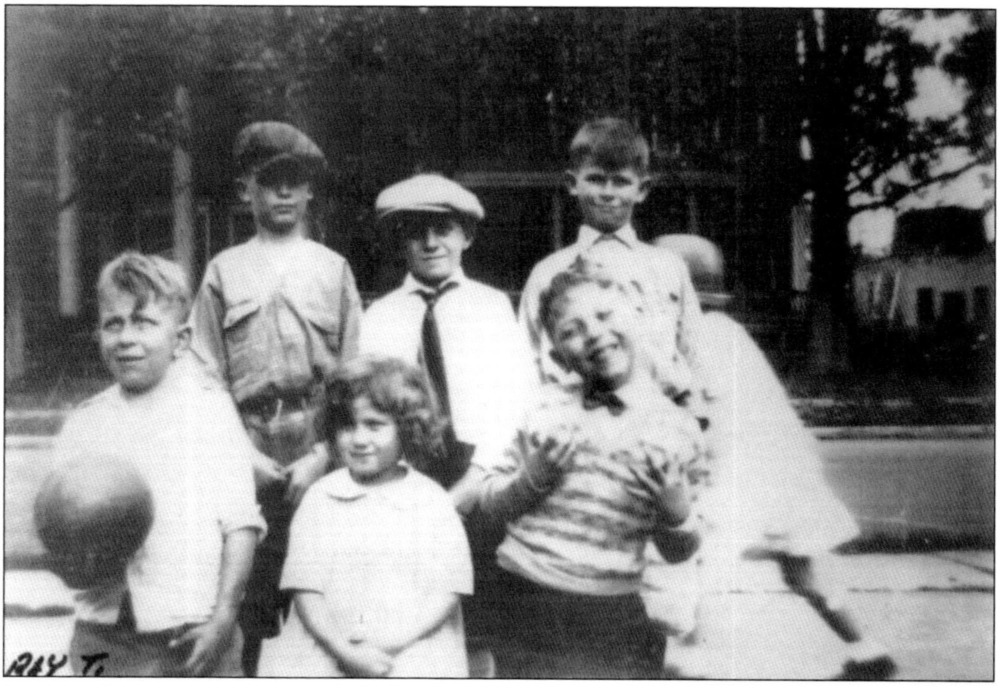

In 1900, the grand opening was held for a new building at 50976 Washington Street. Called the Chesterfield Hotel or the Hotel Chesterfield, it was the hub of sporting and social activities for many years thereafter. In the era of the interurban railroad, before automobile and paved roads took over, it was popular to take vacations in large resort hotels such as the Chesterfield. The hotel was near where the town movie theater was in the 1950s and 1960s. Today, New Baltimore Recreation Center is on the site. When the hotel was built, a mineral bathhouse was already nearby, on the corner of Front and Washington Streets.

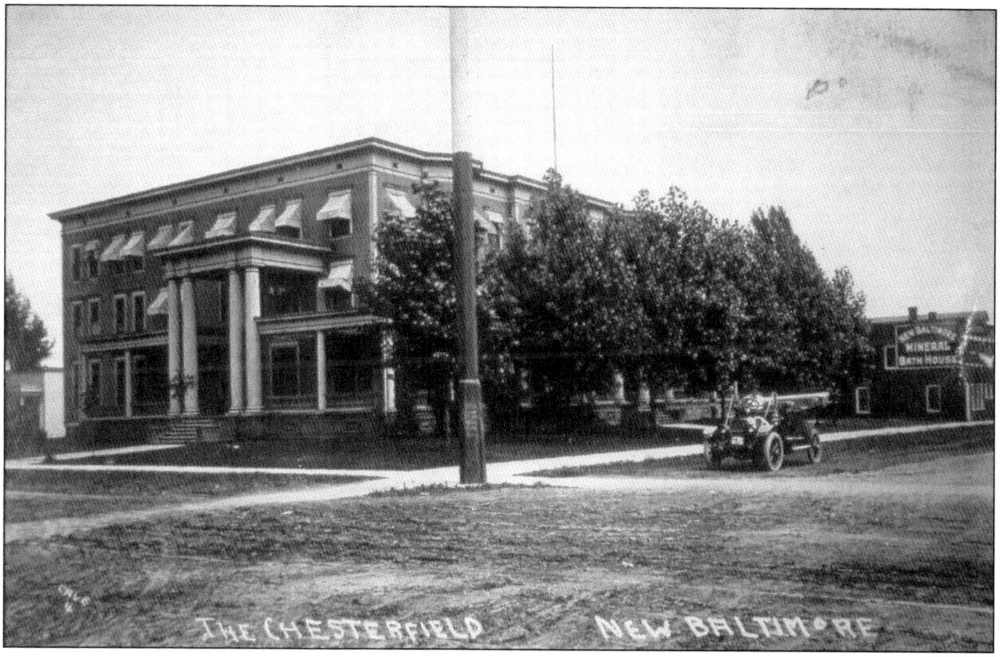

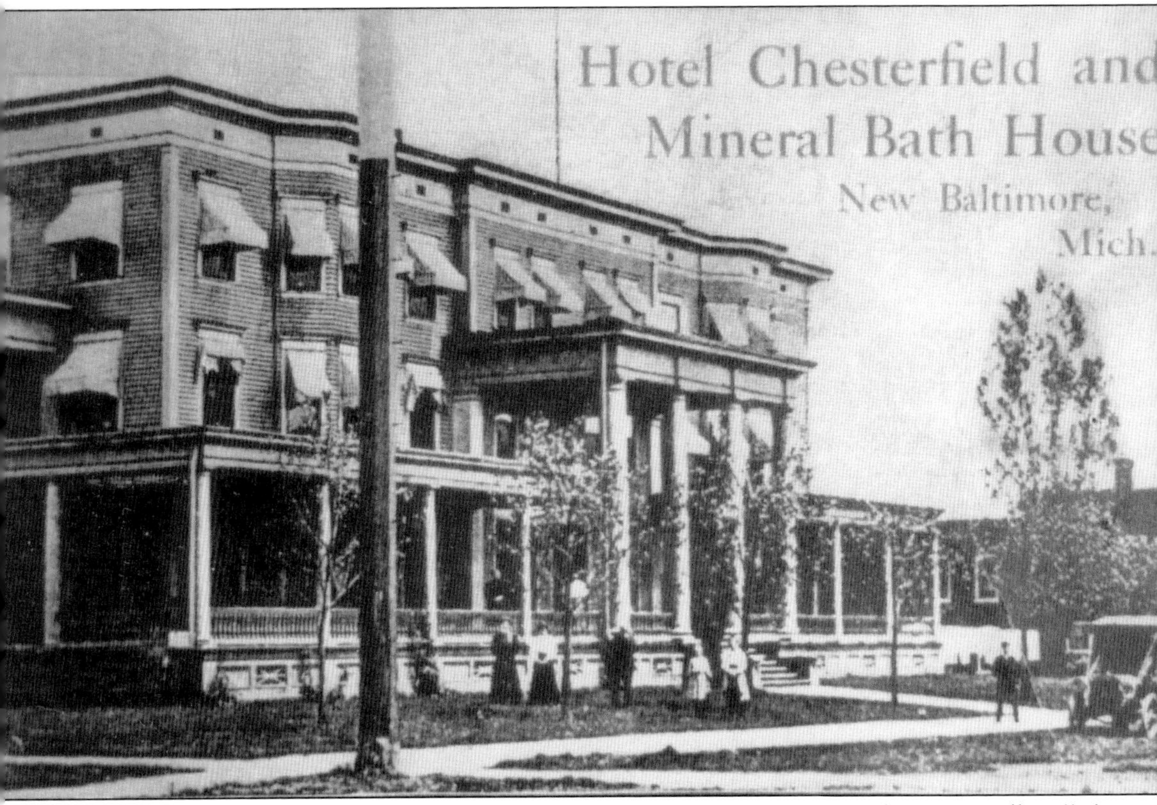

The Mineral Bath House was originally built around 1855 by John Evans, and was originally called the Evans Hotel. It was very popular for a time, and was bought out by a Mt. Clemens businessman, Charles Meldrum, who owned two mineral bathhouses in the Mt. Clemens area. He reportedly did not want the competition, so he capped and closed the New Baltimore mineral baths.

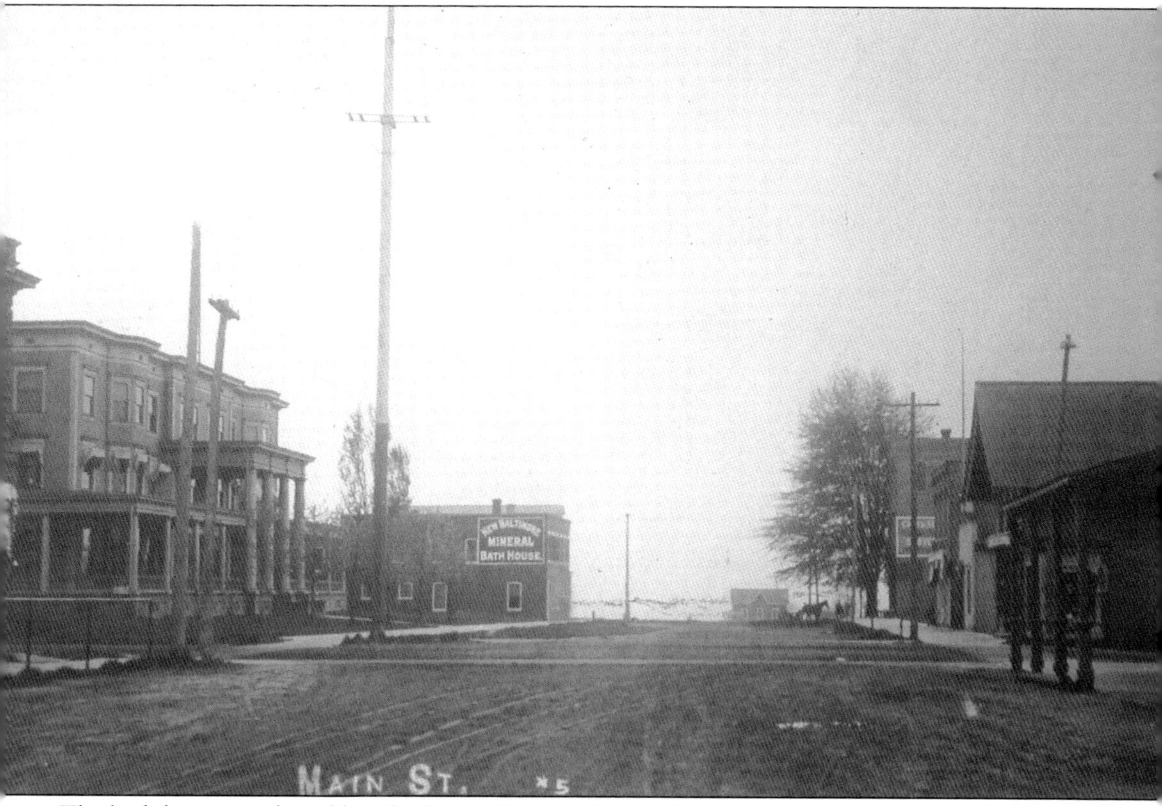

The bath house purchased by Charles Meldrum in New Baltimore provided competition for the Fountain Bath House in Mt. Clemens. It had 70 bath rooms, 40 "cooling rooms," ladies' and gentlemens' parlors, and even a physician's office. It was started by R.O. Meldrum in 1886 and was operated by his son Charles until 1921.

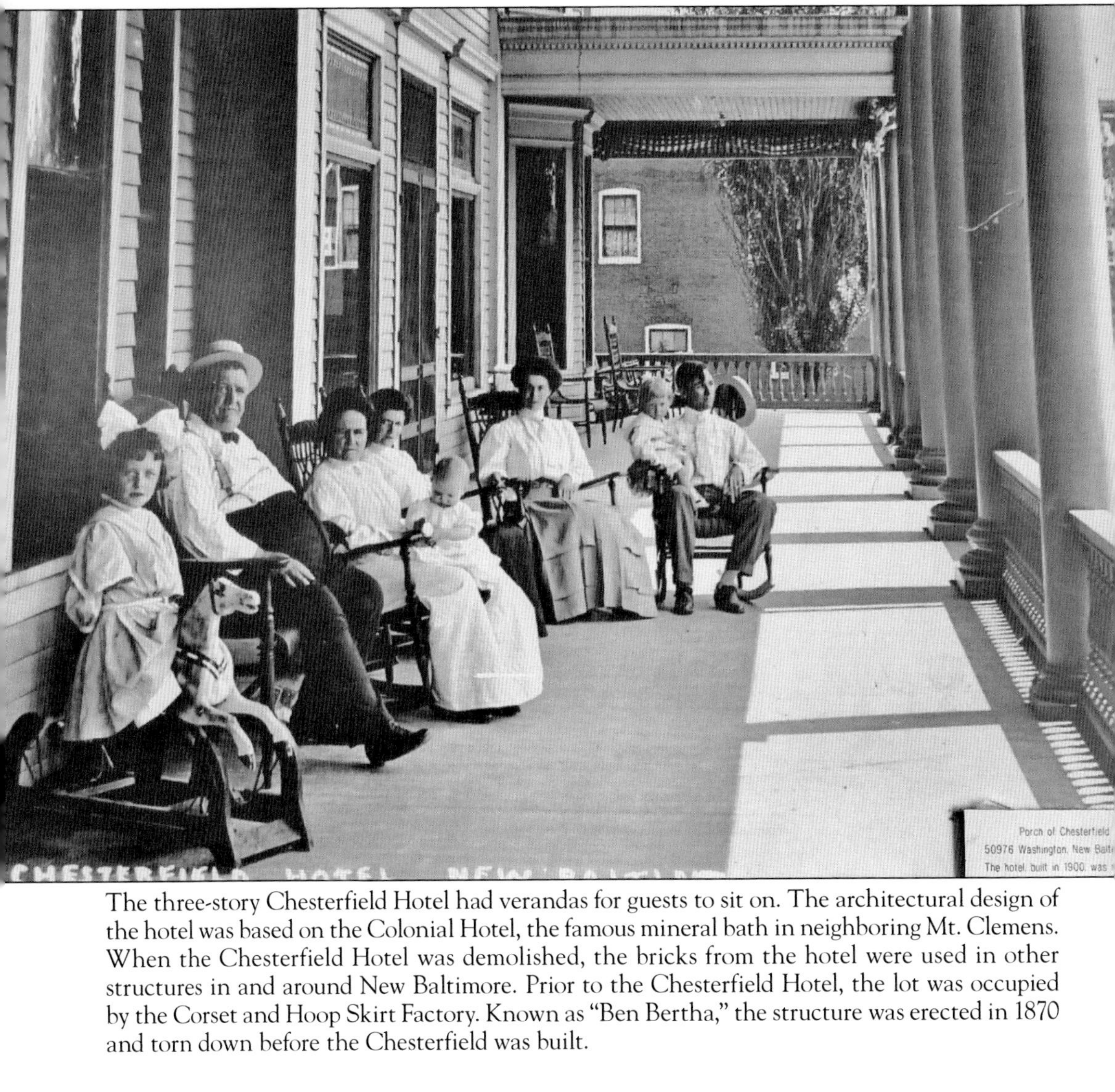

The three-story Chesterfield Hotel had verandas for guests to sit on. The architectural design of the hotel was based on the Colonial Hotel, the famous mineral bath in neighboring Mt. Clemens. When the Chesterfield Hotel was demolished, the bricks from the hotel were used in other structures in and around New Baltimore. Prior to the Chesterfield Hotel, the lot was occupied by the Corset and Hoop Skirt Factory. Known as "Ben Bertha," the structure was erected in 1870 and torn down before the Chesterfield was built.

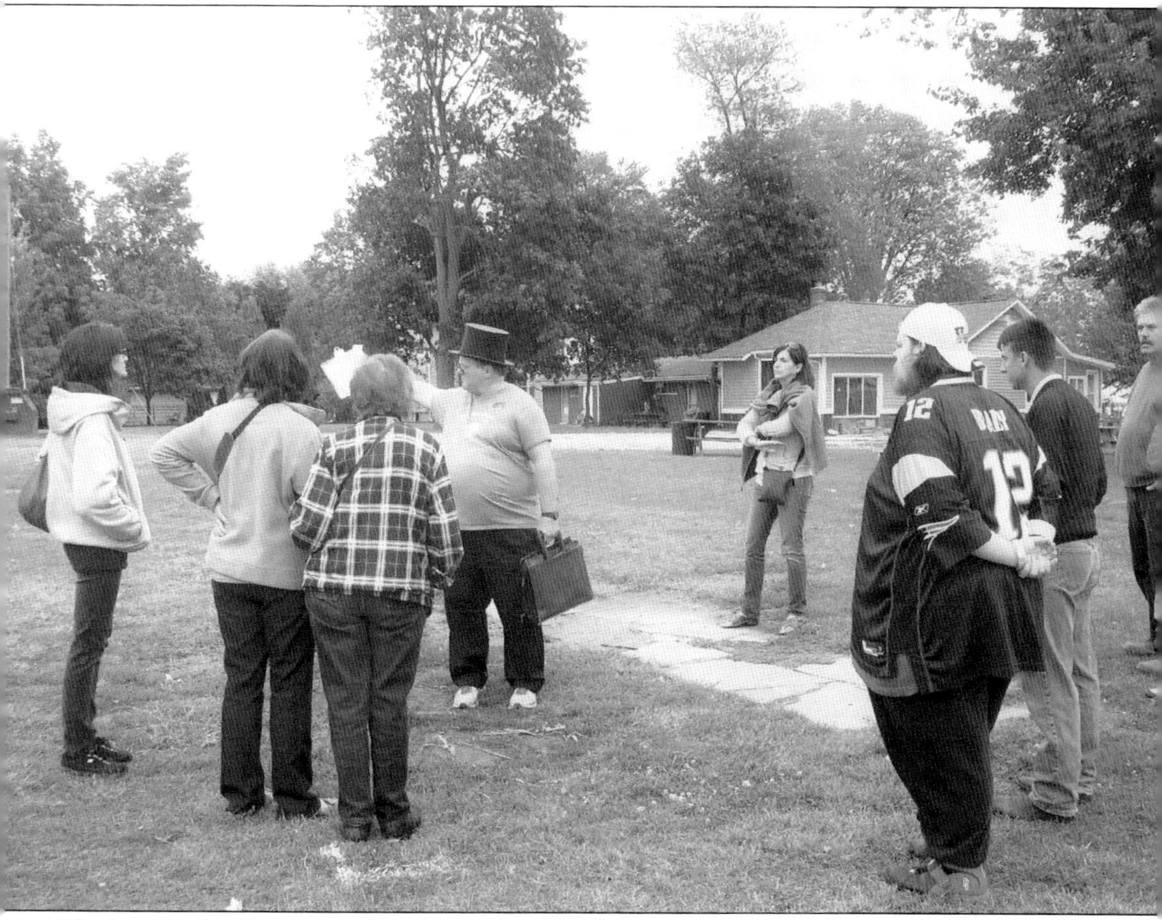

The hotel had well-manicured poplar trees and landscaping until 1934, when a large storm—by some reports a tornado—ripped out all the trees and landscaping. The landscaping was not replaced, which helped bring about the decline of the hotel. The sidewalks of the hotel are now all that remain. They are seen here in 2013, along with participants in one of coauthor Richard Gonyeau's history tours and patrons of the New Baltimore farmers' market.

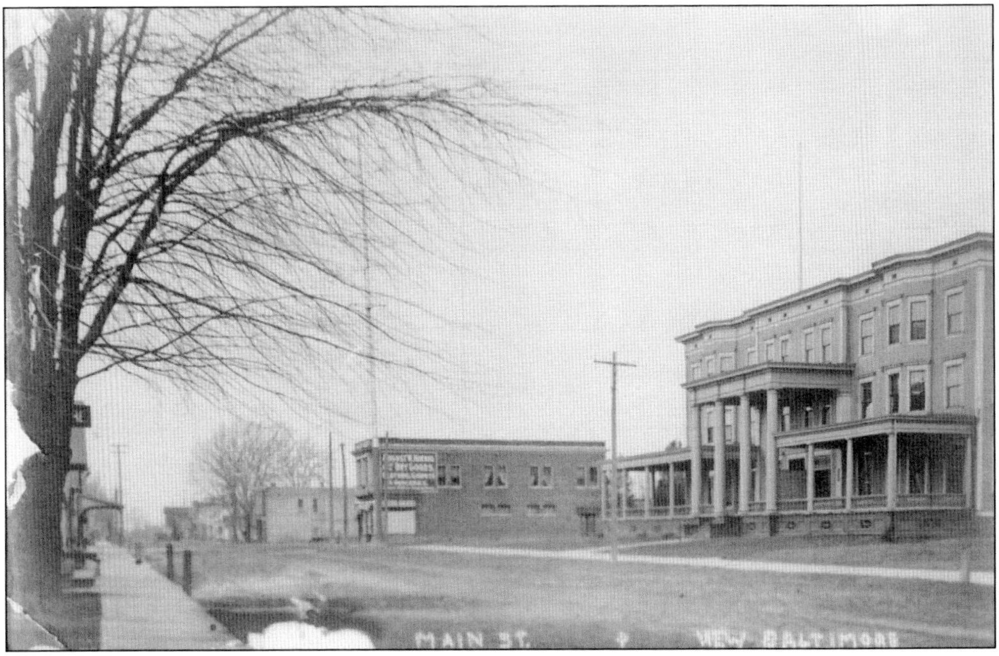

As other vacation options and the Great Depression took hold, the hotel era of New Baltimore ended. The Chesterfield Hotel fell into disuse and then abandonment, as it was no longer in use, except by the occasional squatters who sometimes took up illegal residence in the vacant building. It was demolished in 1937.

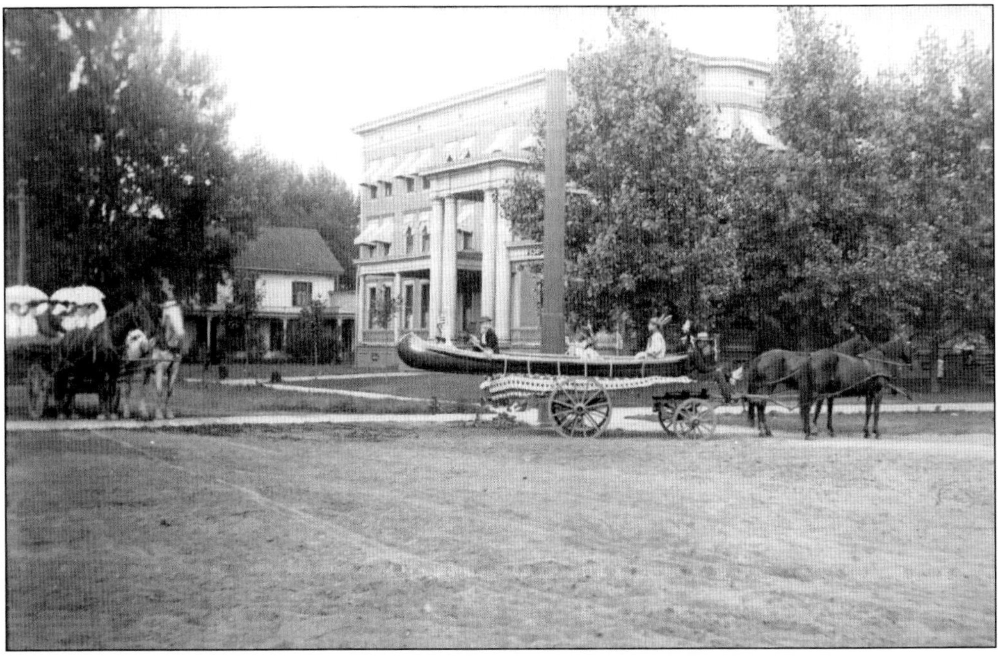

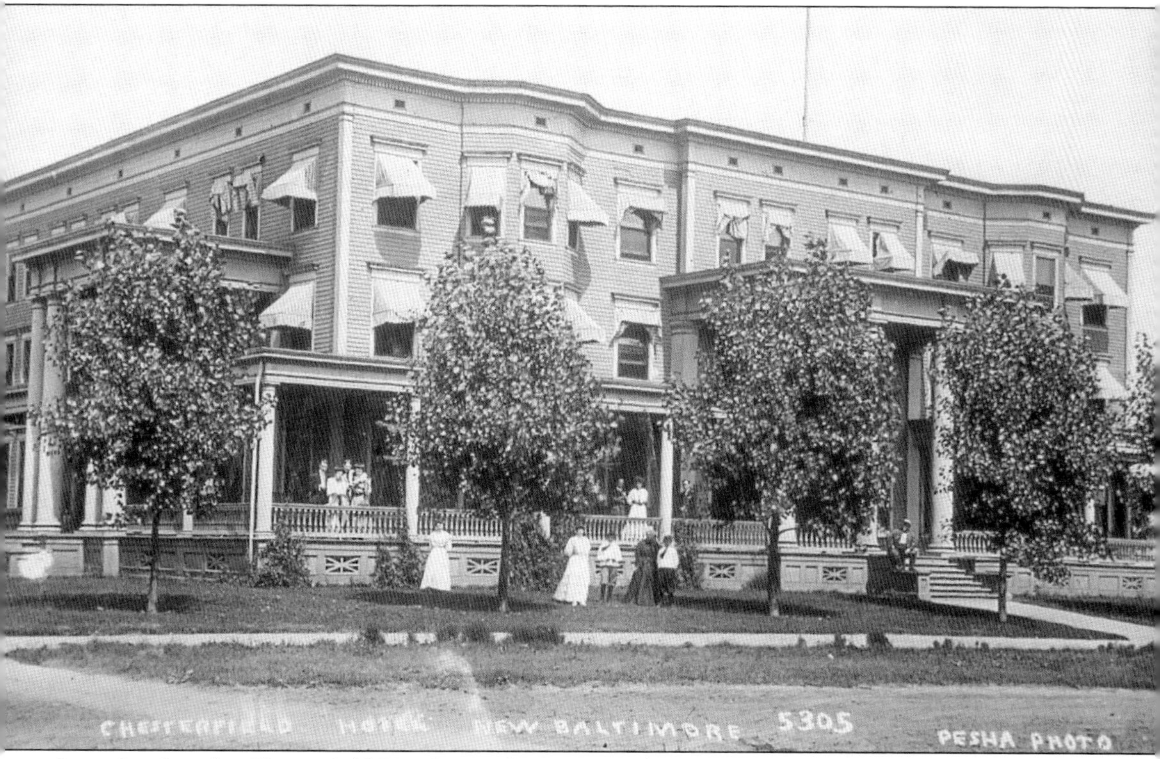

In its heyday, the Chesterfield Hotel was where New Baltimore went to have fun. The Roaring Twenties had its share of unique fads, including phone booth stuffing, goldfish swallowing, marathon dance contests, and pole sitting. The originator of pole sitting was Hollywood stunt man Alvin "Shipwreck" Kelly, who sat on a pole for a record 13 days. Soon, others were trying to break his record, and the flagpole outside of the Chesterfield Hotel regularly had pole sitters between 1925 and 1930.

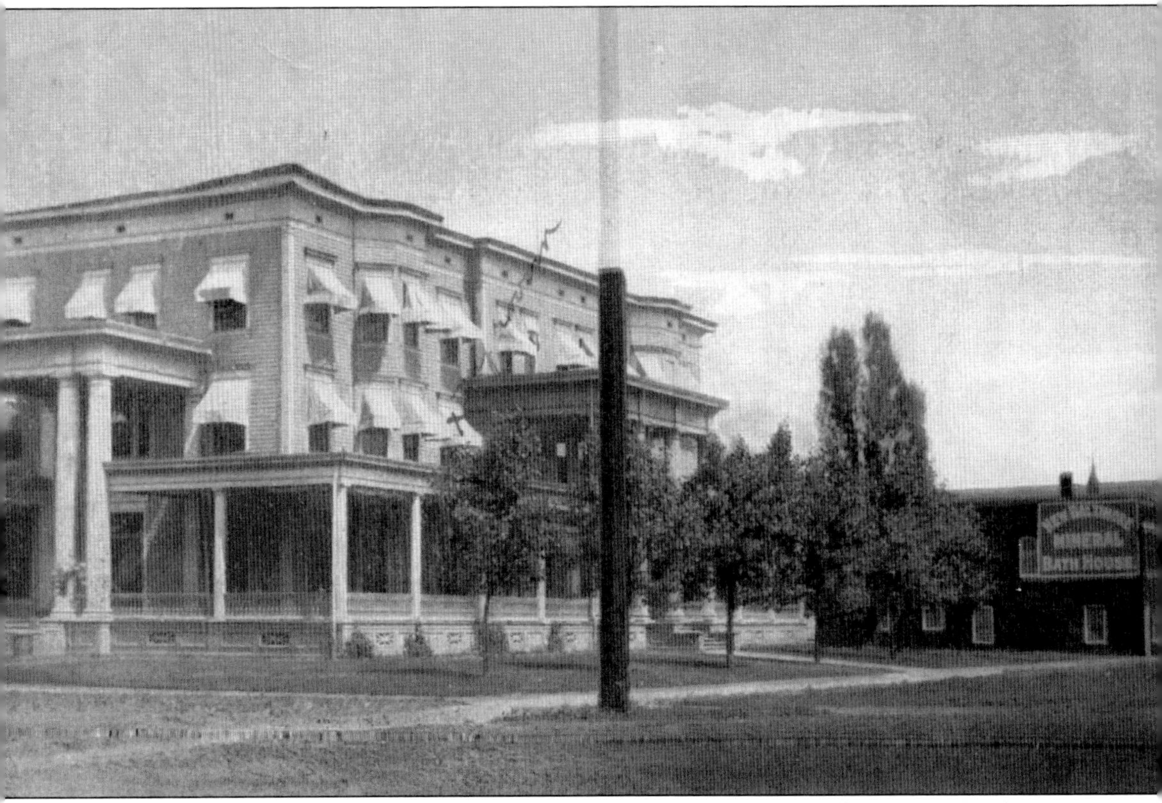

The Chesterfield Hotel had its most famous visitor in January 1904, when Henry Ford came to test one of his new autos, the Arrow, on the smooth ice surface of Anchor Bay in New Baltimore. He brought his auto to the village by interurban rail.

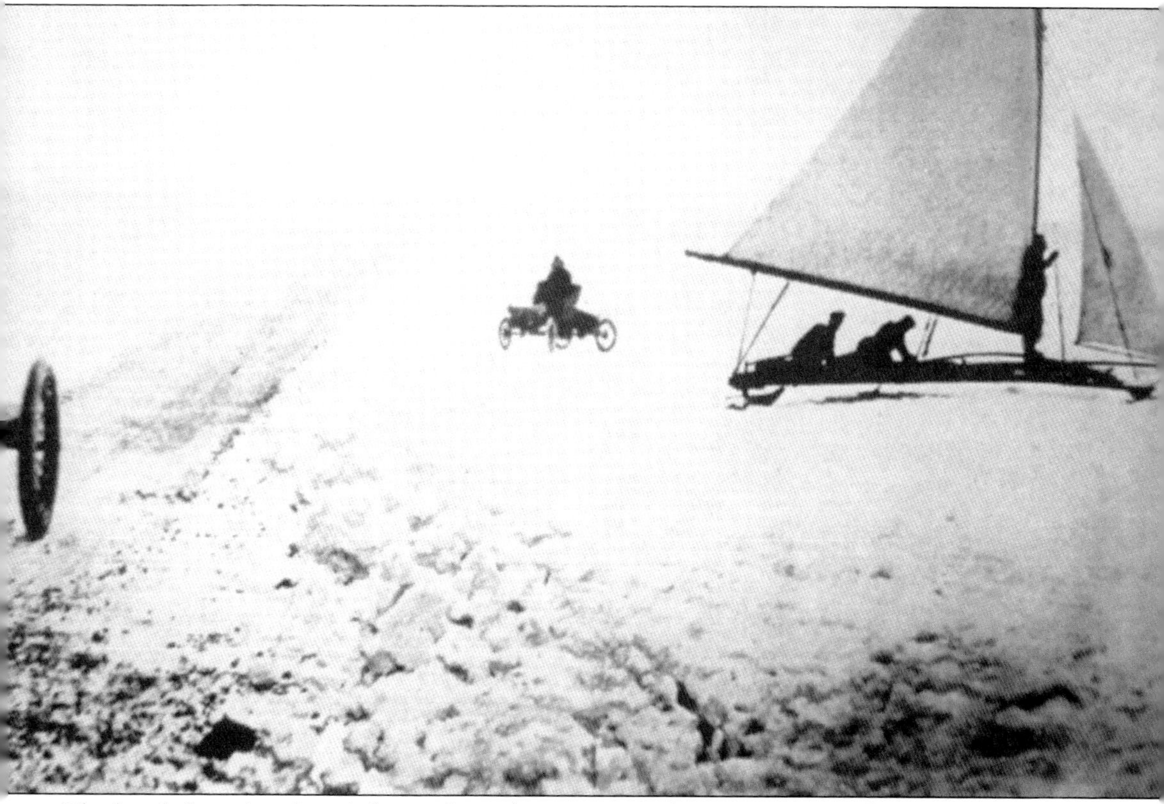

The hotel cleared and sanded a track on the ice on Anchor Bay. Peter Caillet, an early town historian who lived to be 91, claimed that Ford still owed him $5 for hauling cinders to the makeshift racetrack. The Chesterfield Hotel advertised the event by saying that Ford would keep trying until a new speed record was set. Ford did not disappoint, setting a new record of 91.37 miles per hour.

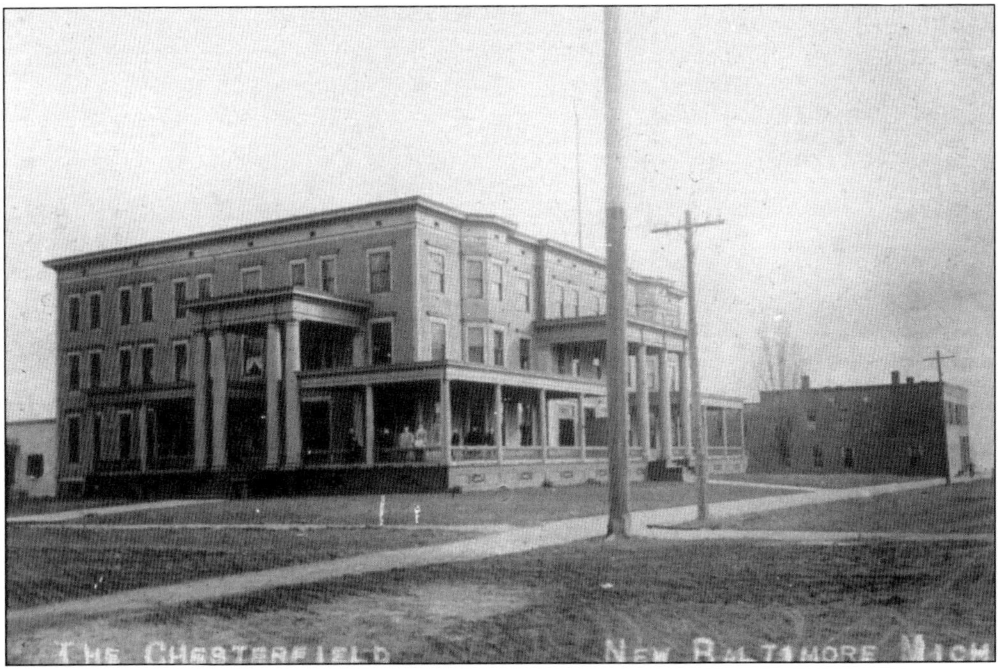

After his record-breaking feat on the ice, Henry Ford and his entourage stayed at the Chesterfield Hotel. While at the hotel, they feasted on roast muskrat. Even though the entrée was not popular with his colleagues, Ford pronounced the feast "delicious." Many years later, to commemorate the speed record and Ford's 75th birthday, the town held a parade, which Ford attended. Also featured in the parade was Old 999, reportedly the car in which Ford set the 1904 speed record.

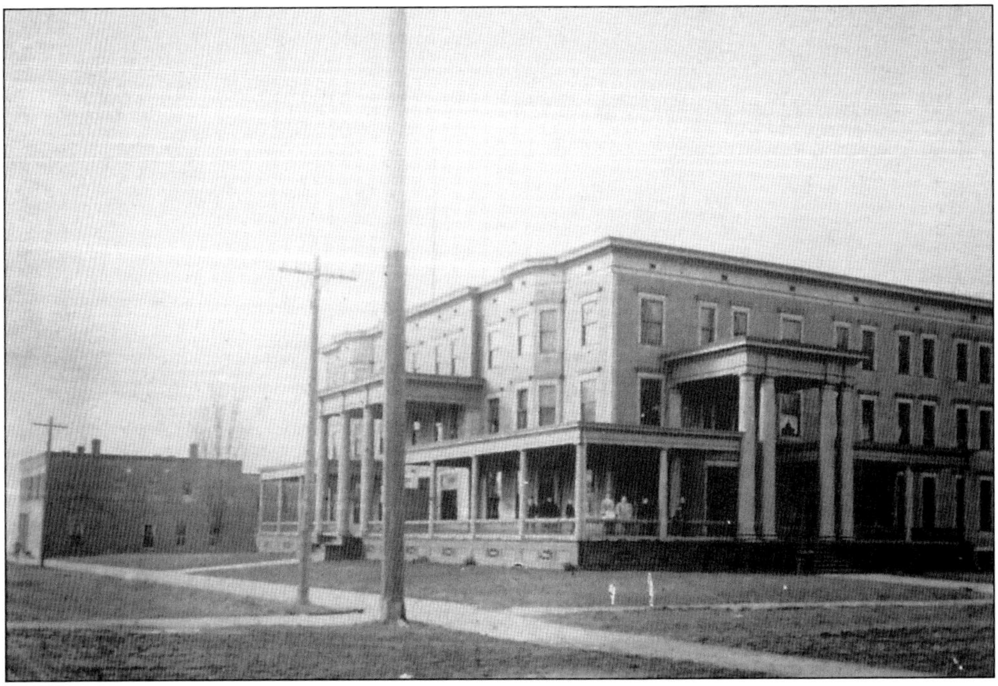

Five

Washington Street

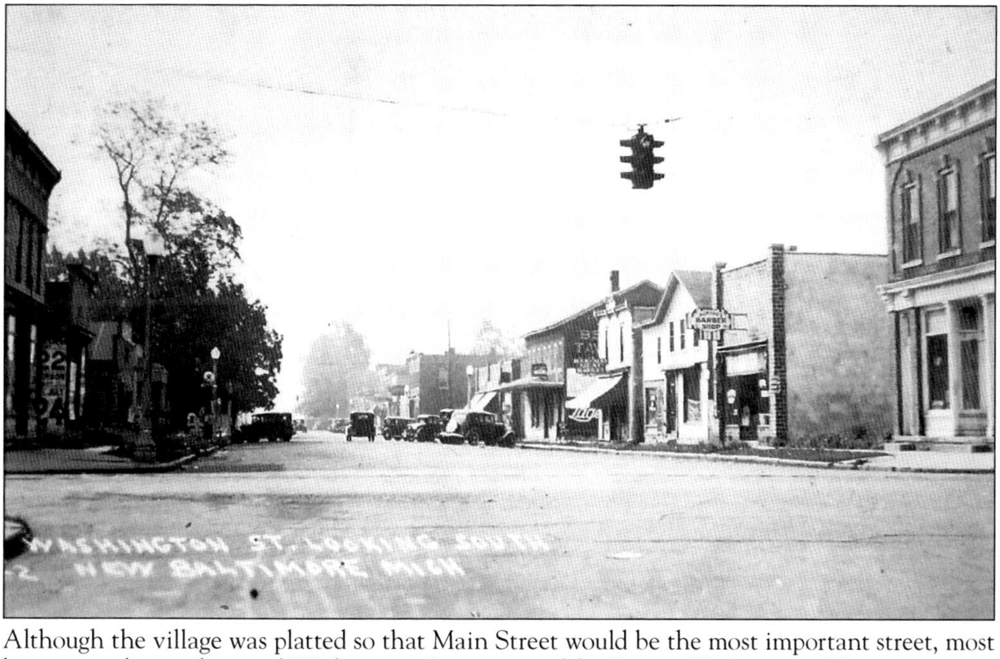

Although the village was platted so that Main Street would be the most important street, most businesses clustered around Washington Street, named for George Washington. The intersection of Washington and Main Streets was long the main crossroads of New Baltimore, and many of the buildings of the last 50 to 100 years are still part of a vibrant downtown.

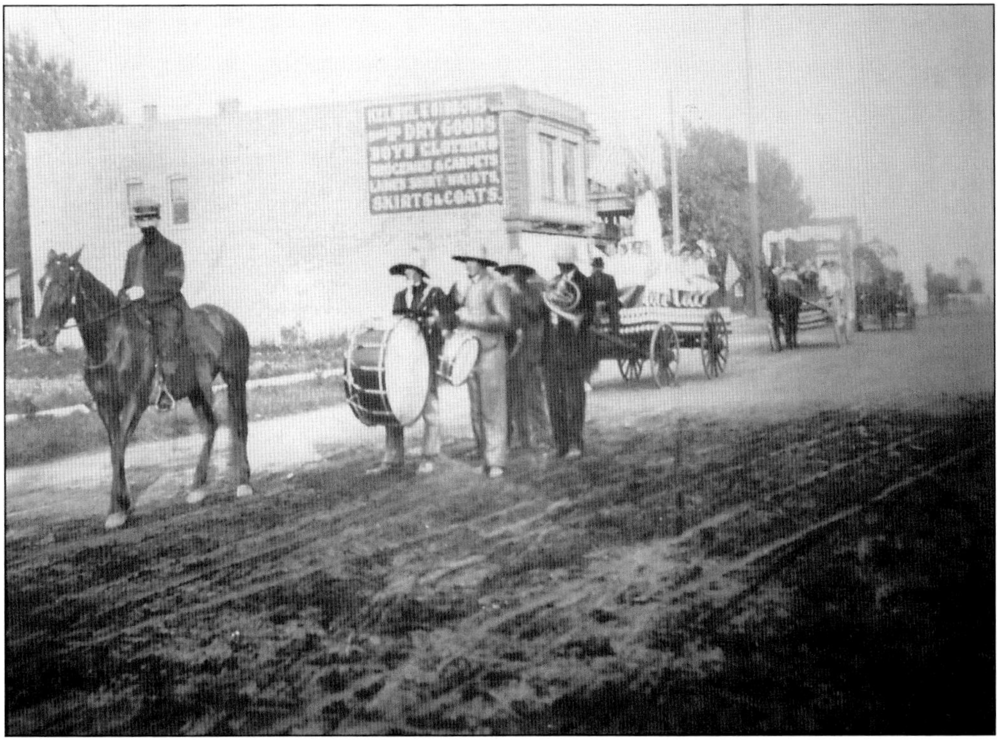

Since its early days, New Baltimore has always loved a parade. One of the first was this 1911 parade, sponsored by the First Congregational Church and featuring the Farmer's Band. In these days, before the widespread use of motor vehicles, floats were horse-drawn. Homecoming and Memorial (Decoration) Day have long been affairs marked by a town parade. The homecoming parade of August 1914 featured the Walpole Island Indian Brass Band and the launch of a hot-air balloon in the vicinity of today's Town Pump.

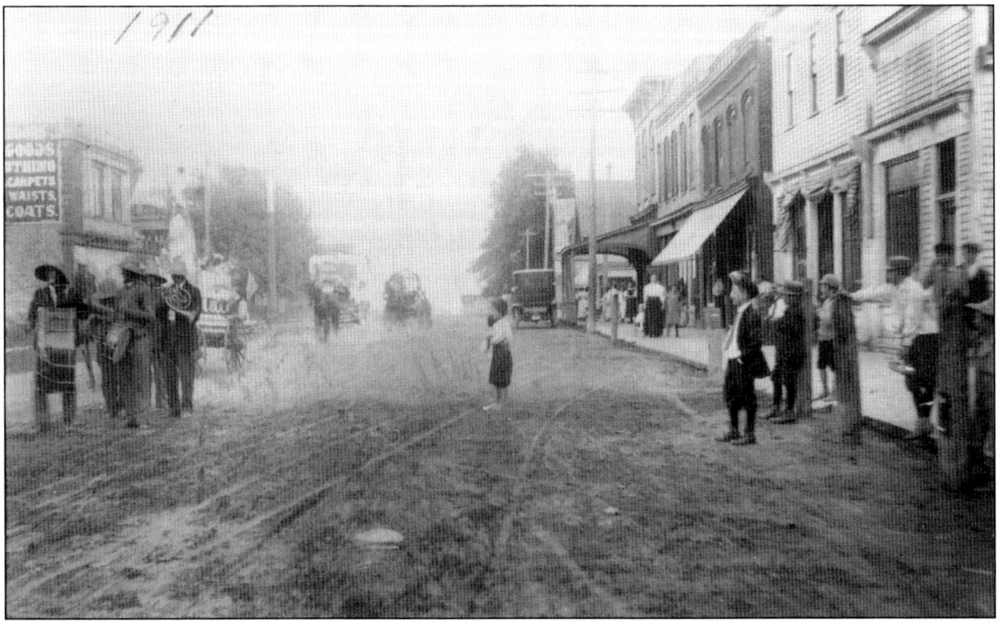

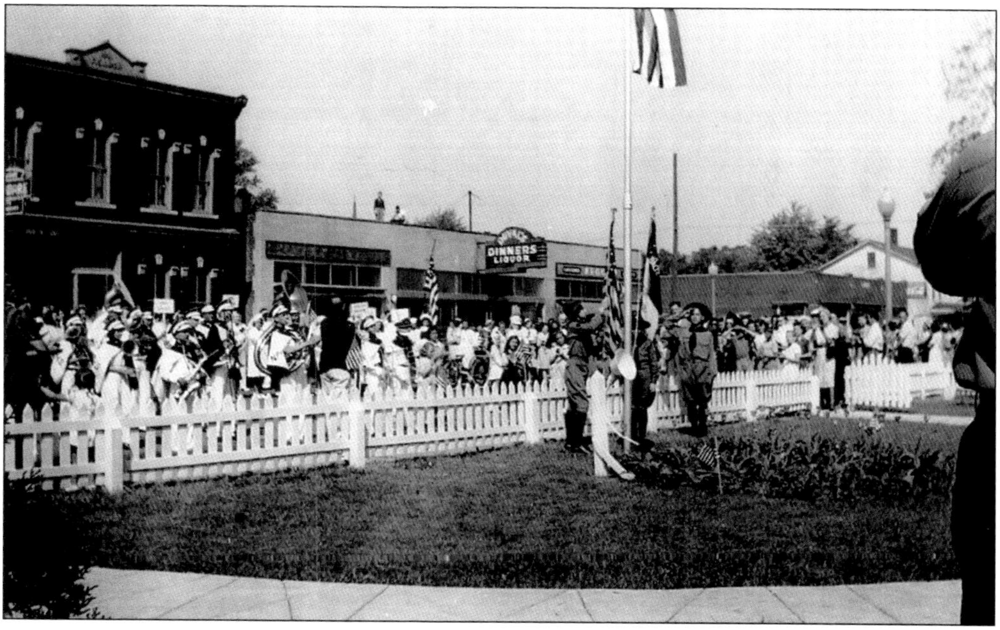

The earliest parades were routed down Washington Street, while Green Street was used more often in later years. In 1955, the Davy Crockett Fourth of July Festival was held. The next year, the festival was named Bay-Rama by Anchorville resident Chet Green. After a brief hiatus, it was reestablished in 1965 and called Bay-O-Rama the first year, and then just Bay-Rama after that. In later years, it became the Bay-Rama Fish Fly Fest because of the swarms of fish flies that usually inhabited the downtown area during the Bay-Rama festival.

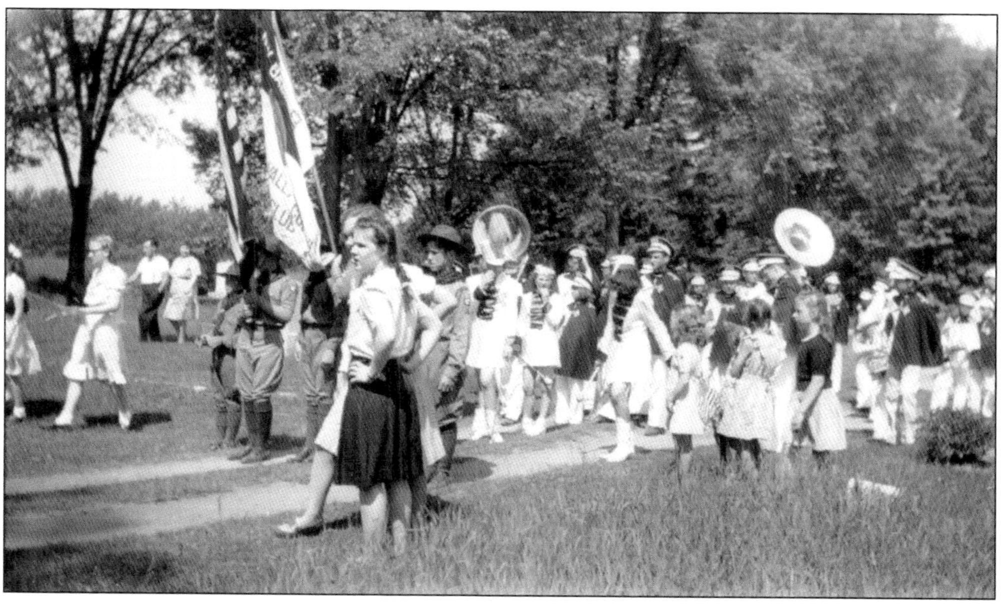

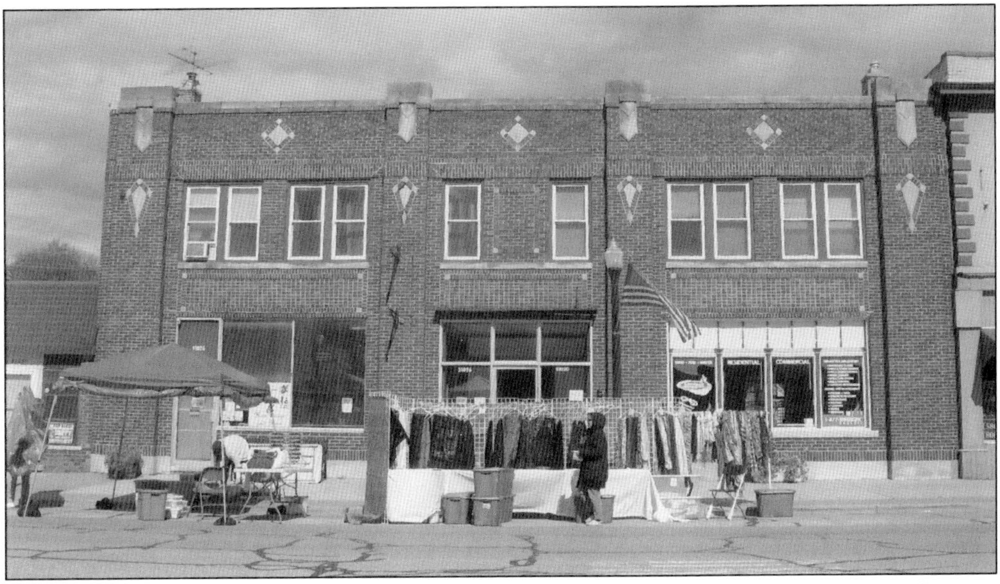

Two of the chief supporters of the festival were Oscar and Mary Socia of Citizens State Savings Bank, which started in 1922 on Washington Street. The bank opened four years after the closing of a previous New Baltimore bank, the W.F. Sandell Bank. The Sandell Bank was located in the building next to the Schlosser Building, which was once Art & Mary's Grocery and is presently the Wine Shoppe. H. John McGill and B.V. Nunneley were the Citizens State Savings Bank's first two presidents. Joseph Suess was the third, serving until 1942, when William E. Bowers took over. The bank, first located on Washington Street near Green Street, moved to the majestic brick building above, across from the Baker Building. The local Detroit Edison shared the building with the bank. A thick bank vault is still located in the basement of this building. The bank was one of the main sponsors of the Goodfellows, pictured below.

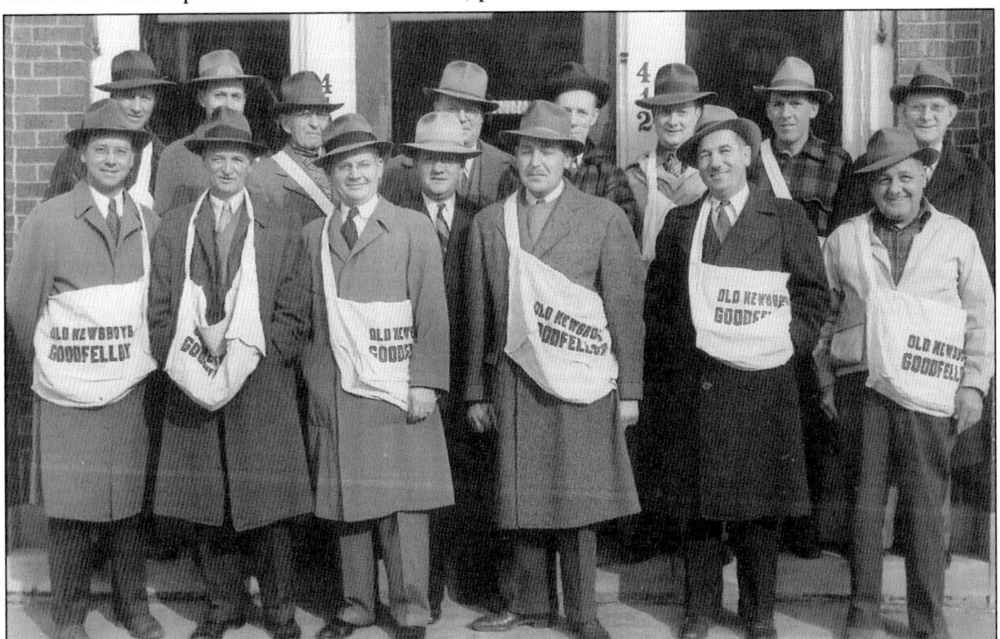

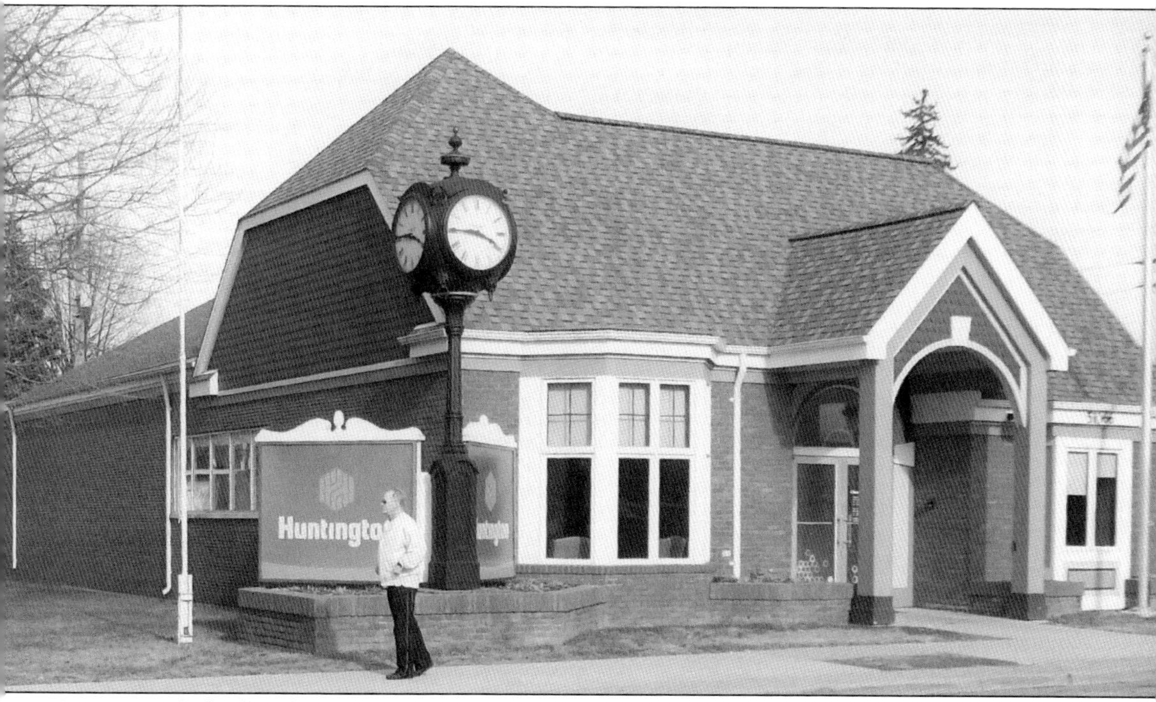

Louis Pingel, the founder of the Citizens State Savings Bank, became its president in 1947. Pingel was a longtime community benefactor and helped establish the town library. When he died unexpectedly in 1955 at the age of 66, Joseph Habarth succeeded him, serving until 1966. In 1957, during Habarth's tenure, a new, state-of-the-art bank building, costing $41,637, was constructed a few doors away from its old location on Washington Street. Following Habarth in 1966, Thomas Stapleton, Mary Socia's father, took over until his death in 1976. Then Oscar Socia, Mary's husband, succeeded Stapleton as president. In 1994, following Socia's stint as president, Oscar and Mary's son Paul Socia became the bank president, serving until the bank closed during the recession year of 2009. Mary Socia started working at the bank in 1945 at the age of 16 as a teller and worked at many other positions for more than 50 years, taking just a brief time off to raise the couple's children, Michelle, Mark, and Paul. (Courtesy of Lynn Lyon.)

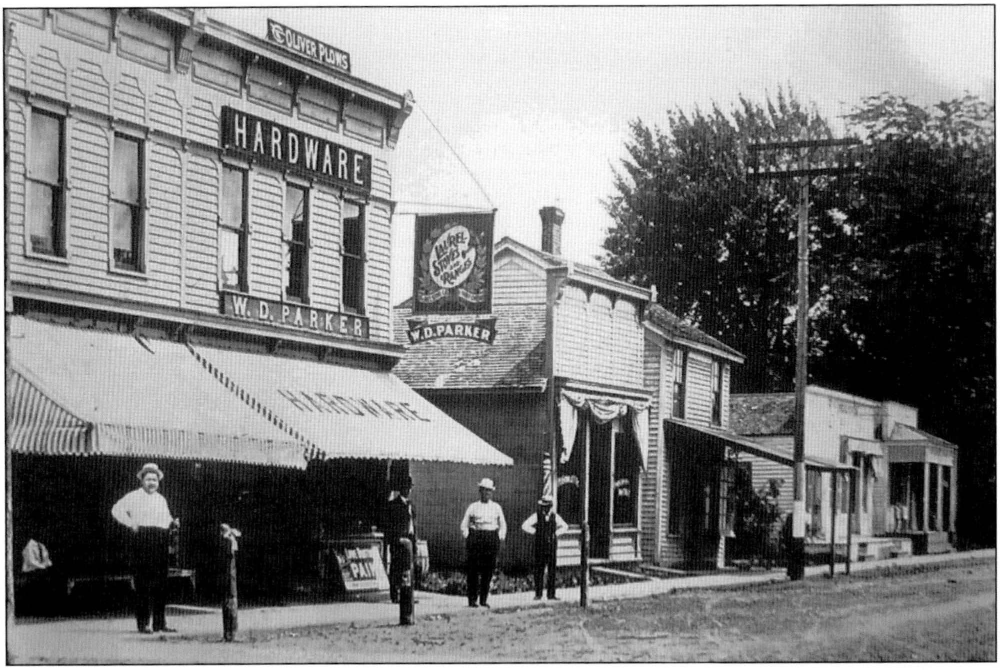

The hardware store of W.D. Parker occupied the building at the corner of Washington and Green Streets around 1930. After it was a hardware store, it was the Homestead Bar. Next door to Parker's was a barbershop. Two stores down was a building that originally housed a car repair shop. It was then used for city storage, and later became the town library. This building was still intact in 2013, and used as an office building. Across the street was a row of buildings that included Nick Socia and William Moore's barbershop, at 51055 Washington Street, a millinery business, and A.F. Reinecke Dry Goods.

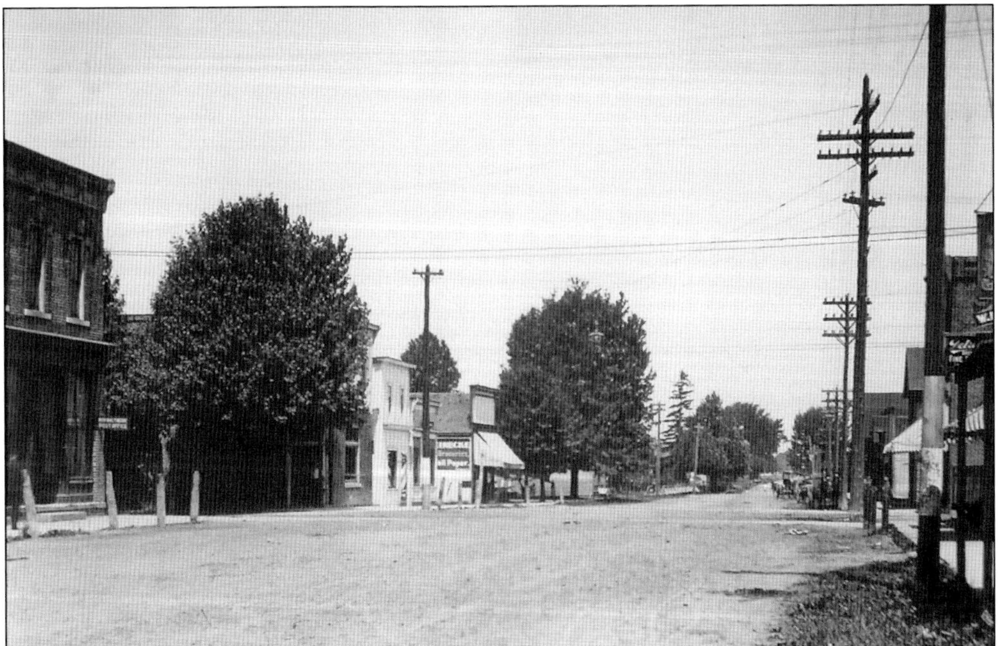

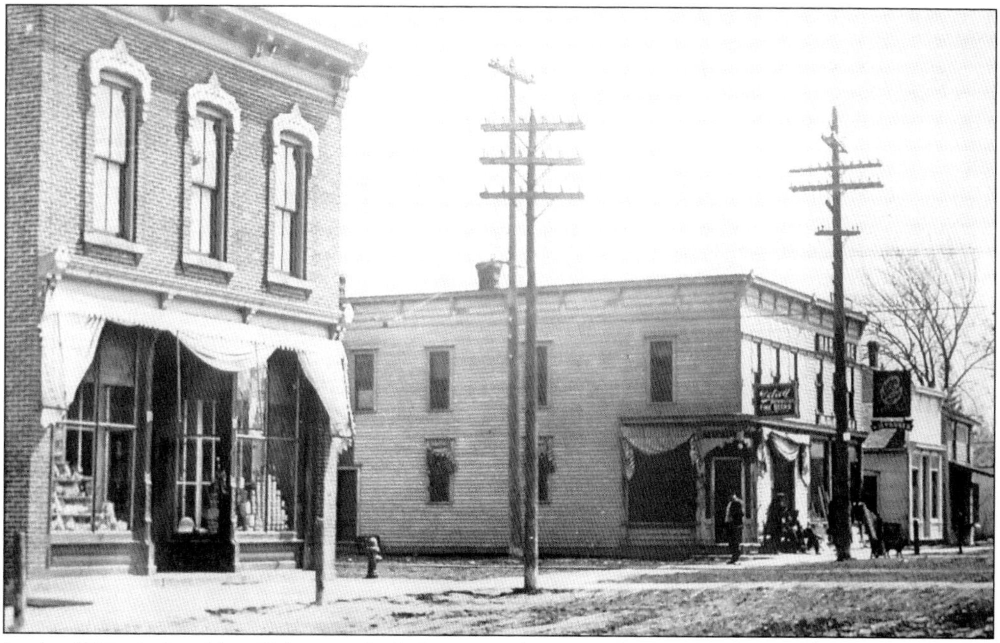

In the 1890s, before New Baltimore had electricity, kerosene lamps were put on the principal street corners of the city. Lamplighters were paid $12 per month to light them. A cart with a ladder attached was used to light the lamps. The first electric power in the city was provided by the DUR powerhouse. In 1900, the Michigan Electric Company provided electricity, and lights were erected in 1901, as well as a switch booth at Washington and Alfred Streets. In 1902, a lighting commission was formed and an electric plant was built. The downtown area had telephone poles supporting electrical wires suspended above the street.

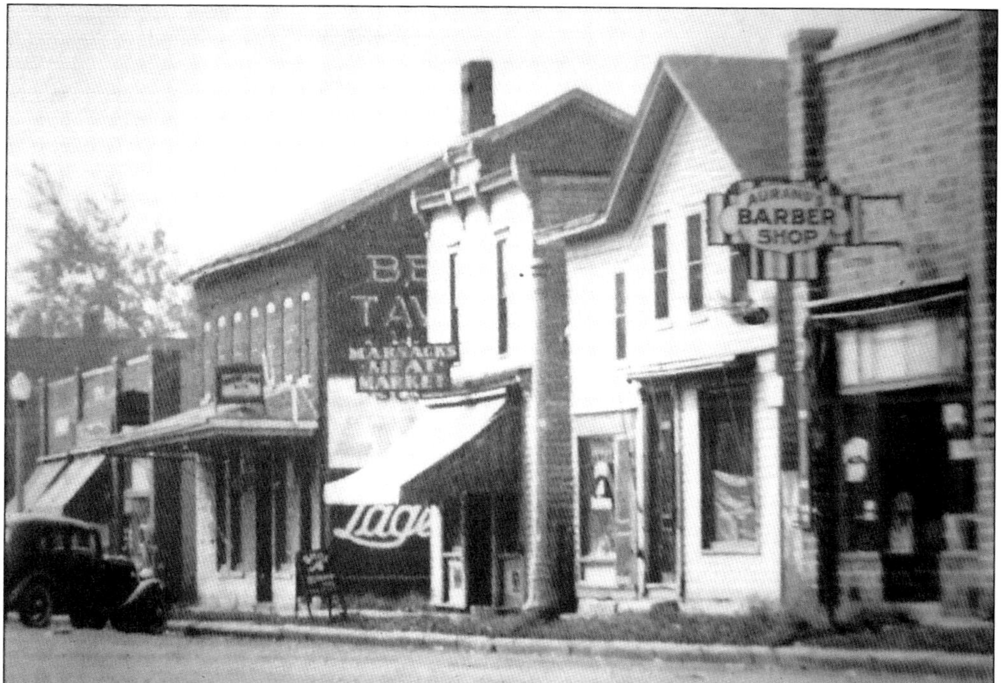

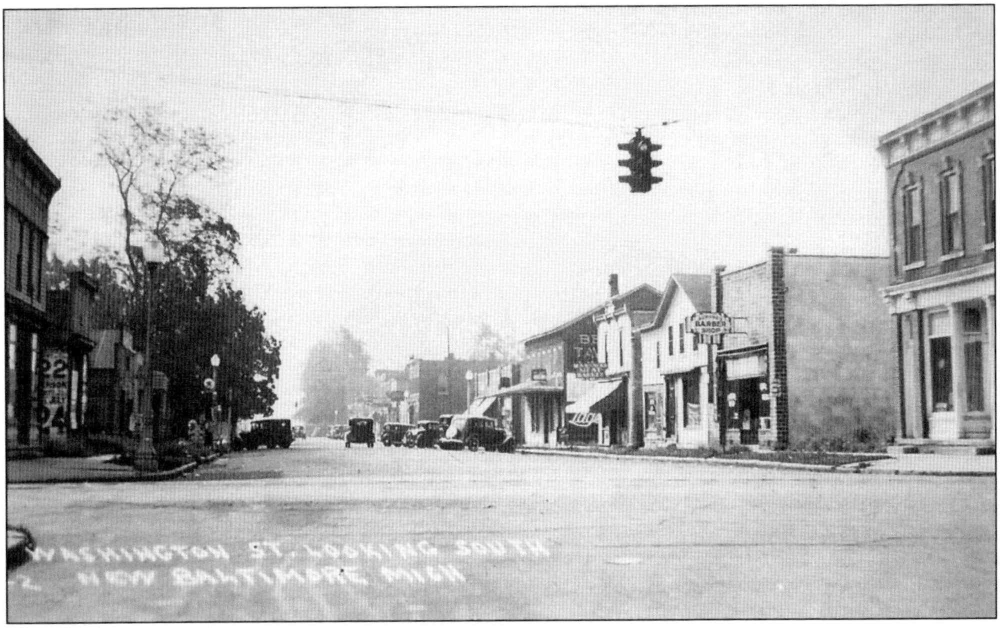

In the 1940s, electrical wires were no longer suspended in the air on telephone poles, and the streets were paved. The Grand Pacific House had by this time progressed from being a hotel to housing Maliskey's Hardware, which would last almost 30 years in the building. Next to it was Duvall's Restaurant and a Kroger grocery store. A few years later, this building was occupied by the Chapoton Clothing Store, and then by the Michael Brothers Men's Store.

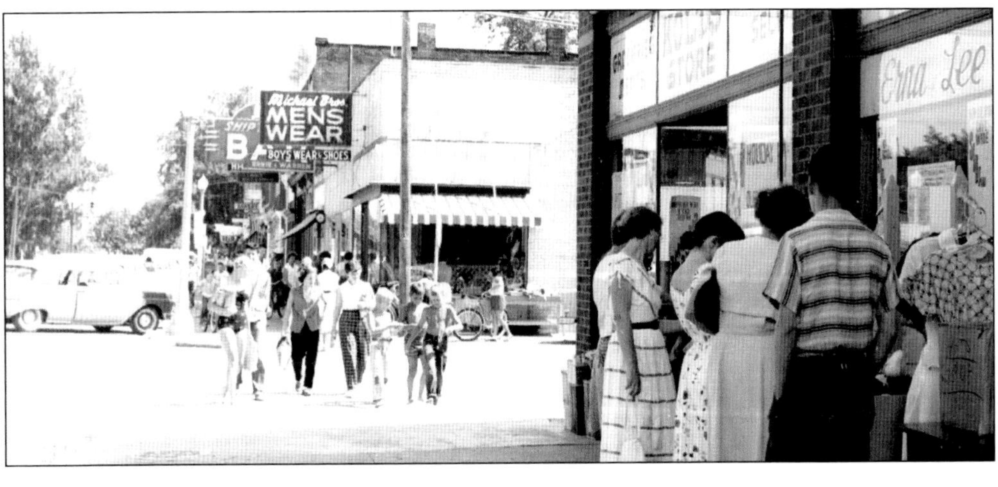

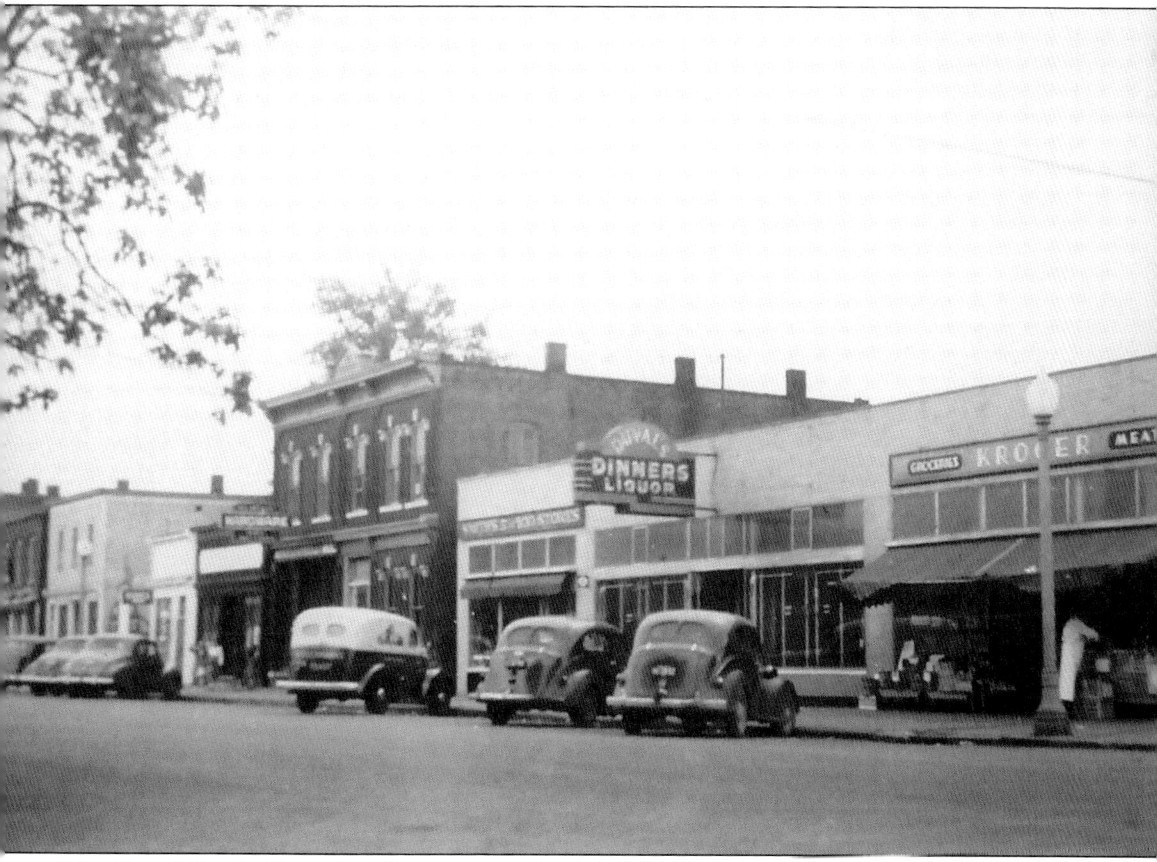

The Grand Pacific House building continued as a hardware store in the 1950s. The buildings near it included restaurants and a laundromat. Today, this same block is once again home to restaurants. For over a decade, Mike's Comics, a comic book and gaming store, has thrived in what was once a dime store.

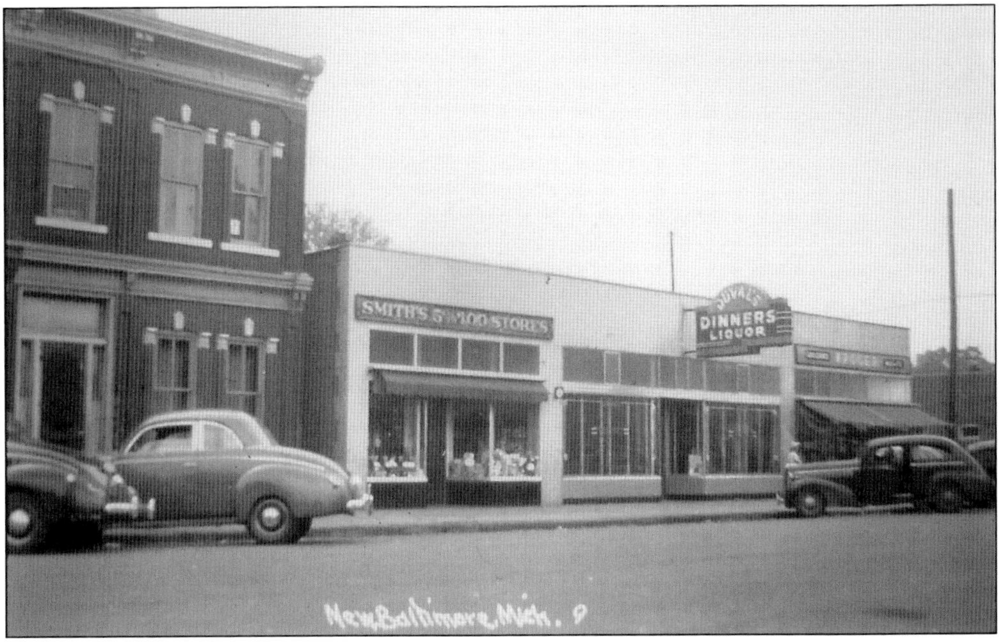

The view above, of Washington Street in the 1960s, shows changes. Kroger's was in the same building that Michael Brothers Men's Store would occupy. Looking east down Washington Street toward the bay in the early 1900s, one could view the DUR train heading down Green Street. The Detroit Brewing Company offices were on the corner, next to the hardware store. Looking farther down the street to Alfred Street, one could see the Fink Building, which now houses Red's Barber Shop. By the 1940s, the area of Washington and Alfred Streets was quite built up, and included Kolt's Market, at the corner next to Duval's Restaurant, and Maliskey's Hardware in the former Grand Pacific House.

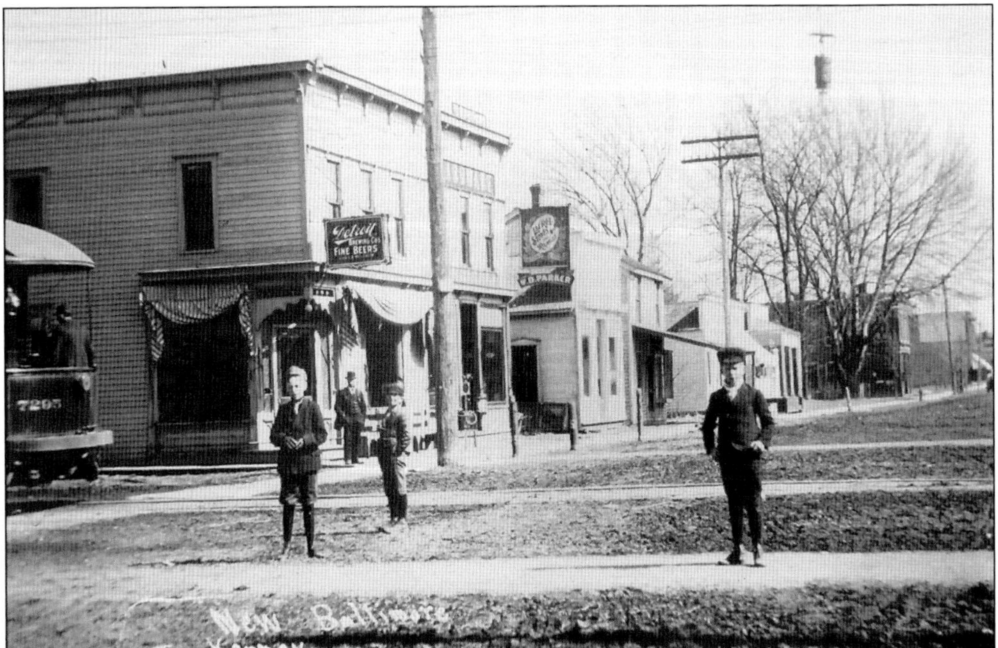

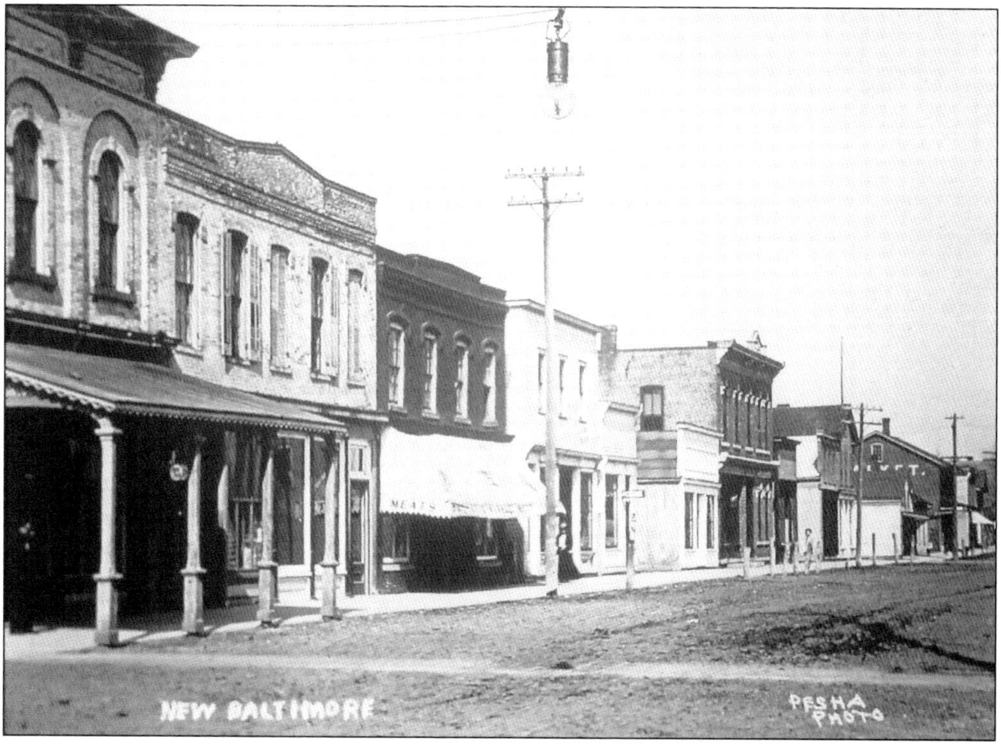

The above view of Washington Street shows a single street light, dirt roads, and hitching posts. Pictured below is the Heath building and the future Schoebel's next to the Koenig barber shop.

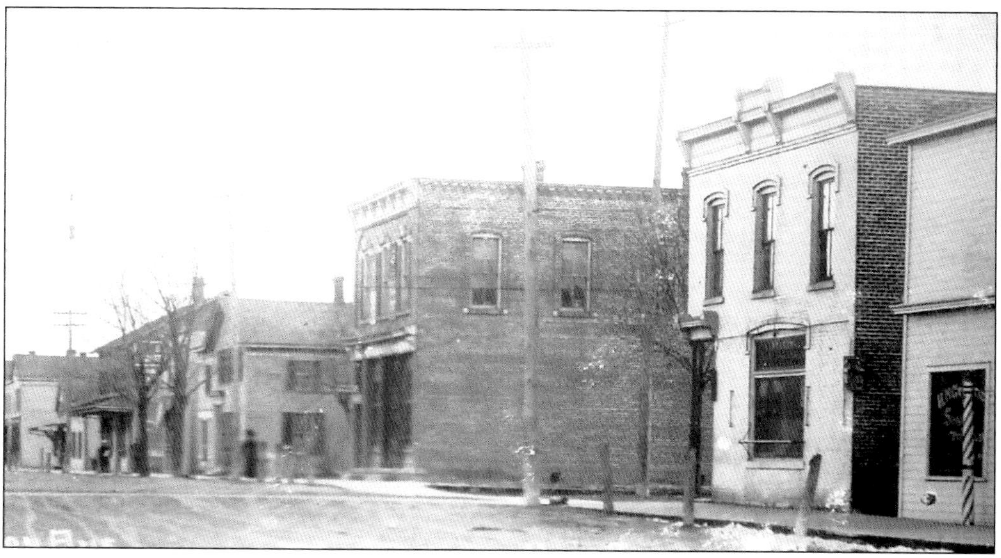

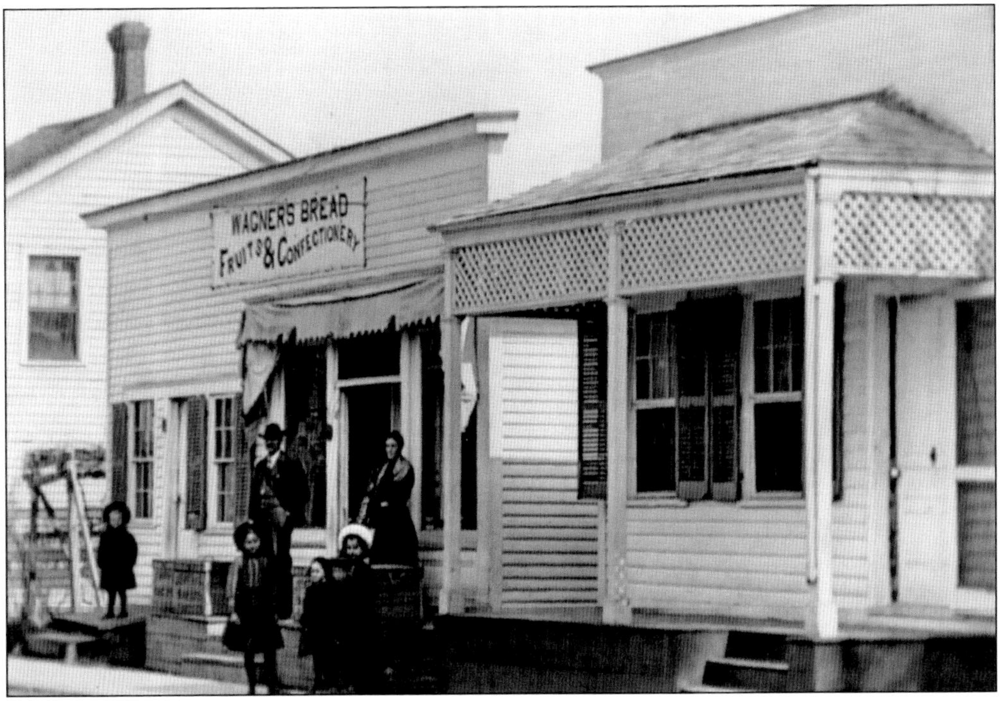

In the 1920s, Wagner Bread also sold fruits and confections. The company was next to the building that would later be a garage, a city storage area, and, finally, the first city library. The building at the corner of Washington and Green Streets was first a blacksmith shop, then a saloon, and then, from the 1940s to the 1980s, Schoebel's Drug Store.

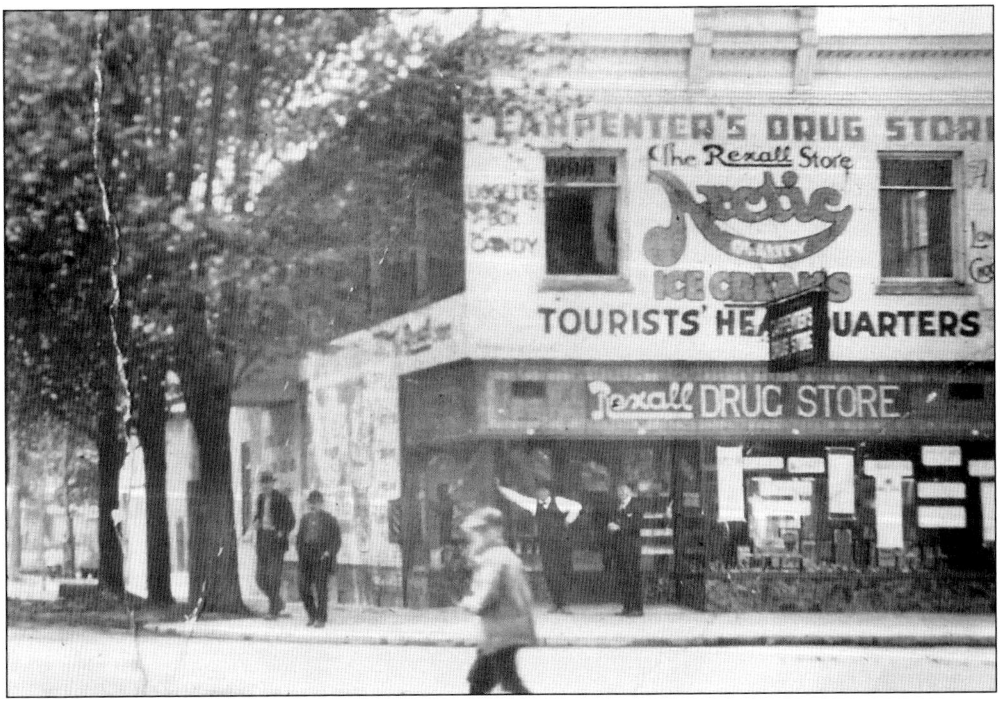

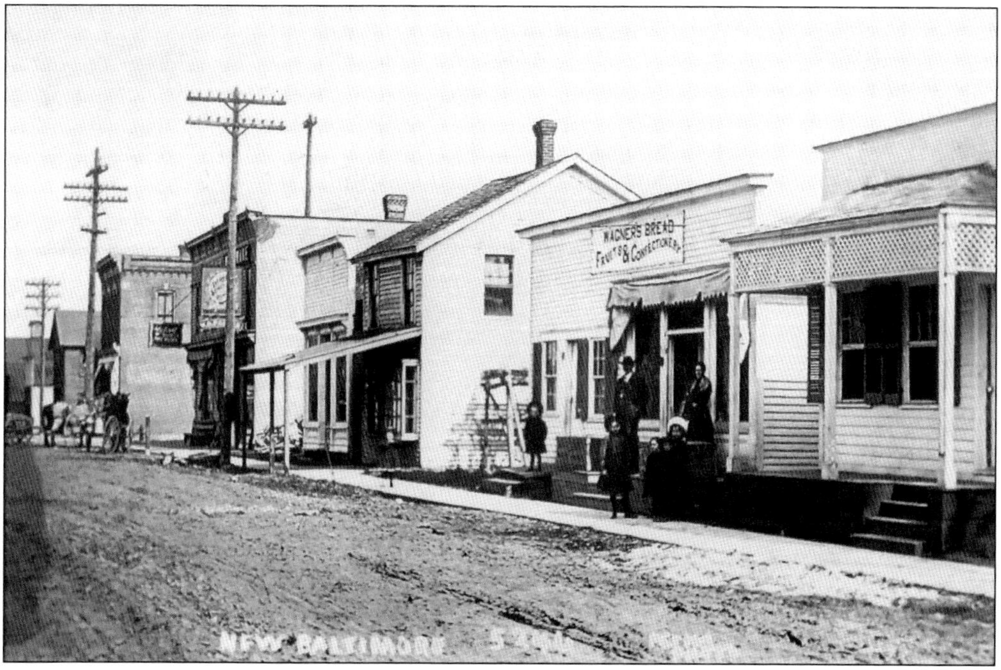

These two close looks at Washington Street in the early 1900s show both hitching posts and electrical poles. While avoiding the muddy streets by staying on the wooden sidewalks, one could get off the interurban train at the corner, do some shopping, and then return to Anchorville, Fair Haven, Pearl Beach, Algonac, Chesterfield, New Haven, or other surrounding towns.

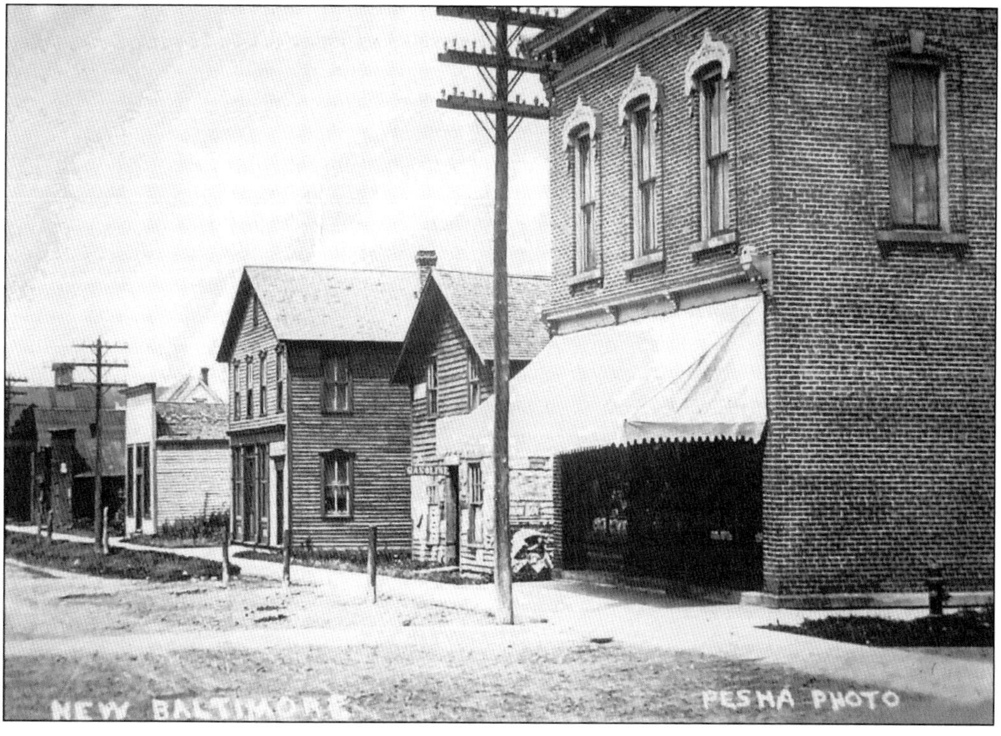

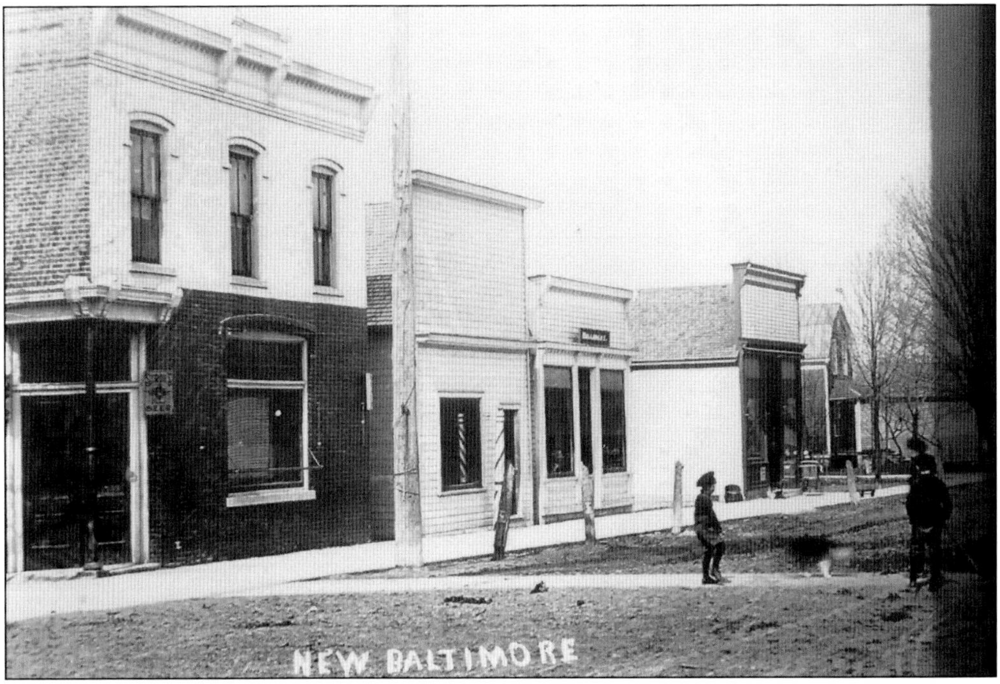

In the early days, a stagecoach ran back and forth from the New Haven depot to New Baltimore via the plank road that Alfred Ashley helped build.

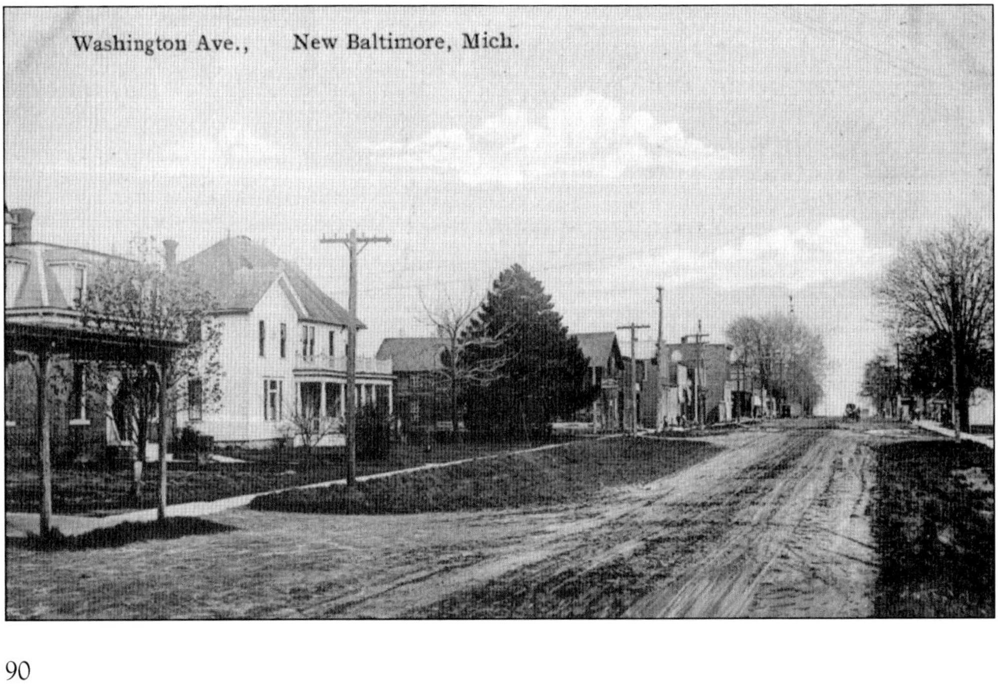

Six

PEOPLE OF NEW BALTIMORE

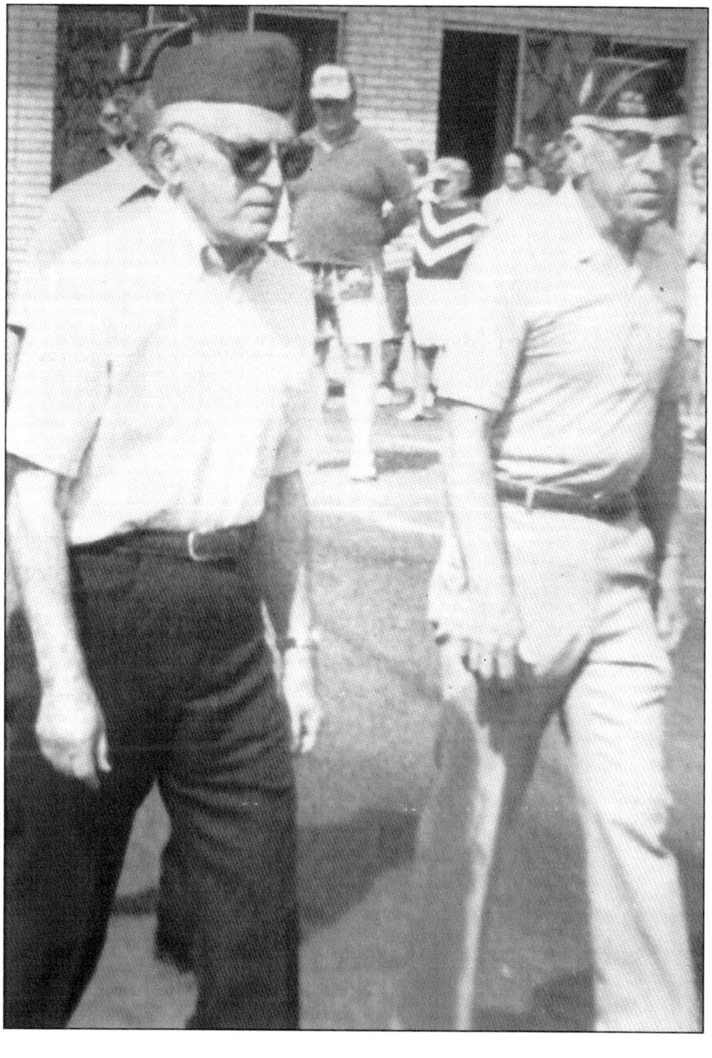

In 1956, Walt and Frank Michael, both World War II veterans, took over Chapoton Clothing Store, the men's clothing store started by their uncle Clarence Chapoton in 1946. They renamed it Michael Brothers Men's Store. The epitome of small-town trust and service, they allowed some customers to take clothes home for people who did not have time to make it to the store to try on before they bought them. Walt was a local celebrity, known for his support of the local high school athletic teams, the Anchor Bay High School Tars, his sportswriting for the *Anchor Bay Beacon*, and for never missing a high school basketball state tournament. He was appointed a city councilman because he and his wife, Norma, never missed a meeting.

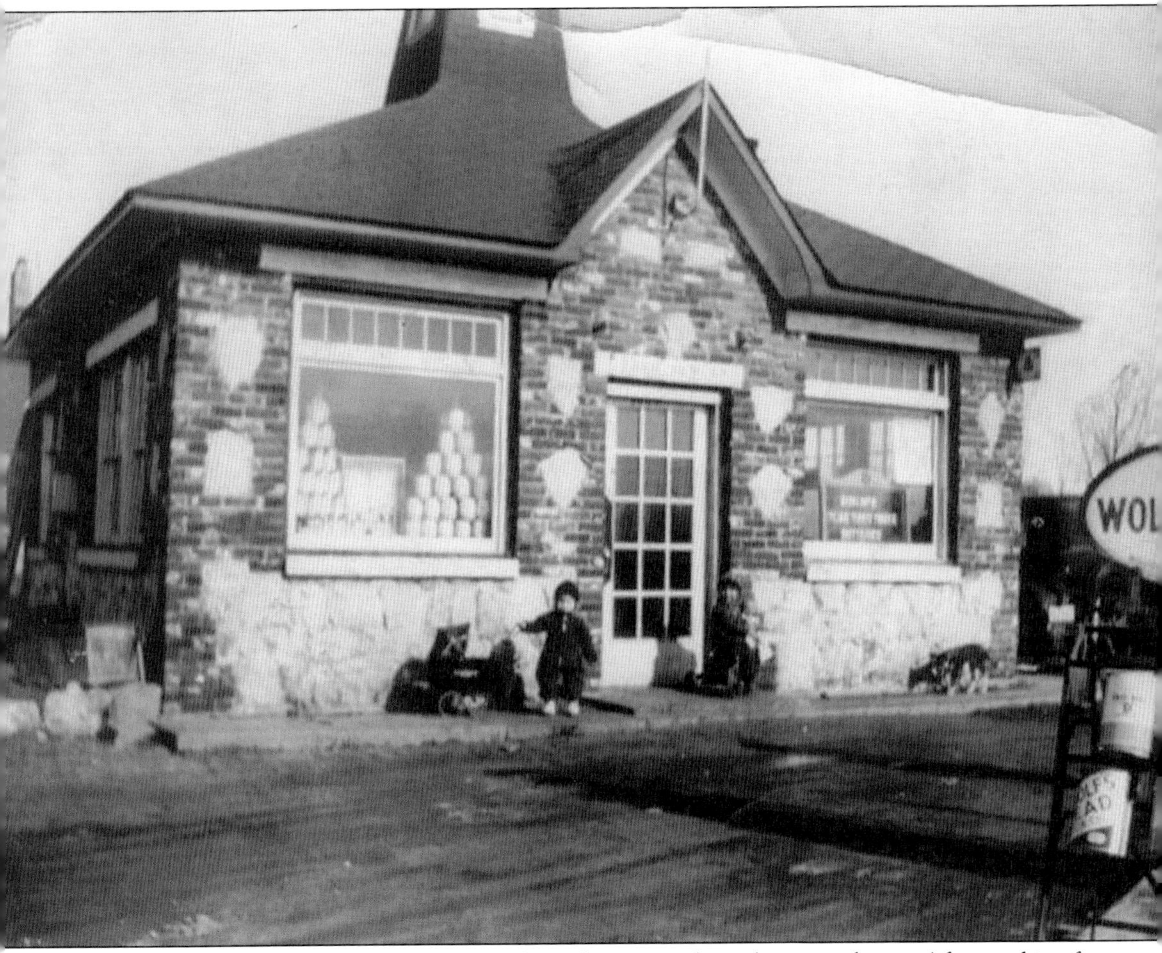

Born in 1902 in Bad Axe, Michigan, Fred Dunlap was orphaned at an early age. After working for US Rubber and doing a stint in the Army, Dunlap moved to New Baltimore at the age of 27. He opened his first gas station at the corner of County Line Road and Main Street, now the site of a trailer park. County Line Road was the border between Macomb County and St. Clair County, although this changed in 1931 when New Baltimore became a city and incorporated land that had been in St. Clair County. Dunlap opened a second gas station near the old Engelman Broom Factory and also operated the Wayside Restaurant in the same building.

Fred Dunlap met his future wife, Lucille, at the Engelman Broom Factory, where she was an employee. They got married in 1933 and had five children: Bette, Duane, Fred, Charles, and Nancy. About that time, Dunlap built a Standard gas station at County Line Road and Green Street, using a design he had seen at the 1933 Chicago World's Fair. Dunlap later built the family home on the corner of Green Street and County Line Road with bricks from the demolished Chesterfield Hotel. In 1954, Dunlap retired from private business and went to work for Anchor Bay Schools. He was a member of many of the city's civic organizations, including the Anchor Bay Sportsmen's Club and the UGOIGO Club, which he helped found.

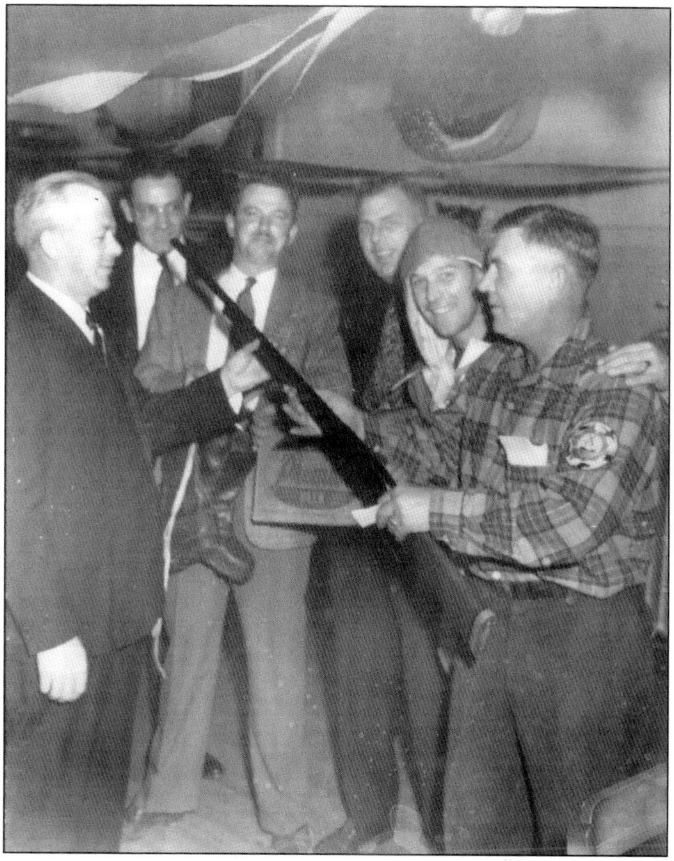

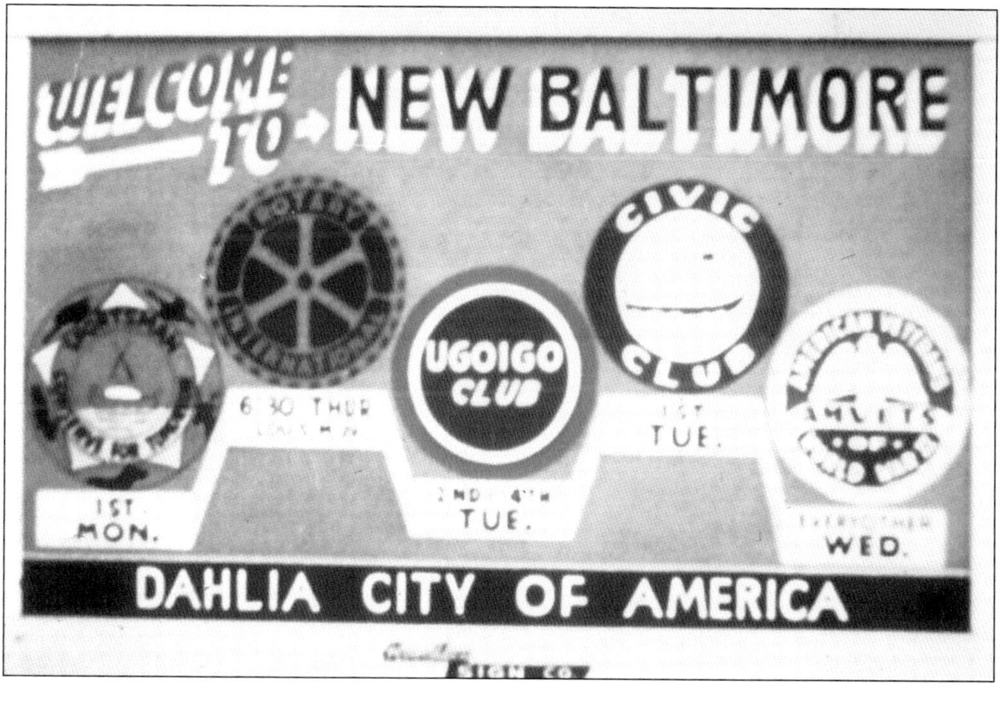

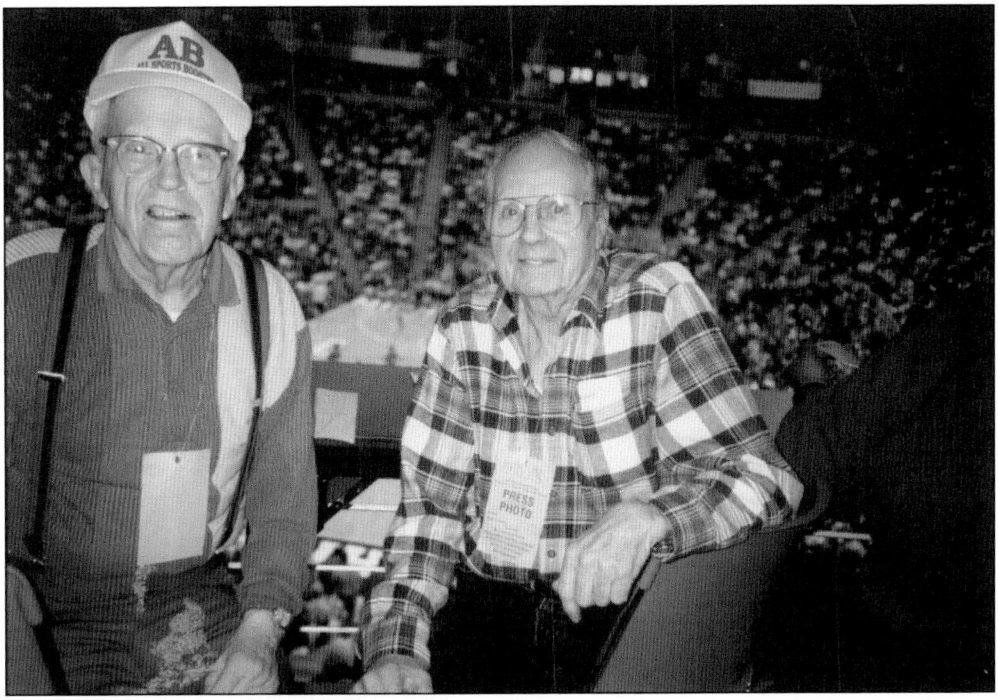

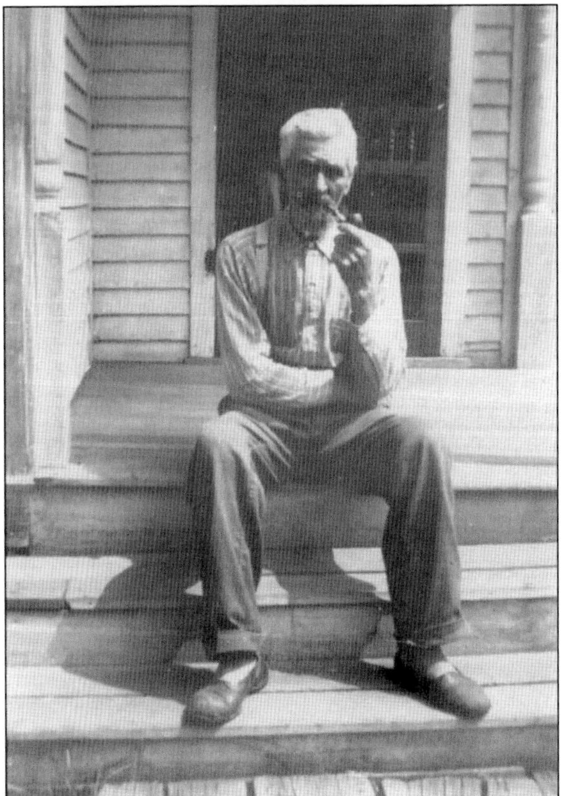

Above, Walter Michael and William Woehler hold the record for the most high school state championships attended in the state of Michigan. They viewed hundreds of games over more than 60 years. Both were active in many New Baltimore organizations. Patrick Dubay (left) was the oldest living World War I veteran from New Baltimore and was an early source of historical information.

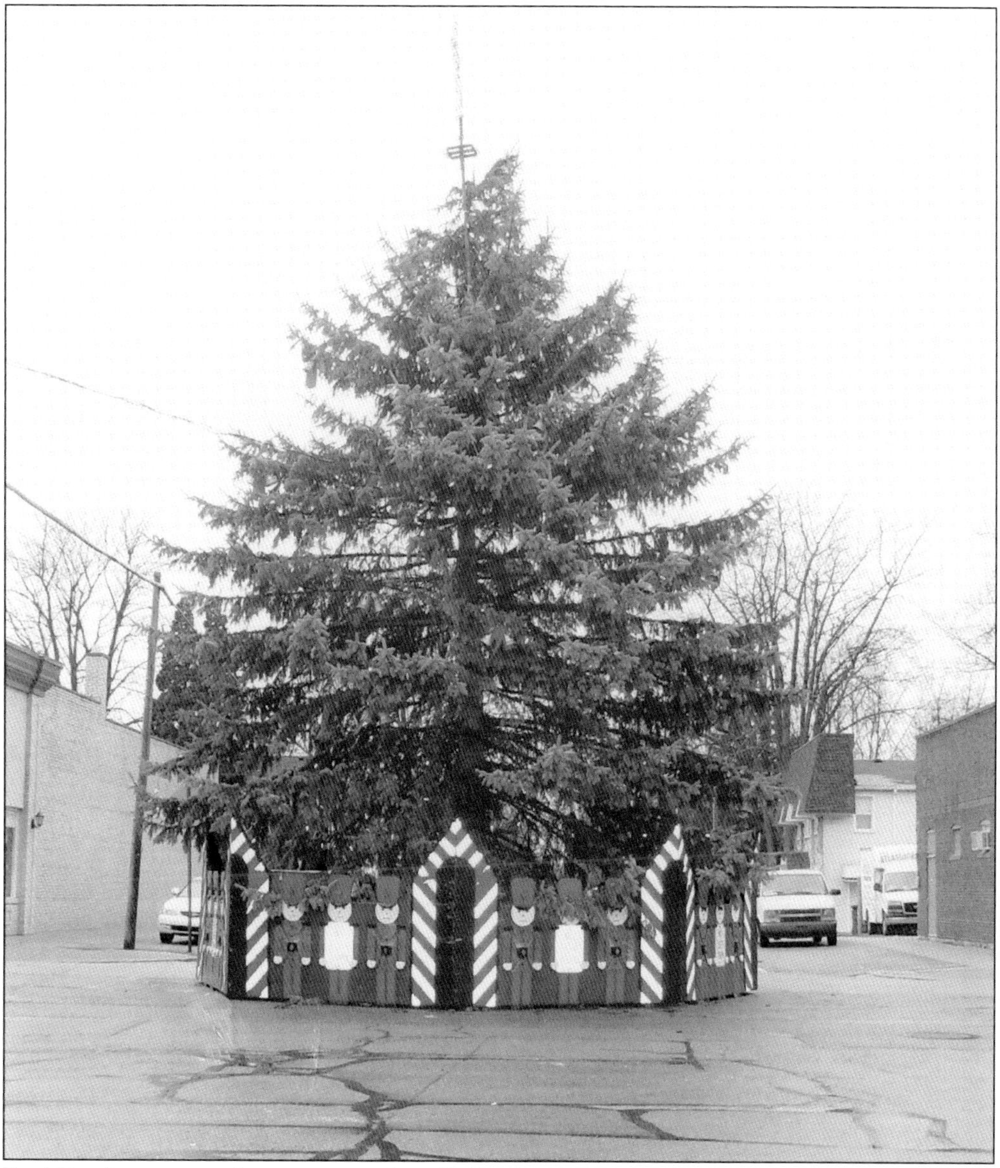

Fred Dunlap was on the city council in 1965 when a city proclamation was issued to erect a Christmas tree in the center of town. This unique town precedent has caused a lot of attention. The only incident involving the tree was when heavy winds blew it over one year. The tree is anchored in a manhole in the center of the intersection of Washington and Alfred Streets.

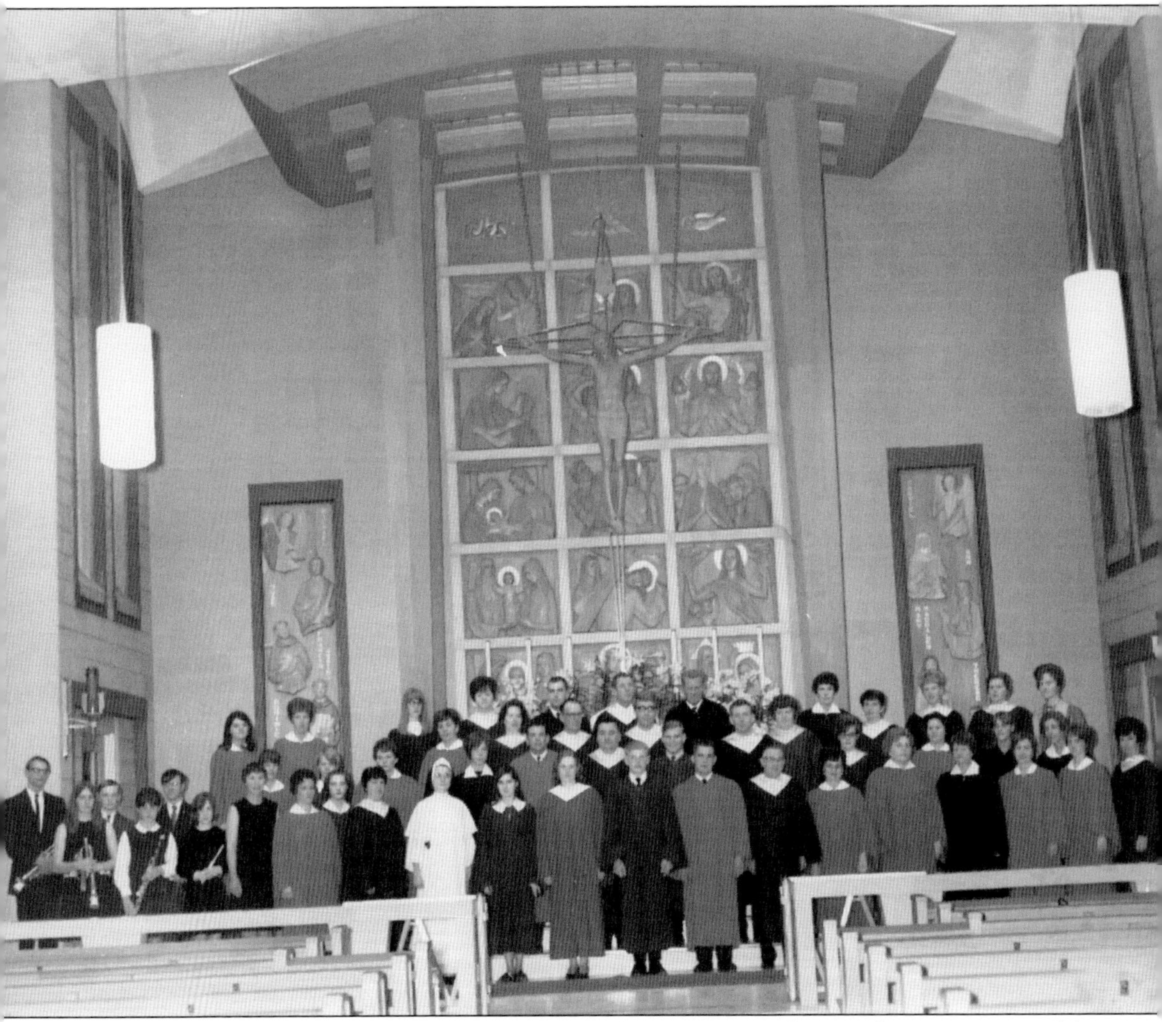

The lighting of the tree is a city ceremony at the beginning of December, accompanied by townsfolk singing Christmas carols. Often, they are joined by the Interfaith Choir, which was organized by Fred Dunlap's daughter Bette Carrothers around 1966. The choir was organized from multiple local church choirs to enable the performance of musical pieces requiring large ensembles, such as Handel's "Messiah." They have performed at countless civic events and venues in the years since. At times, they have had as many as 80 members, and they have sung with the International Symphony in Port Huron, the Michigan Opera Theater, and on WDIV Channel 4 and WJR radio in Detroit.

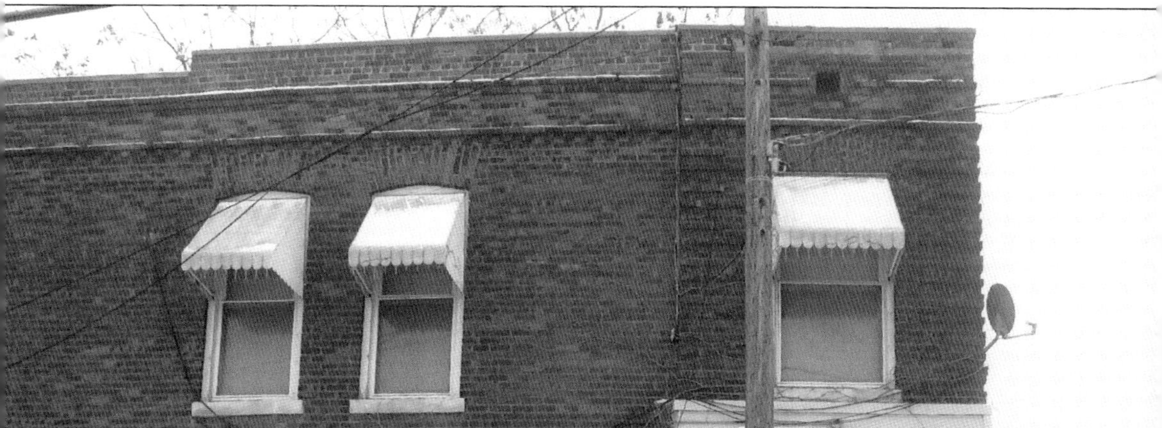

Red Aurand began one of New Baltimore's long-standing businesses, Red's Barber Shop. The barbershop, still at the corner of Alfred and Washington Streets, is now headed by Red's grandson Tim. It has been in the Fink Building for over 50 years. The corner has long been a home to barbershops. The Fink Building replaced a building that burned down in 1899 that housed Chase's Barbershop. One of New Baltimore's few fire fatalities was a barber who died in the fire. John Fink, a tailor who made men's clothes, also occupied the building, as did many businesses in the space next to the barbershop. Fink was also the city treasurer and postmaster, and ran the post office from this building.

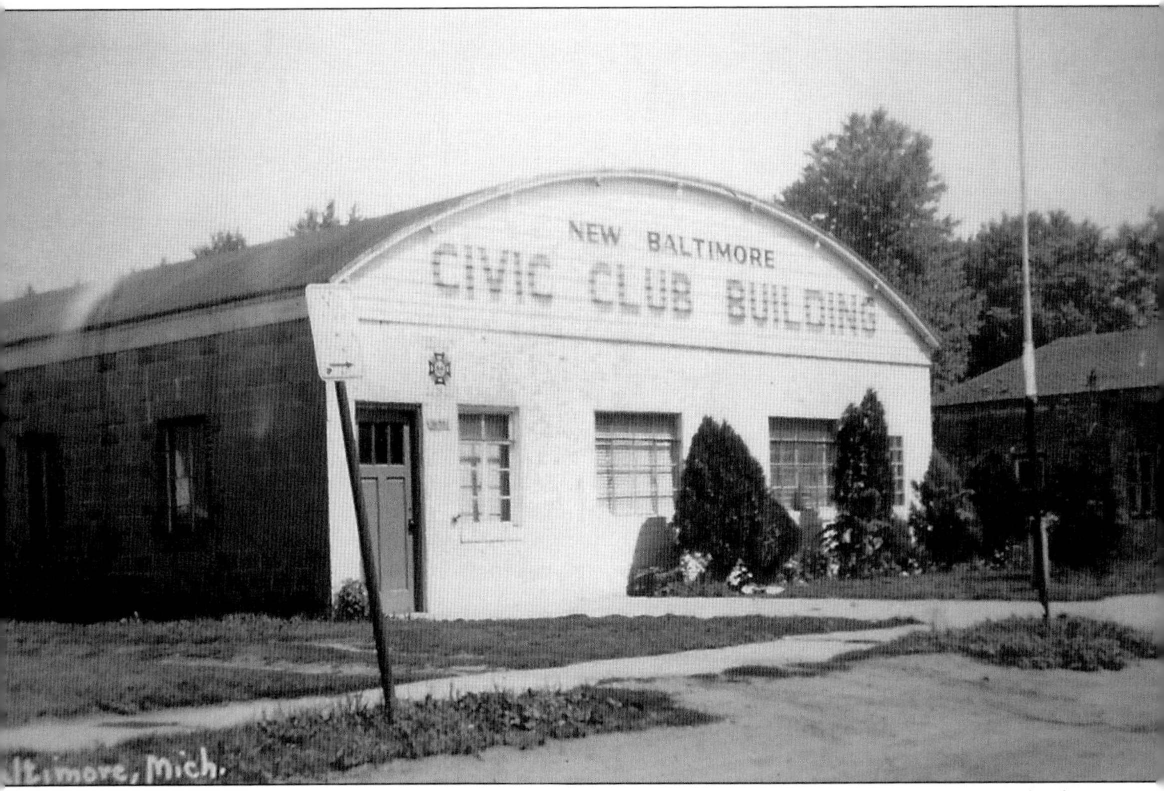

The Exchange Club, an early New Baltimore civic group, was established in 1926. By the late 1930s, it had evolved into the Civic Club, and it has long been one of the premier civic groups in the city. Just a few of its activities over the years have been co-sponsoring Bay-Rama events, Little League, Boy Scouts, scholarships for local students, and also the town Christmas tree. The club moved into its building at 36551 Main Street on September 2, 1950. The building had previously been owned by the V.L. Graff Company, which occupied the building as the St. Clair Manufacturing Company.

Seven

Schools and Libraries

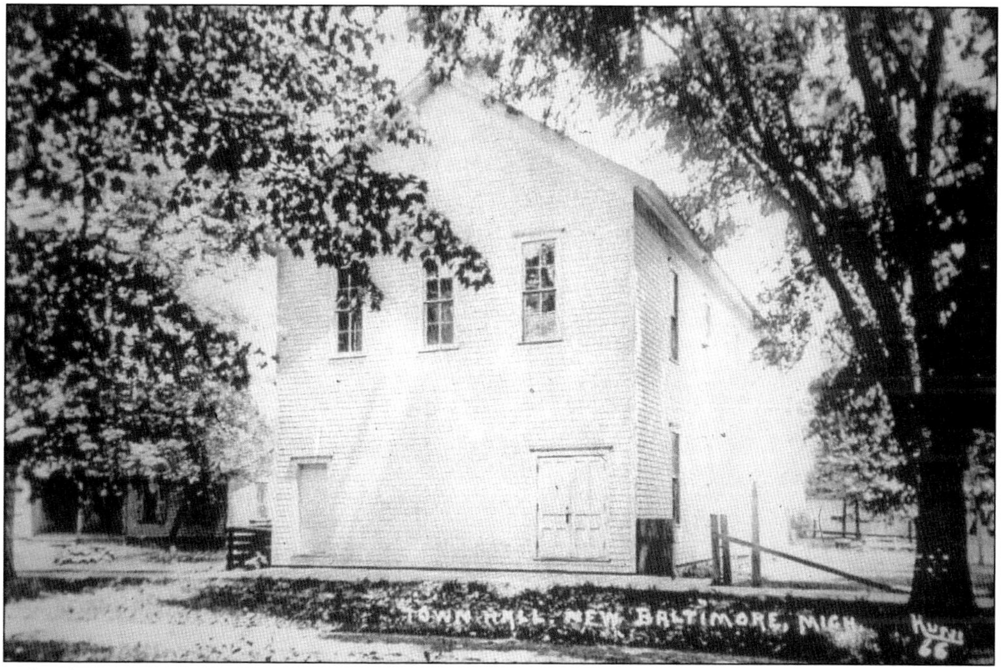

Schools in New Baltimore included the Chapel school (Chesterfield Fractional District No. 2), at 51204 Washington Street near Green Street, and the Old Town Hall school (Chesterfield Fractional District No. 3), at Maria and Alfred Streets. Another nearby school was the Salt River school (Chesterfield Fractional District No. 4), on 23 Mile Road by the Salt River. Other schools in Chesterfield Township included the Weller school (Chesterfield Fractional District No. 1); the Green school (Chesterfield Fractional District No. 6), on Sugarbush Road; the Burdon school, also called the Log Cabin school (Chesterfield Fractional District No. 5), at 25 Mile Road and Burdon Street; and the Brooks school (Chesterfield Fractional District No. 7), at 36795 Marine City Highway. Pictured is the Old Town Hall school.

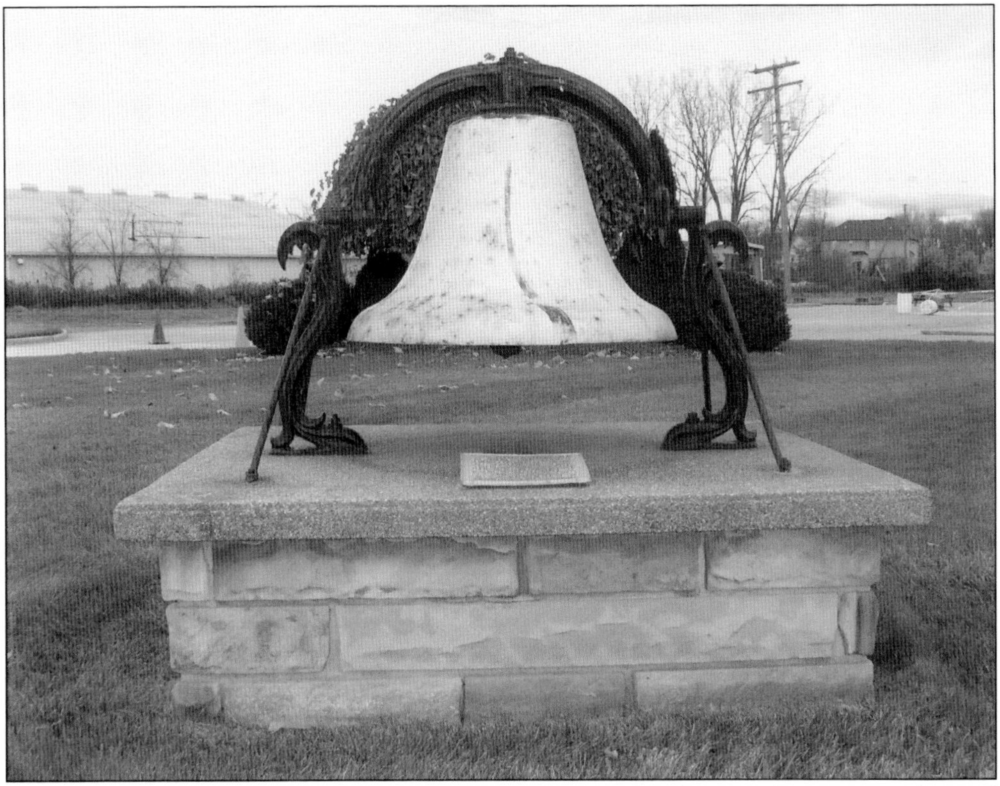

The old town hall, besides being used to teach the upper grades of New Baltimore, was also used for town meetings and to store firefighting equipment. After it was torn down, the bell was saved and placed in front of the VFW building. The 500-pound bell had been purchased in August 1890 for $33 and was used to sound fire alarms. It also rang at 12:00 p.m. and 6:00 p.m. every day, a practice that was curtailed after too many complaints from tired volunteer firefighters, who would hear the bell and immediately take off for an imagined fire.

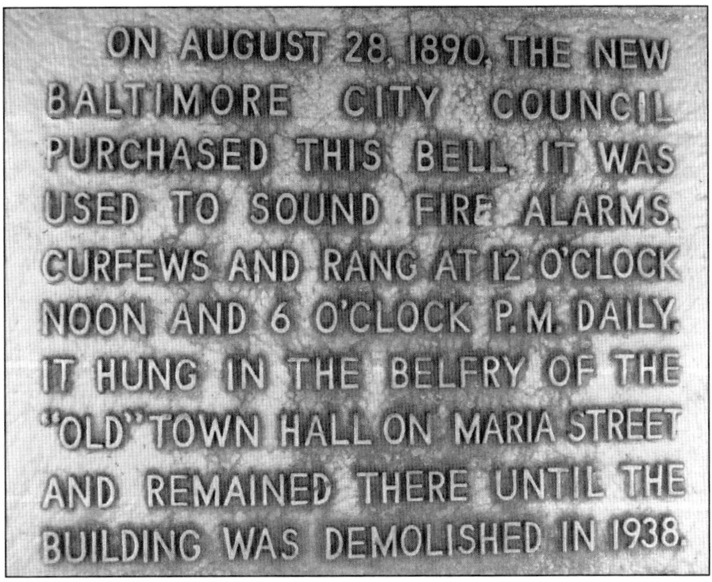

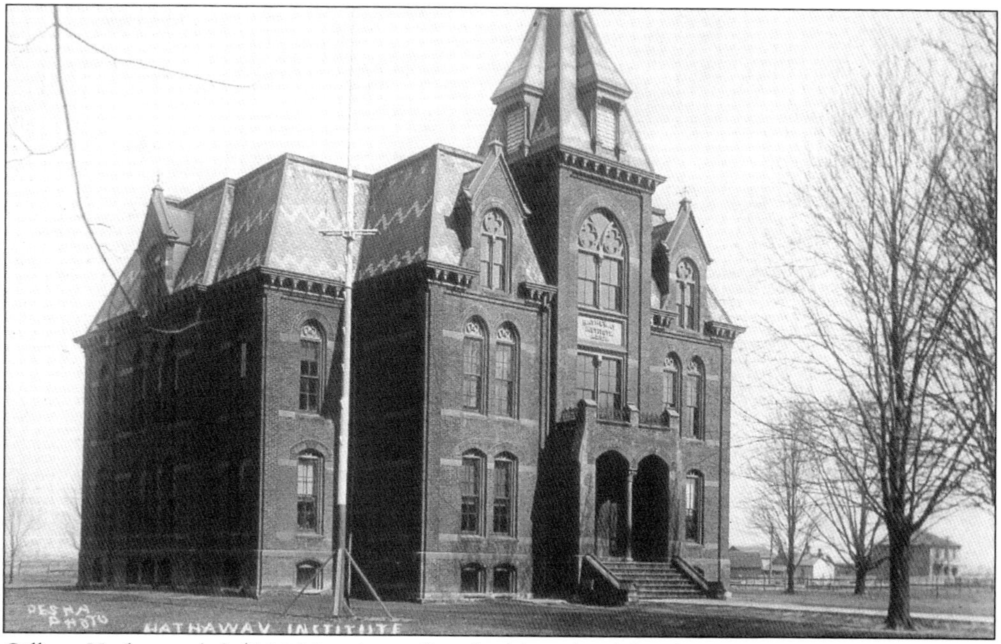

Gilbert Hatheway left $15,000 in his will to build a school for the New Baltimore community. His son James, an attorney, challenged the will all the way up to the Michigan Supreme Court, where he lost two years later. In the interim, the money had grown to about $22,000, and was all used to construct a new school in 1875 and 1876. Before the new school was built, high school students had to go to Mt. Clemens. The Hatheway Institute, as it was known, had grades 9 through 12 and also facilities to train teachers. Basketball games and other town sporting events were held in the gymnasium on the third floor. The gym was notorious for having support poles in the middle of the floor, causing players to have to dribble around the obstructions during games. On the bright side, it put Anchor Bay at a distinct advantage over visiting teams who were not used to the obstacles.

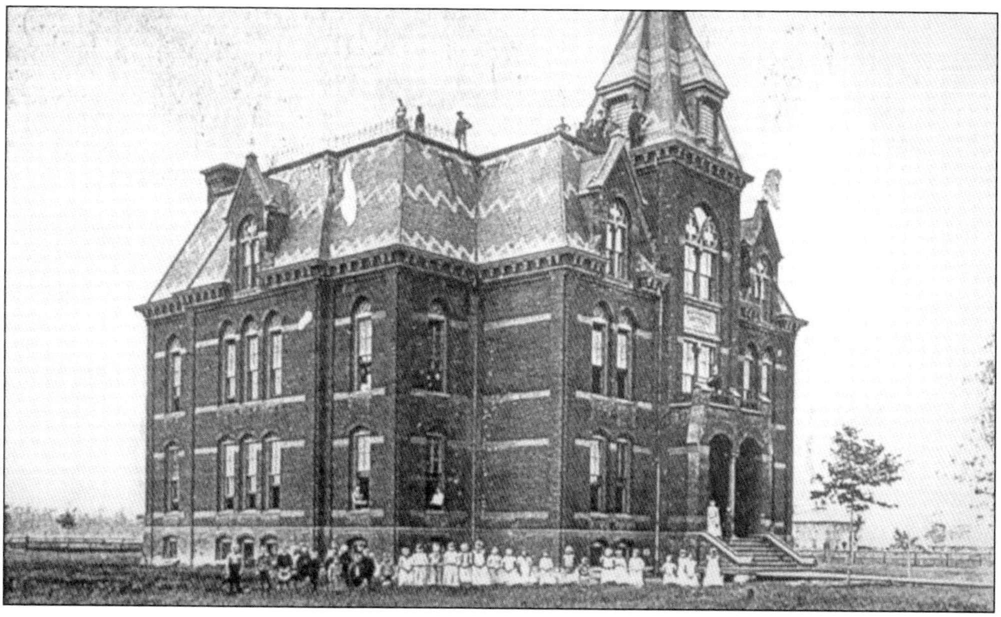

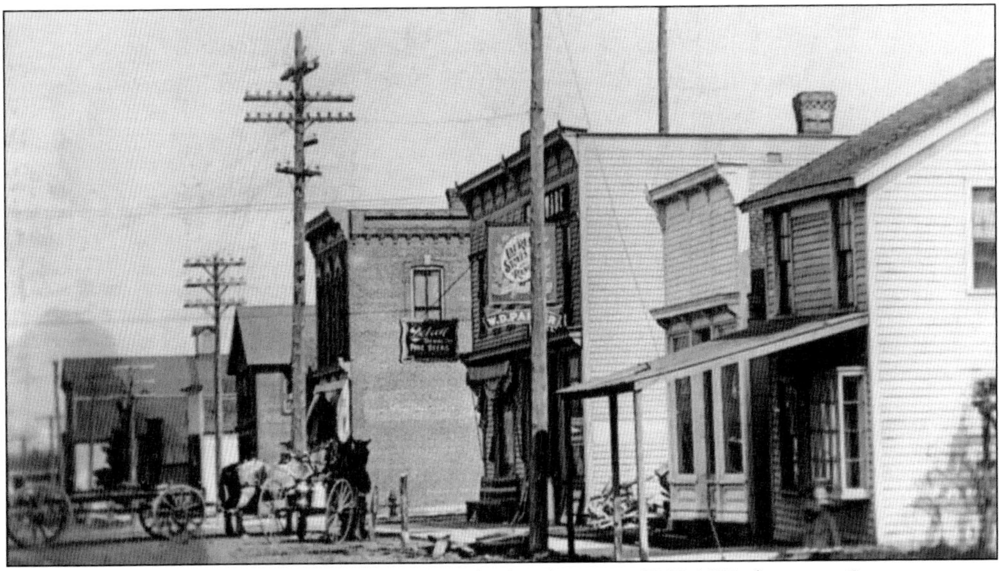

The Chapel Building, which held the Chapel school, was at 51204 Washington Street, next to the granary and not far from the hardware store. The school covered the lower grades while the Old Town Hall school covered the upper grades. This building was later moved to the rear of the nearby Marsack's Meat Market and used as an icehouse. In 1948, the Anchor Bay School District was formed through a coalition of the various one-room schoolhouses and organized under the Rural Agricultural Act. In 1949, a bond issue was passed that was used to build a new high school. This school, built on Washington Street by Will Lee Boulevard, was in the vicinity of the Anchor Bay Airpark, a small airport on Ashley Street north of Crappeau Creek. By 1956, all of the schools were under the umbrella of the Anchor Bay School District.

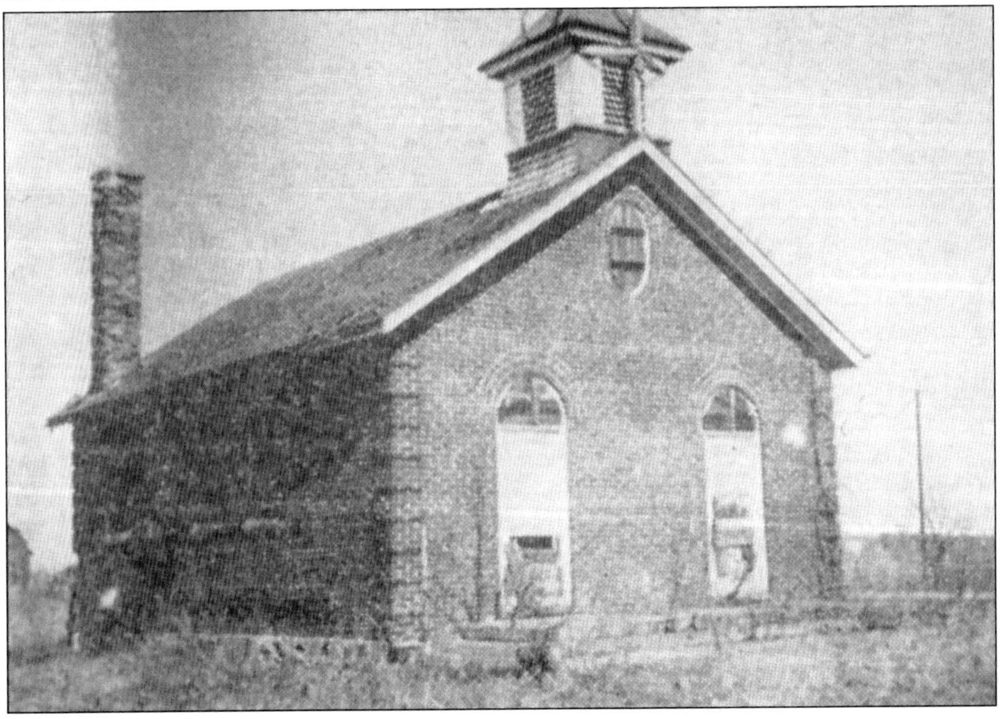

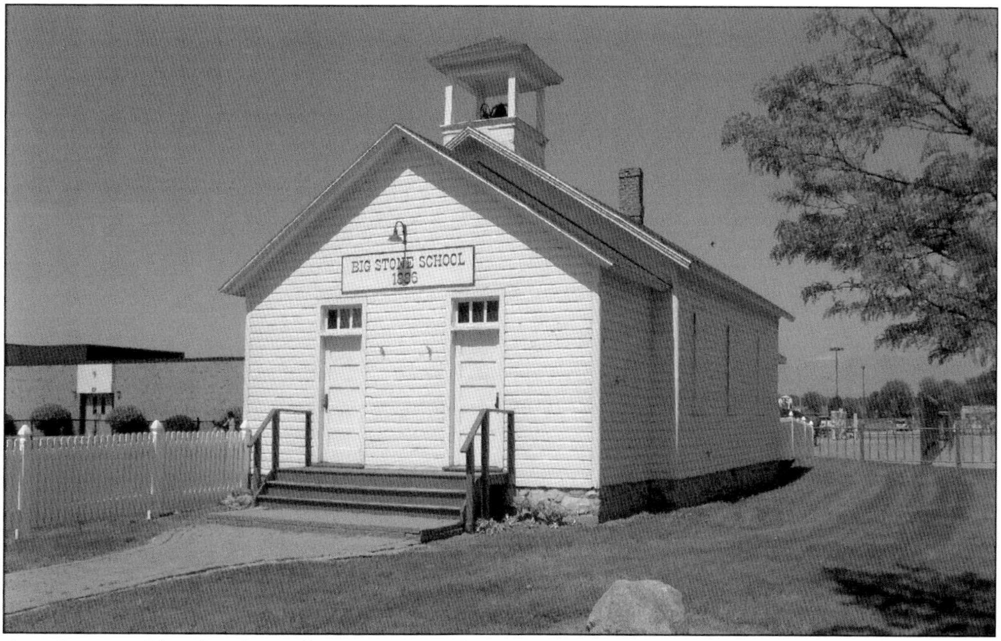

Another notable school was the Big Stone school (above), on Frost Road near 27 Mile Road. This school was once used for storage behind what is now Lighthouse Elementary. It was moved to the front of Washington Street at Will Lee Boulevard. The first libraries in the New Baltimore area were contained within the one-room schoolhouses of the era. Books were required to be purchased from a list prepared by the state librarian and the superintendent of public instruction. Schools could also apply to the state librarian for a bookcase of 50 books, which could be borrowed for six months, at which time it would be returned or exchanged for another bookcase with 50 different books. The participating schools only had to pay for shipping. The repurposed town garage, converted to the town library, is pictured below.

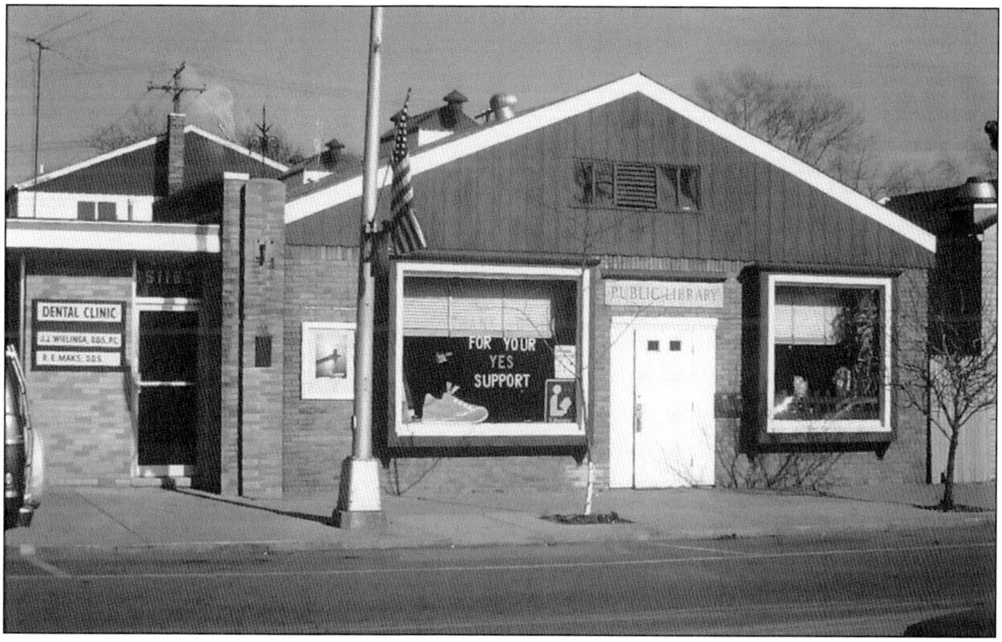

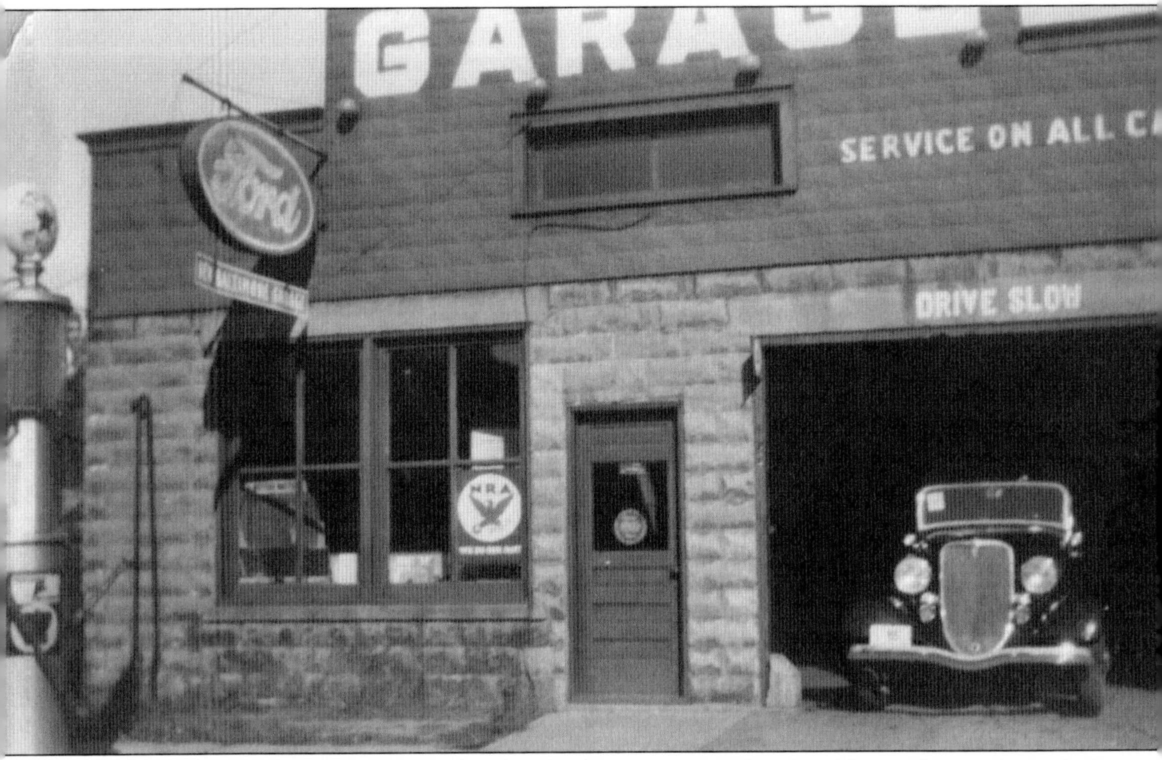

New Baltimore did not have an official public library until 1941, when Elmer Skinner invited all "clubs, churches, schools, and civic organizations" to attend a meeting at the municipal building on Front Street on March 11. The meeting resulted in the formation of the New Baltimore Public Library Association. Temporary quarters for the library were provided by New Baltimore mayor Harold Engleman in the city garage on Washington Street. As money was raised and books were donated, new temporary librarians Marie Marsh and Jane Miller inaugurated the library by checking out the first book to Mayor Engleman. Marsh's "temporary" assignment would last 41 years, until her retirement in 1982. She continued to volunteer at the library for many years until her death at age 101 in 2010. The library directors after Marsh were Beth Bagley-Stanton, from 1982 to 1987, and Margaret Thomas, from 1987 to the present.

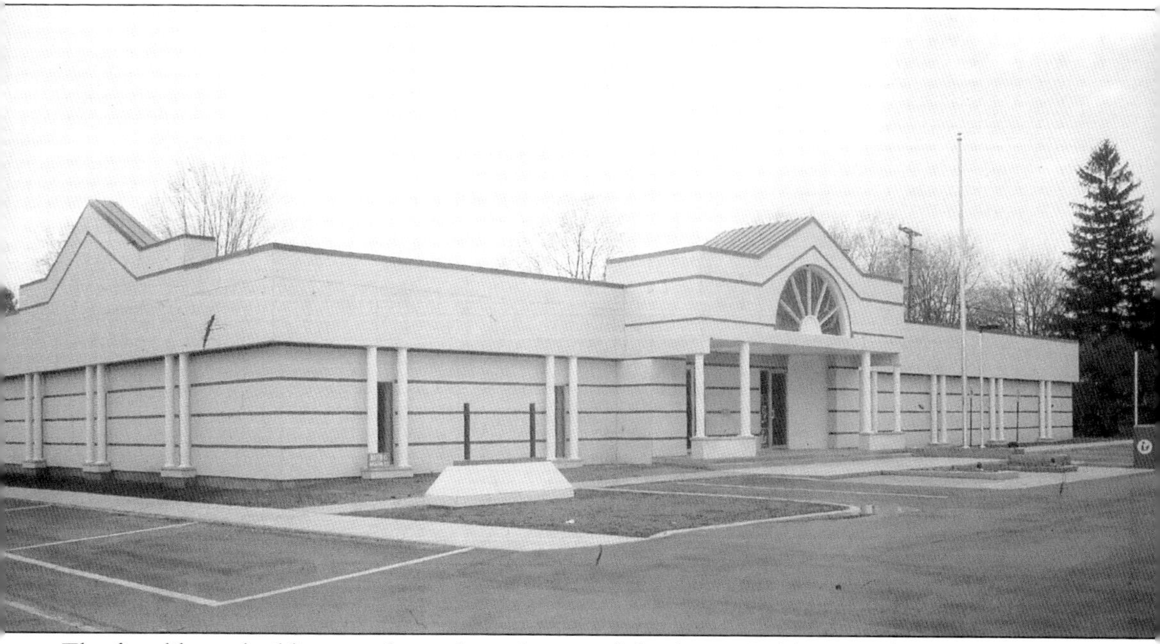

The first library building was located on the site of the former Tubby's Candy Store, which burned down around 1910. That building was replaced by a cement-block building constructed by Arthur Vossen of St. Clair. In the early 1920s, the building was a Dort automobile dealership before becoming the city garage, and its first library. Stuart and Velma MacDonald, owners of MacDonald Manufacturing, a plastics manufacturing plant, donated the second library building, which was constructed at Bedford and Main Streets in the late 1940s as a Pontiac dealership. It then became Becker's Department Store before housing Chapman boat builders. The property had at one time been the site of a corset and hoop skirt factory, and then, in 1917, the area's first modern garage, built by auto pioneer Alfred Helwig. When that building burned down in 1939, Helwig's grandson Harold and granddaughter Georgina Kristiansen built the present building, now called the Stuart and Velma MacDonald Public Library.

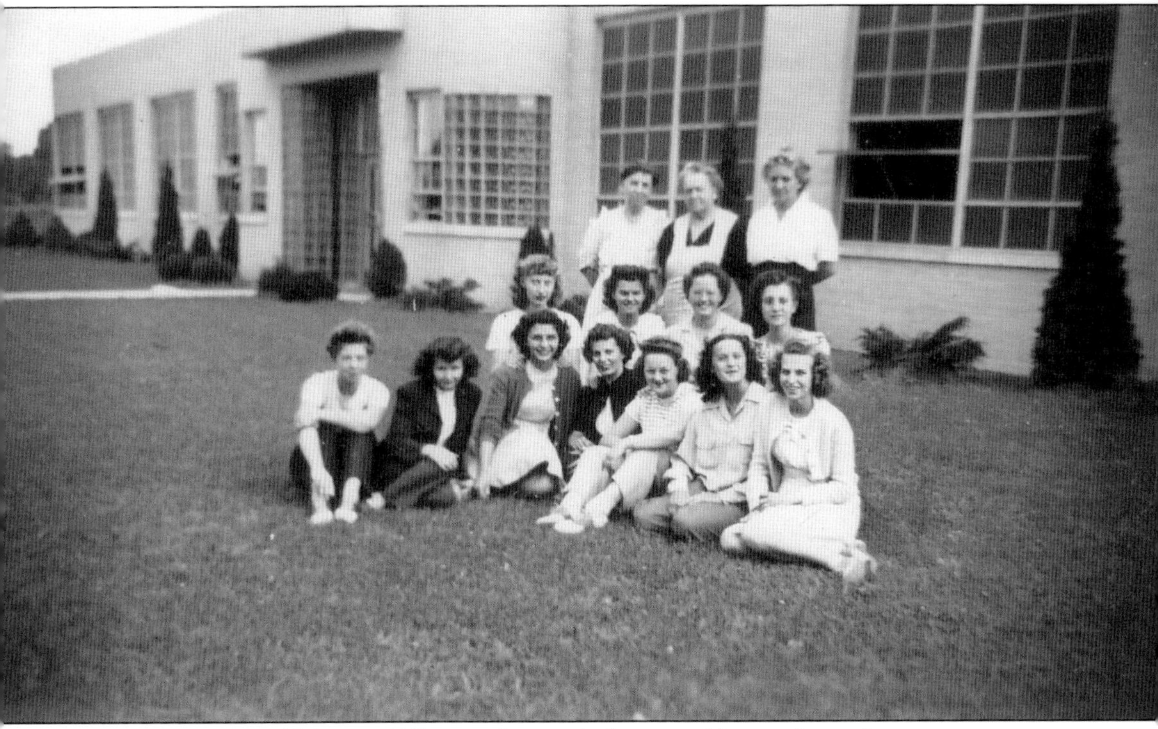

Stuart MacDonald (1914–1997) owned several plastics, rubber, and metal-stamping companies. He first established MacDonald Manufacturing Co. in New Baltimore in 1943, and expanded with a new plant in 1946. MacDonald was a pioneer in polystyrene processing and also owned a company in Georgia that molded rubber car mats. In the New Baltimore area, he also operated a metal stamping and tooling firm and a factory that made wheel weights for cars. He was the area's largest employer and taxpayer for many years. MacDonald was also a community benefactor and promoter of the city, as well as one of the original organizers of the Bay-Rama festival. He donated and renovated the building that became the Stuart and Velma MacDonald Public Library. MacDonald Manufacturing Co. was a popular employer, and, in a show of workplace camaraderie, employees often took group pictures in front of the factory building, such as this one from 1946. They also had company picnics, charity drives, and more.

Eight

Notable Buildings and Businesses

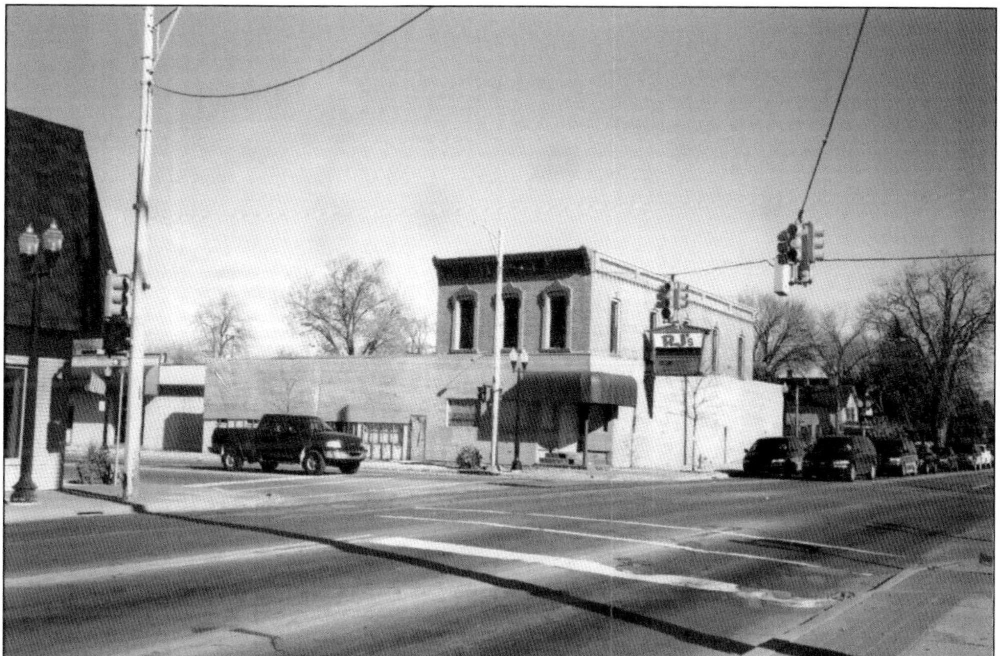

The buildings at the corner of Washington and Green Streets have varied histories. The building that is now Town Heating and Supply was built in the building boom of 1896 to 1906, when many downtown buildings were constructed. Known as Schoebel's Drug Store during much of its history, it was built by George Gallop, who operated a blacksmith shop there. Later, Peter Socia had a saloon there, which, like many of the drinking establishments of the day, provided free food as long as the person was drinking. Since women and children were not allowed in saloons back then, a separate room was provided for them.

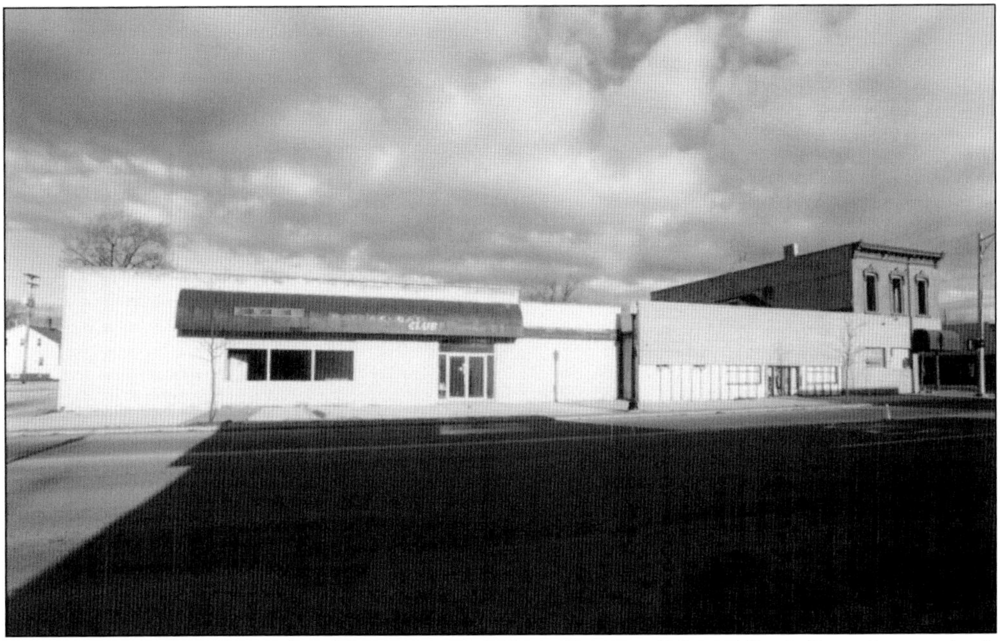

Peter Socia's saloon was replaced by Carpenter's Drug Store and then Allen's Drug Store, which was bought by Frank Schoebel, who ran Schoebel's Drug Store. Across the street from Schoebel's was the town's first movie house, run by Adolph De Stiger. In the 1890s up until the advent of sound motion pictures in 1928, a pianist was usually hired by the theater to accompany the film. According to local movie attendees, the pianist at New Baltimore's first theater was sometimes more engaging to watch than the movie. He was very animated, and would bounce up and down, show obvious emotion, and react in accordance with the action on the screen.

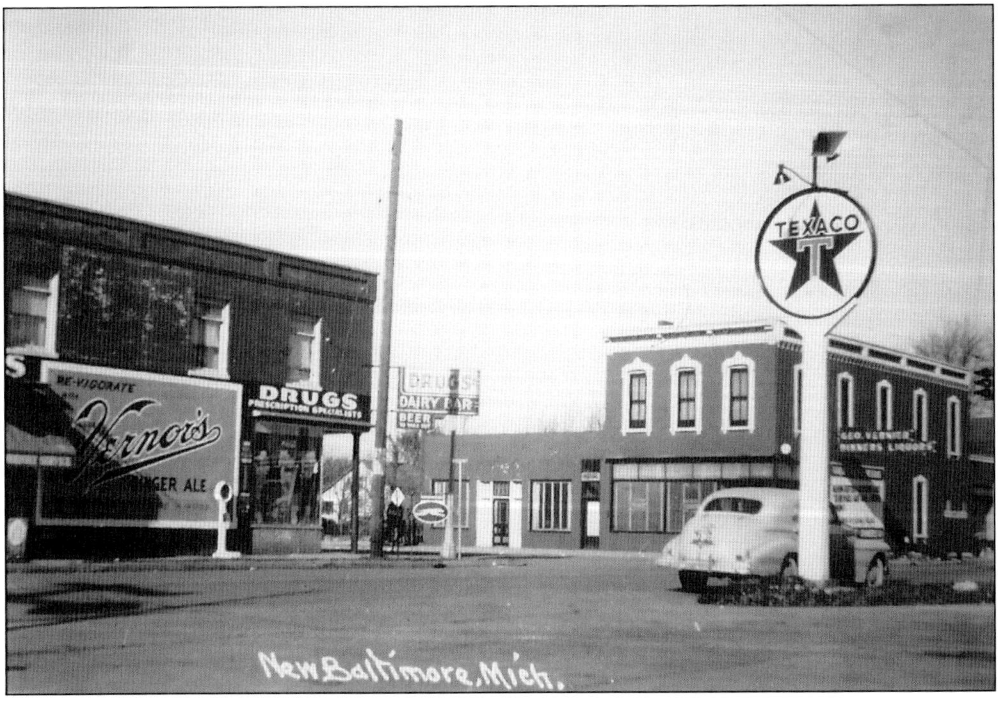

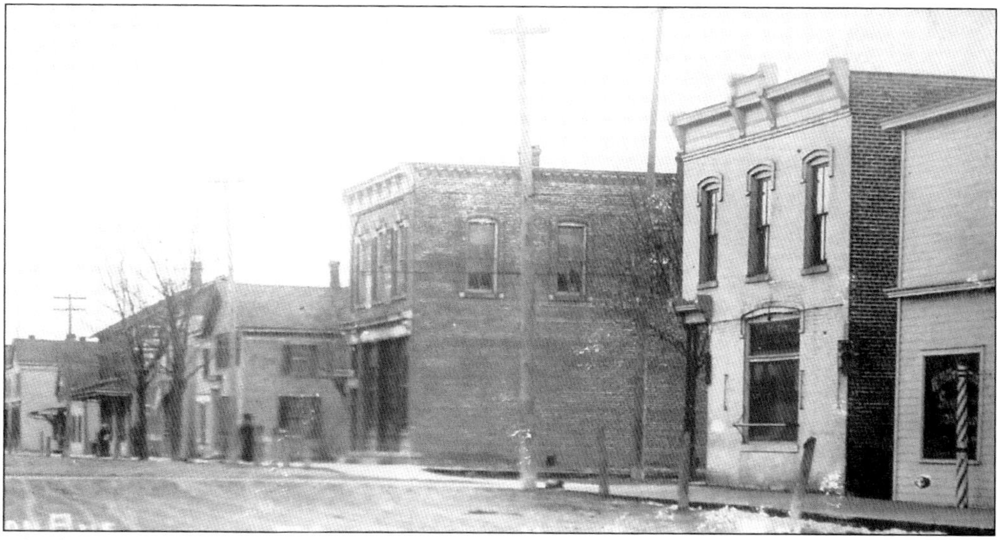

The former movie house served many other roles in later years. It was a telegraph office, but was most well known as a restaurant and tavern. In the 1920s, former Fair Haven postmaster George Vernier moved to New Baltimore and managed the Chesterfield Hotel. Later, he opened a restaurant called Vernier's in the old movie house building. In the 1950s, Jack Hortos, who was very active in the community, added a bowling alley to the building, calling it Bay Lanes. The weekend entertainment at Bay Lanes in the 1960s was often the rock band Unholy Beasts. Ollie Whitney (1901–1972), a former RKO theater circuit vaudevillian and New Baltimore resident, was a New Year's Eve entertainer for many years. The bar portion of the bowling alley was still called Vernier's Grill. Later renamed RJ's, it became an entertainment venue for well-known musical acts of the mid-1970s, including Chubby Checker and Herman's Hermits.

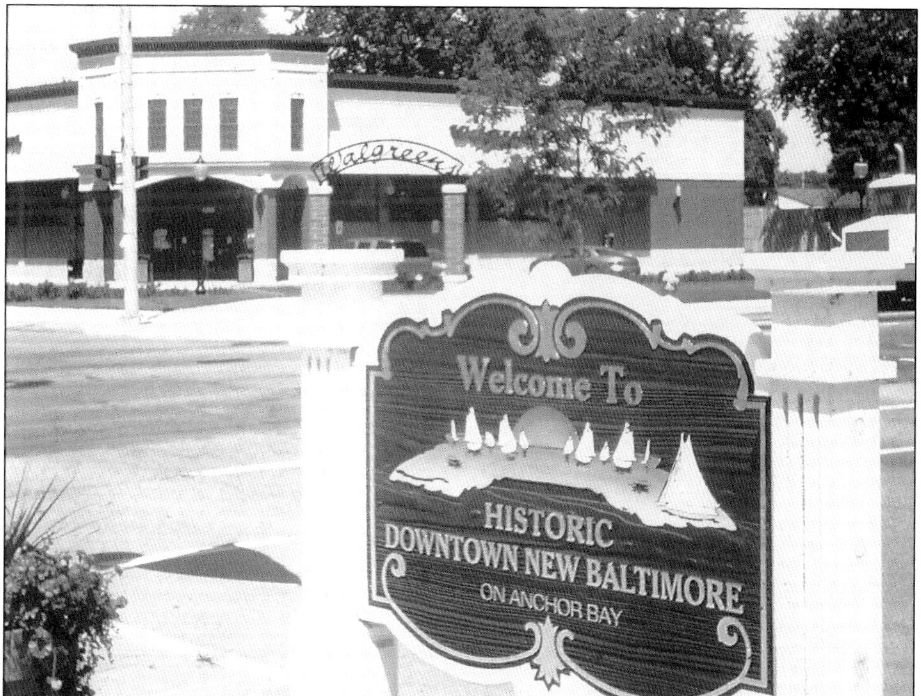

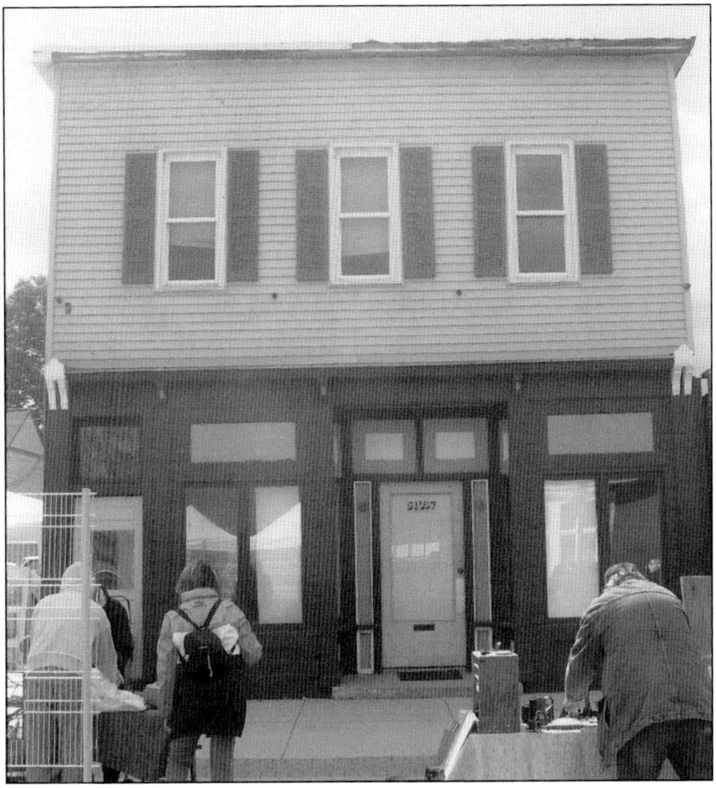

The Baker Building side of Washington Street included a building known as the Miller Law Building, which had many proprietors who practiced law, including Macomb County probate judge Frederick C. Miller, his son Mead Miller, Kurt Ciske, and John MacDonald. During Prohibition, the front of the building was a candy store and the back was a "blind pig." It was also one of the many locations of the town post office and also housed an undertaking business.

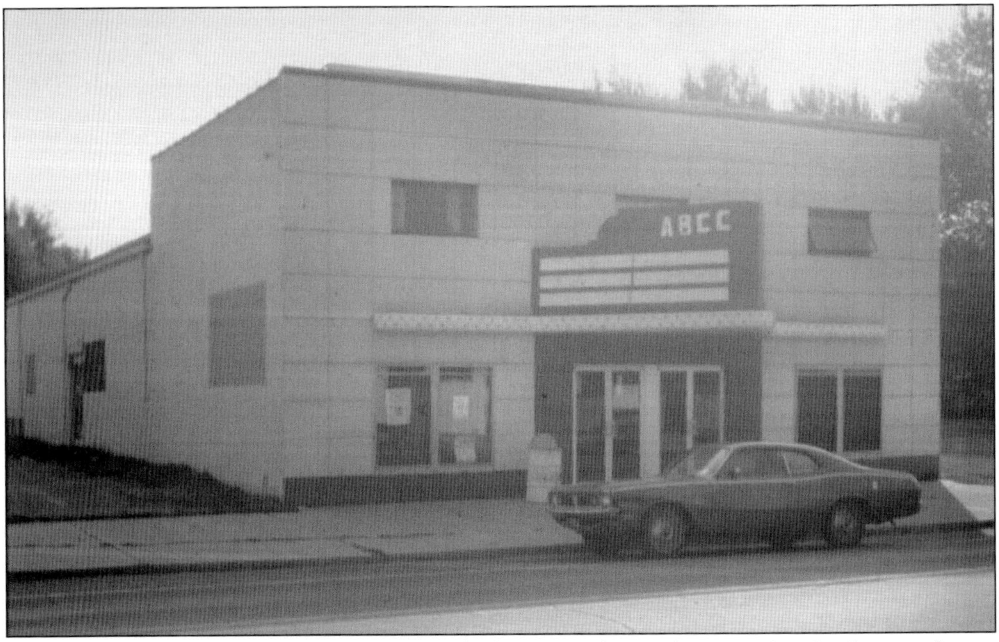

On the former site of the Chesterfield Hotel, the New Theatre became the third movie house in New Baltimore in the 1950s. In the late 1960s, the building was repurposed as the town recreation center, and then briefly served as an entertainment venue for rock bands in 1971 and 1972, including The Frost and Iggy and the Stooges.

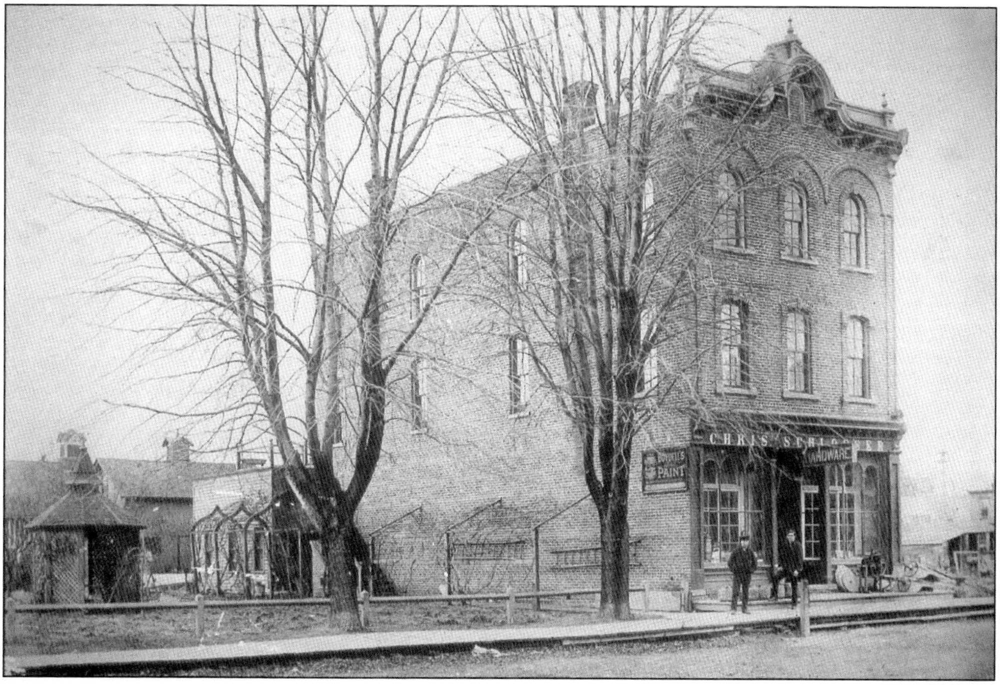

On Washington Street between Front and Main Streets is the building first known as the Schlosser Block. The handsome building originally held the Schlosser hardware store and was erected by J.P. Hension around 1870. In 1872, Chris Schlosser started working for Hension, and later took over the business. He was succeeded by his son Fred, who built replicas of the Old Town Hall and Hatheway Institute that are now in the Grand Pacific House Museum. Over the years, the building has housed an IGA grocery store, a candy store, a soap business, a gift store, and the headquarters of Davey International.

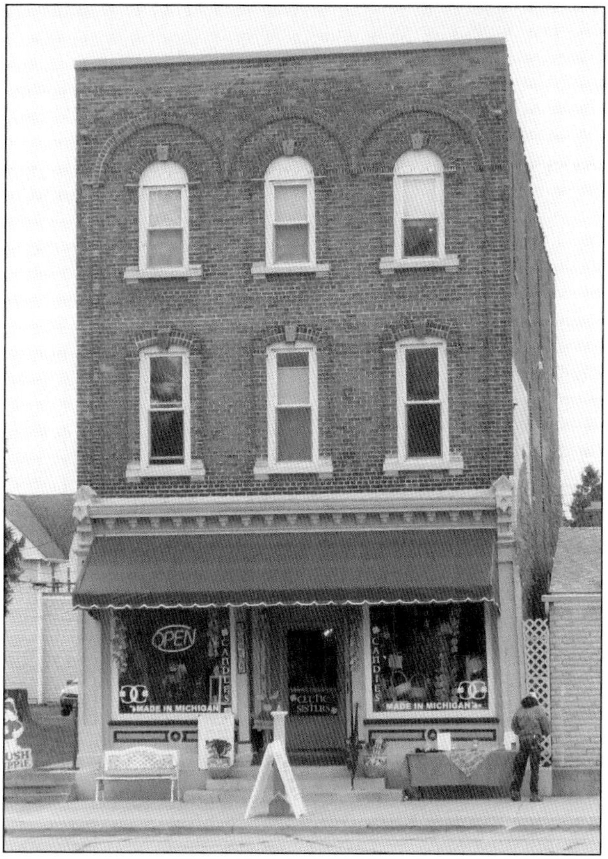

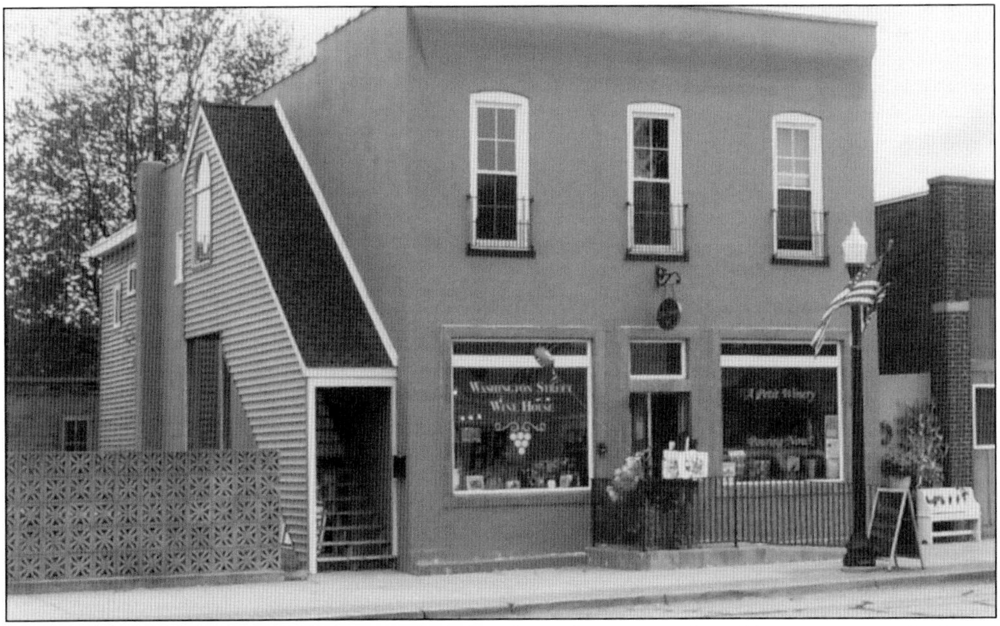

The building next to the Schlosser's Block has been home to a lot of businesses, including a few grocery stores and the wine store that currently inhabits the building. In 1896, it housed the town's first bank. After that, the building became known as the Jewel Saloon. Although the building was known to house a pool hall at one time, it managed to conceal its illegal beer brewing operation on the second floor until the day when the concoction overflowed and leaked onto the first floor. Another alcohol establishment was run by Lou Reidel, who started his first speakeasy during Prohibition in the still-standing structure on Bedford Street, across the street from his first legal establishment, the Town Pump. He probably got away with the illegal bar in his basement for so long because he was a neighborhood benefactor.

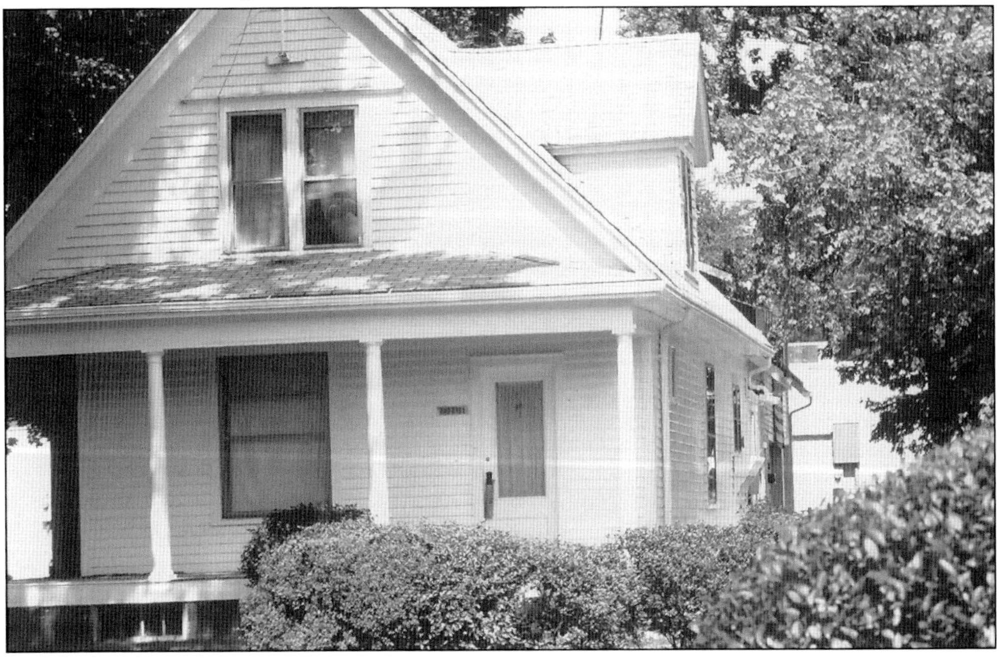

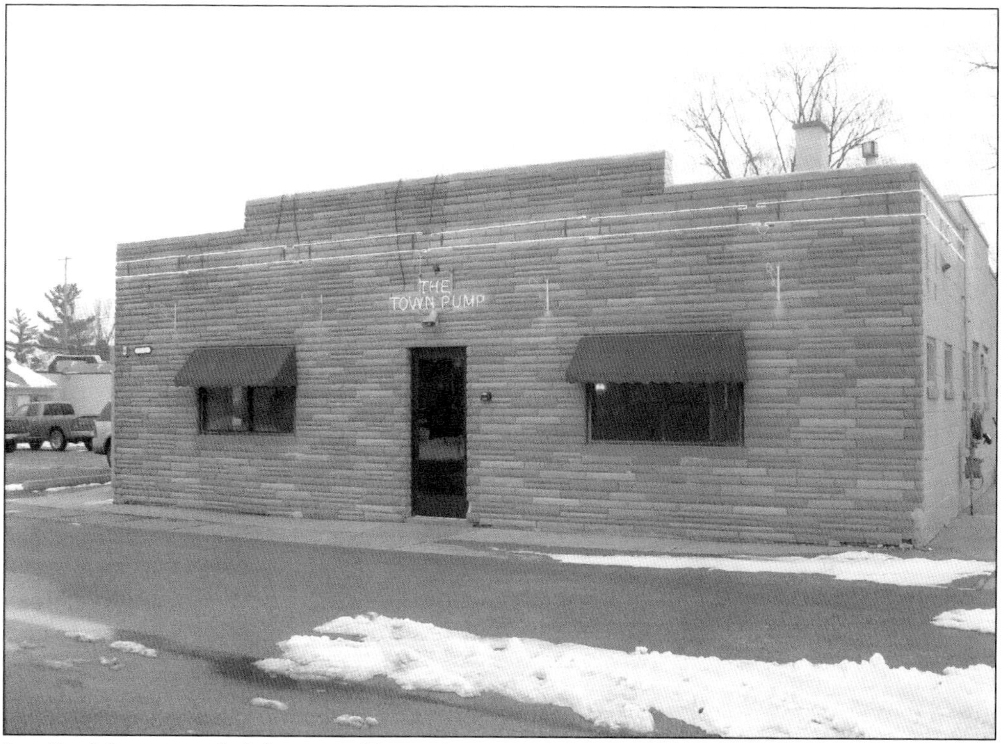

Lou Reidel was awarded the second liquor license in Macomb County after Prohibition; the first went to an establishment in Mt. Clemens. In 1941, he moved his operation across the street to his other establishment, the Town Pump. When he lost the Town Pump due to gambling, he moved back into the basement of his house.

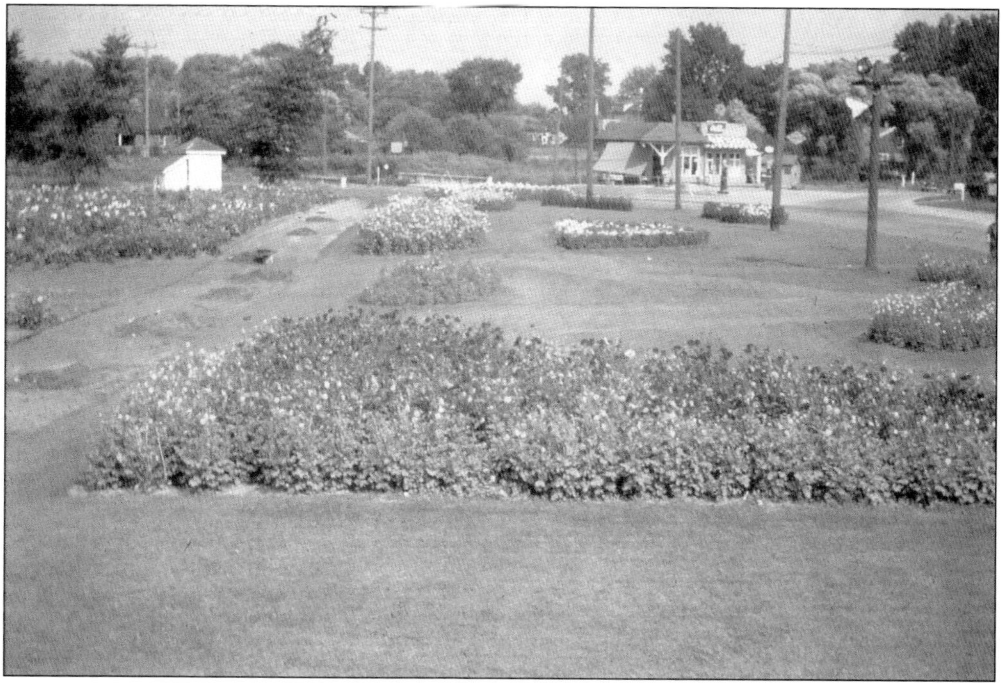

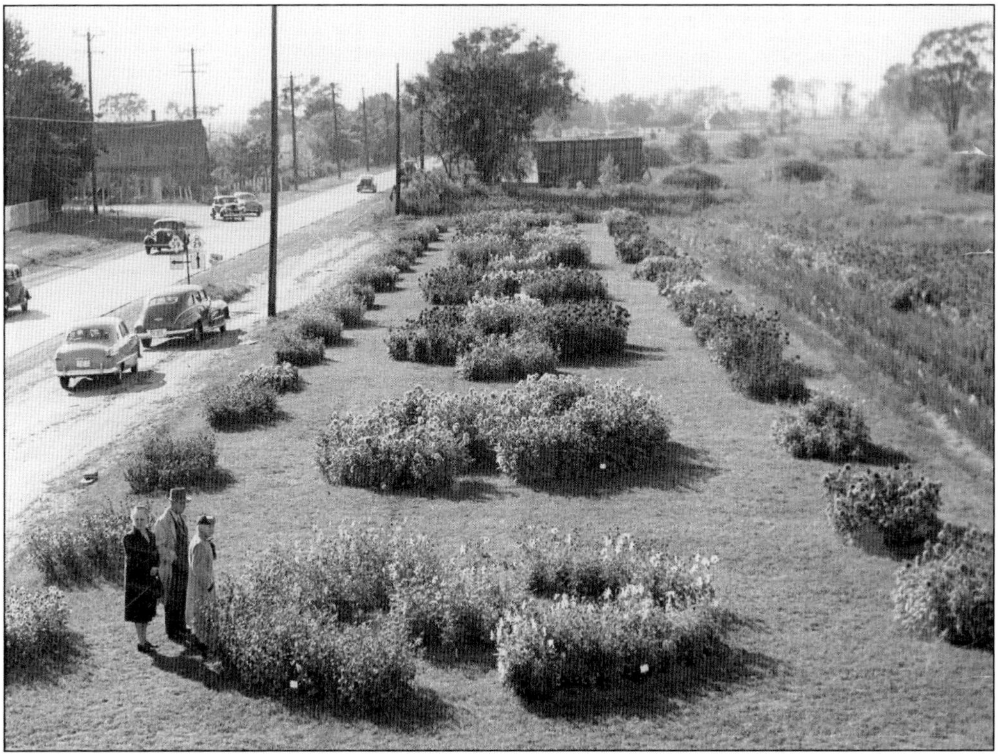

The main road leading to New Baltimore has chiefly been 23 Mile Road, which changes names many times. As it approaches New Baltimore, it divides into two, and the road to the left becomes Green Street, while the one to the right becomes Main Street. Later known as M-29, it is also known as Dixie Highway as it leaves New Baltimore, when Main and Green Streets once more combine. In addition, mainly because of the cheap whiskey sold at the Wayside Inn, on 23 Mile Road near Gratiot Road, it was once known as Whiskey Road. Other names included the New Baltimore Highway and Telegraph Road, because the telegraph lines ran along it.

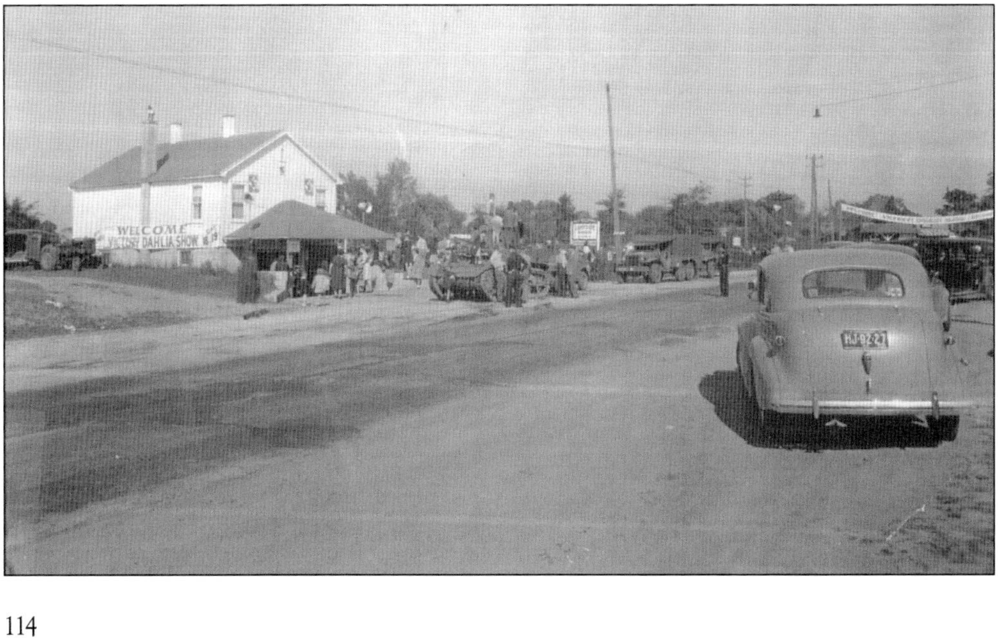

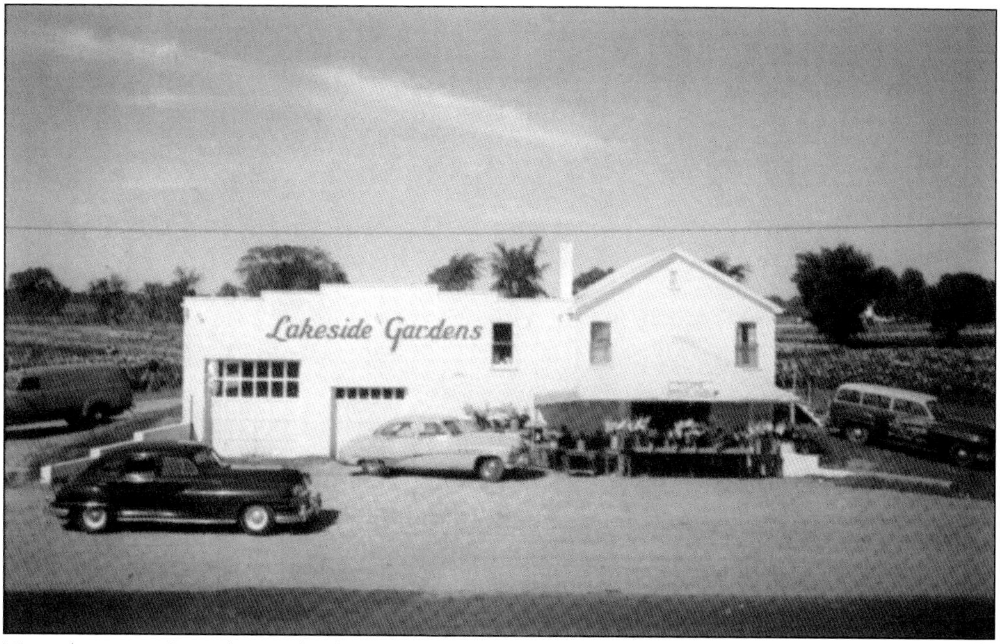

Near the area where the road splits in two was the nursery responsible for giving New Baltimore the name Dahlia Capital of the World. Owned and operated by the Koenig family, they created new strains of dahlias and named them after their grandchildren. For many years, there was a celebration when the dahlias bloomed, complete with a Dahlia queen. The city of New Baltimore honors the Koenigs with a monument to them at the Walter and Mary Burke City Park. It is surrounded by dahlias that were planted and are maintained by the third generation of the Koenig family.

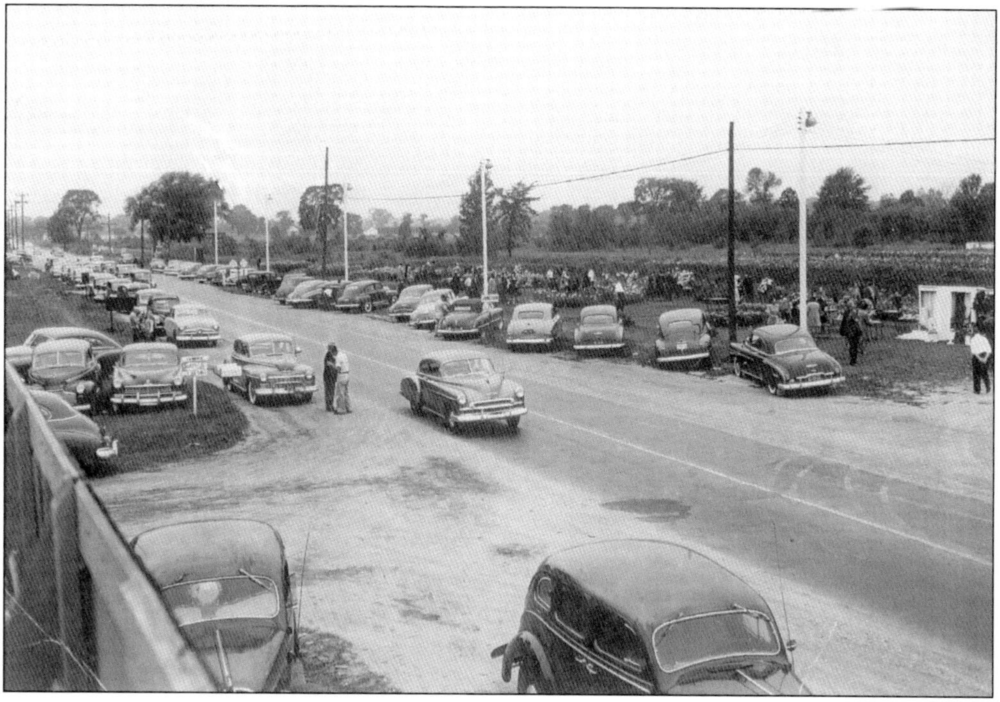

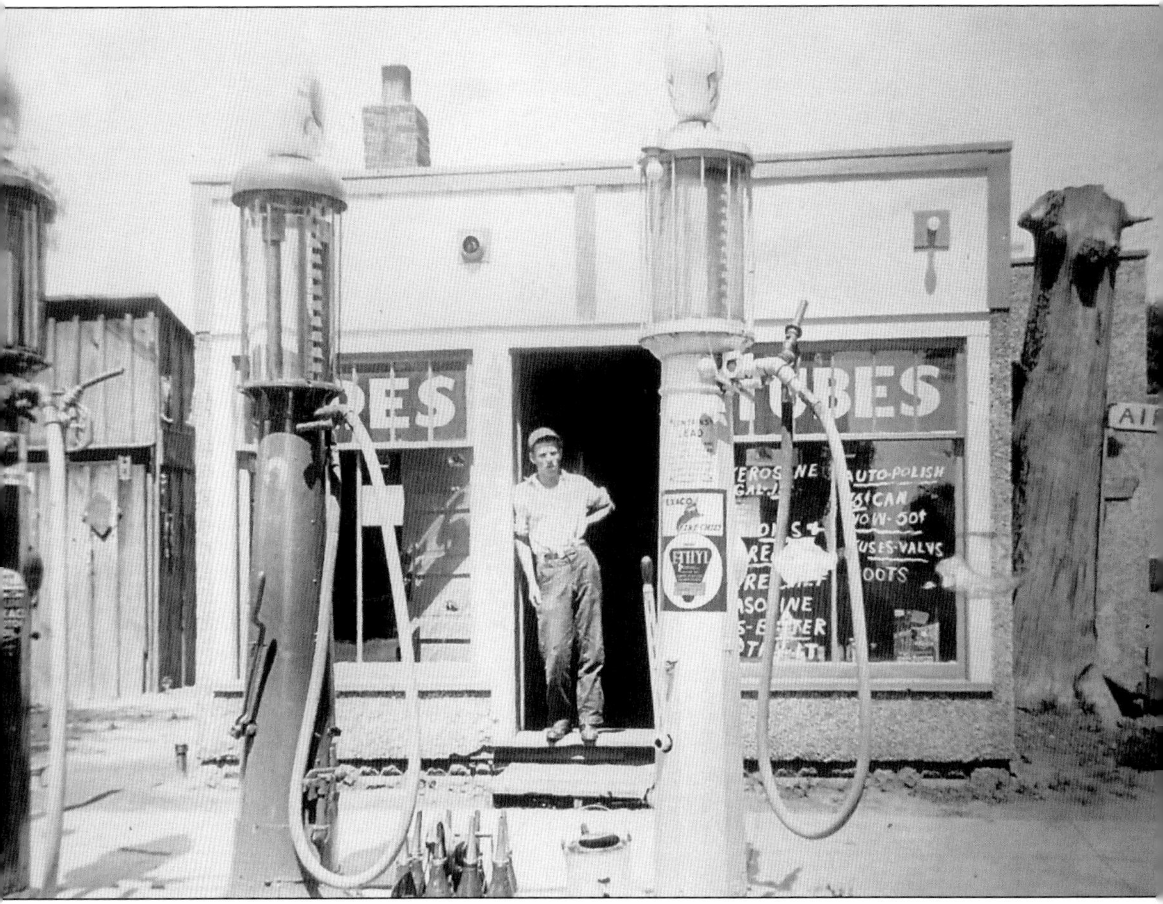

Probably due to its proximity to Detroit, businesses that cater to the automobile have been prevalent throughout New Baltimore's history. There have been quite a few gas stations in various areas of downtown New Baltimore, including the two gas stations owned by Fred Dunlap; the city garage, which became the city's first library; the Helwig garage, which became the present library; Max and Jim's, across from the Hatheway Institute; Kret's Garage; and the Texaco station on the corner of Washington and Green Streets. Other auto-related businesses included the Dort and Hudson dealerships that were once in the city. The gas station was located by the Koenig building, between the building and the alley.

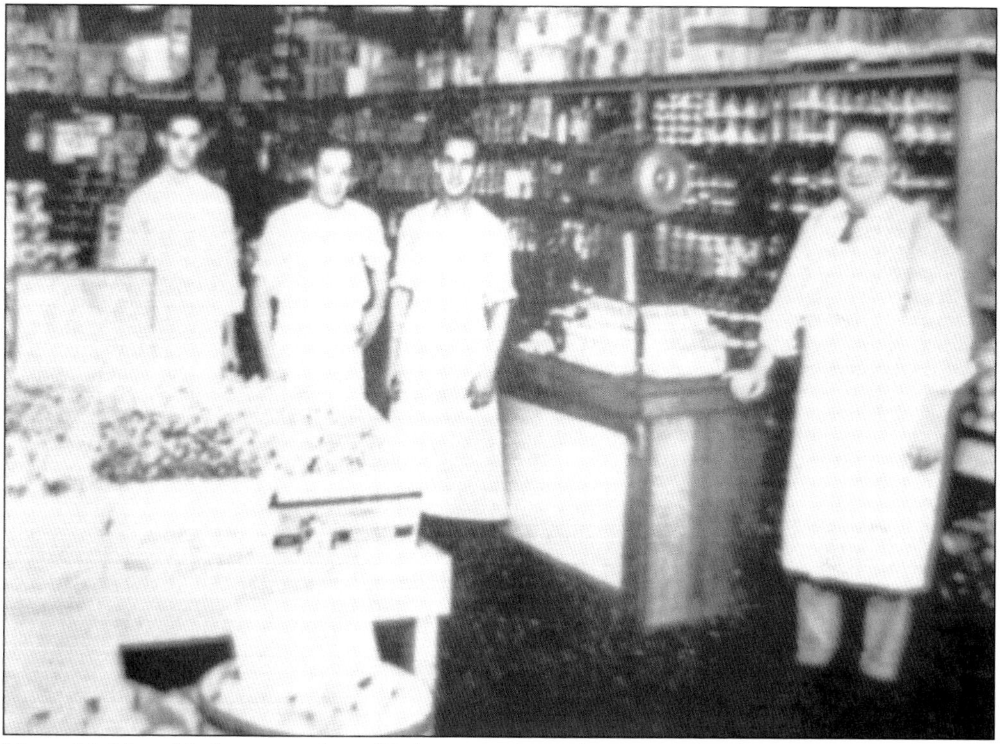

Marsack's Meat Market started on Washington Street between Alfred and Green Streets, and later moved to the building next to the Baker Building, which was erected in 1869 by Frederick Miller. Apprentice butcher Jack Rehfuss doubled as the trombone player in the city band. Below, one of the earliest businesses was the Gallop Blacksmith, in the future Schoebel's building.

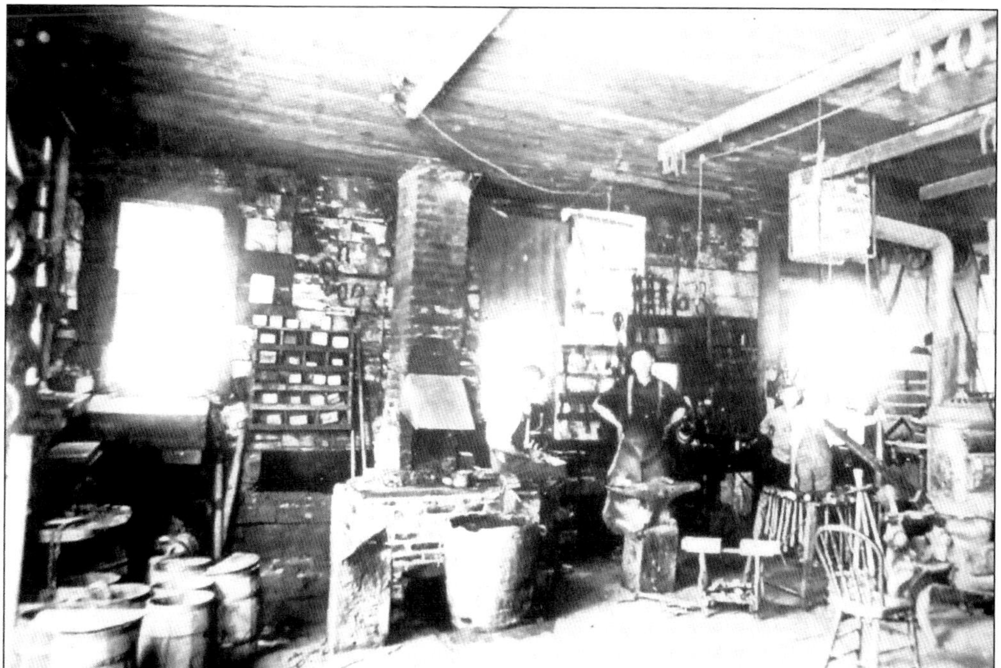

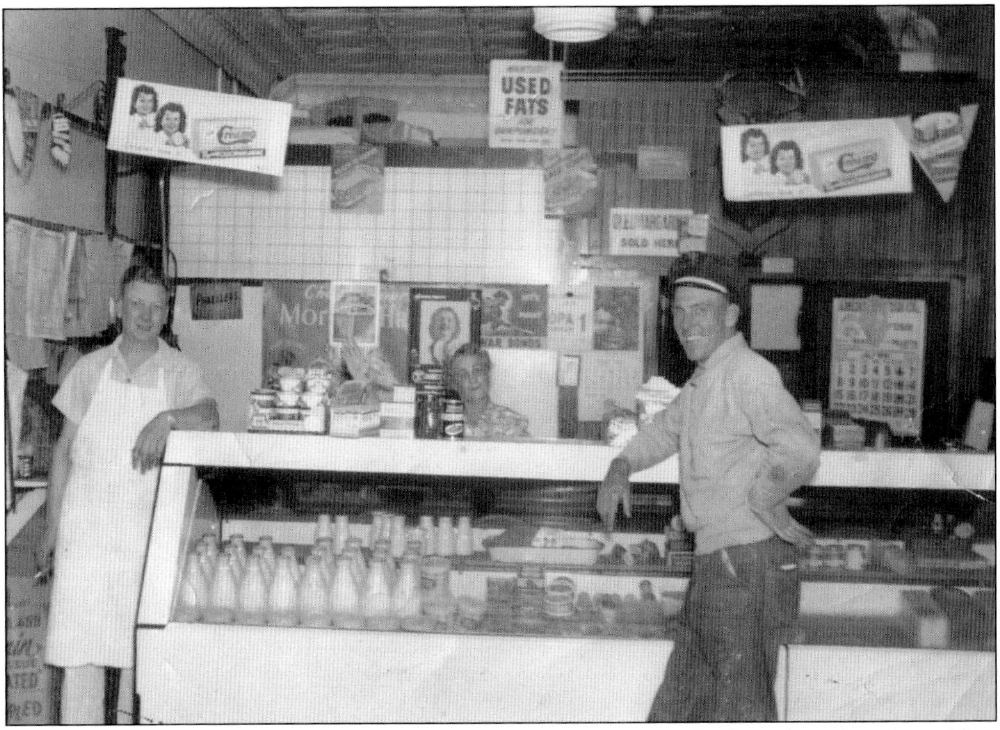

Traditional meat markets, overseen by a butcher who cuts meat and sells it, have long been New Baltimore commercial mainstays. A prime example was Harry's Meat Market, run by Harry Spiekhout on Washington Street from the 1940s through the 1970s. Some of the signs in these 1940s photographs of the butcher shop recall the era of meat rationing during World War II. (Both, courtesy of Sue McPhedran.)

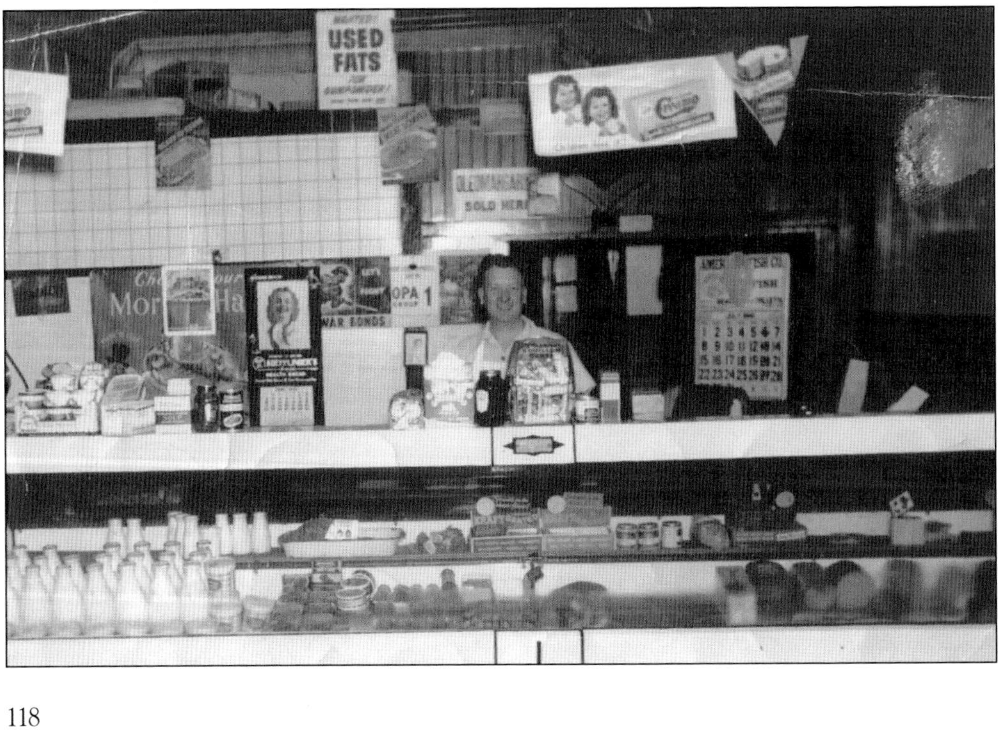

Nine

Floods, Great Fires, and the Fire Department

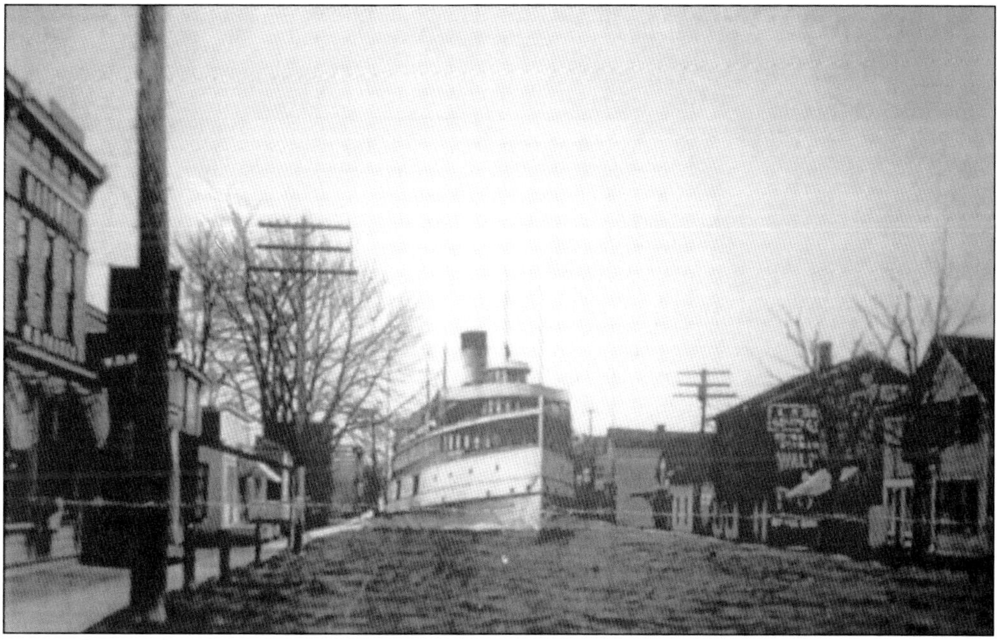

New Baltimore has seen its share of natural disasters. In 1938, a tornado struck, causing considerable damage. Due to its location on the water, many floods have also occurred. In 1955 and again in 1958, floods did most of their destruction along the Anchor Bay shoreline's south end, including parts of neighboring Anchorville. The Dew Drop Inn dropped into Lake St. Clair after heavy storms.

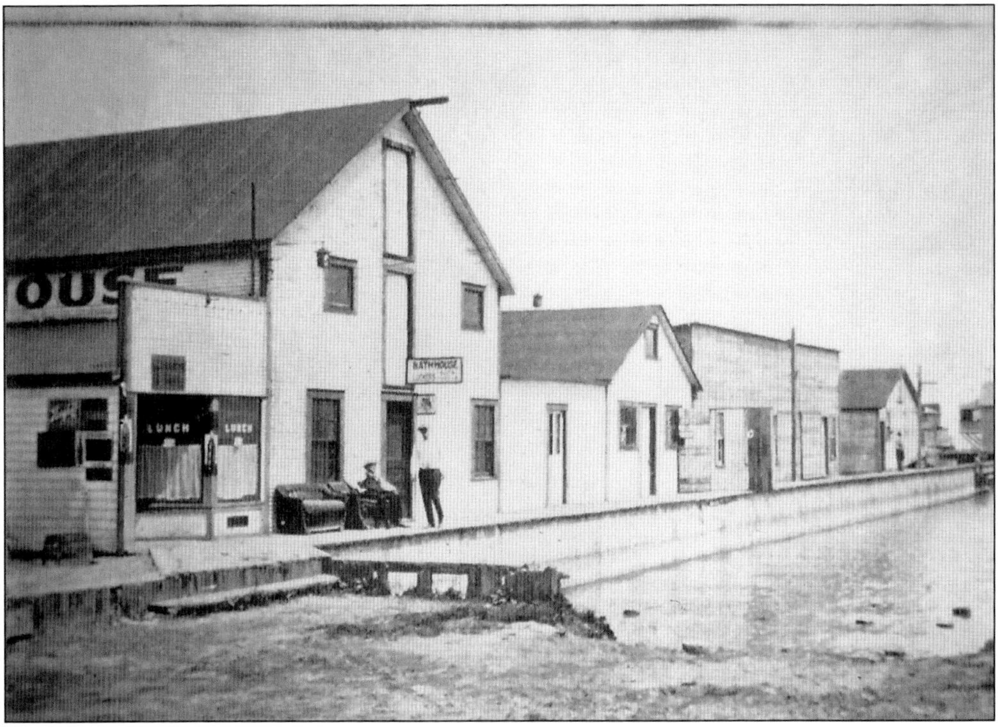

In the 1920s, a dock was erected at the end of Ashley Street that was large enough to hold several businesses, bathhouses, and fishmongers. This dock was known as Spier's dock, and it was where most of the community went swimming. At the end of the dock was a small island, about 100 yards from the pier. On the island was a brothel. Potential customers rang a bell on the dock, and then stood at the end of the dock while the proprietors of the establishment looked them over. If all seemed okay, a boat would be sent over to pick the person up.

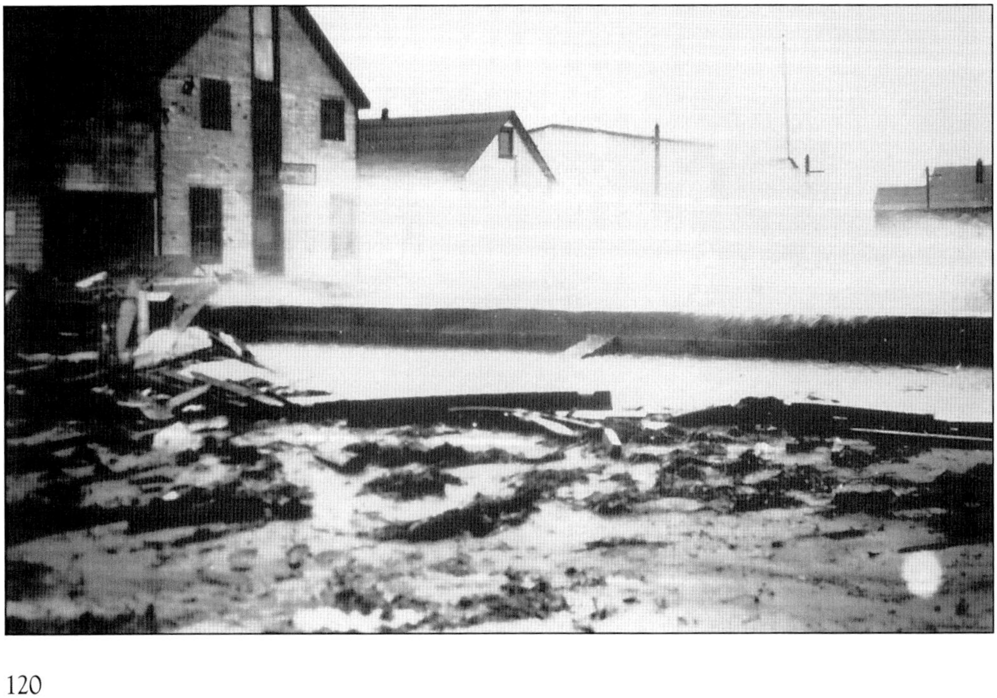

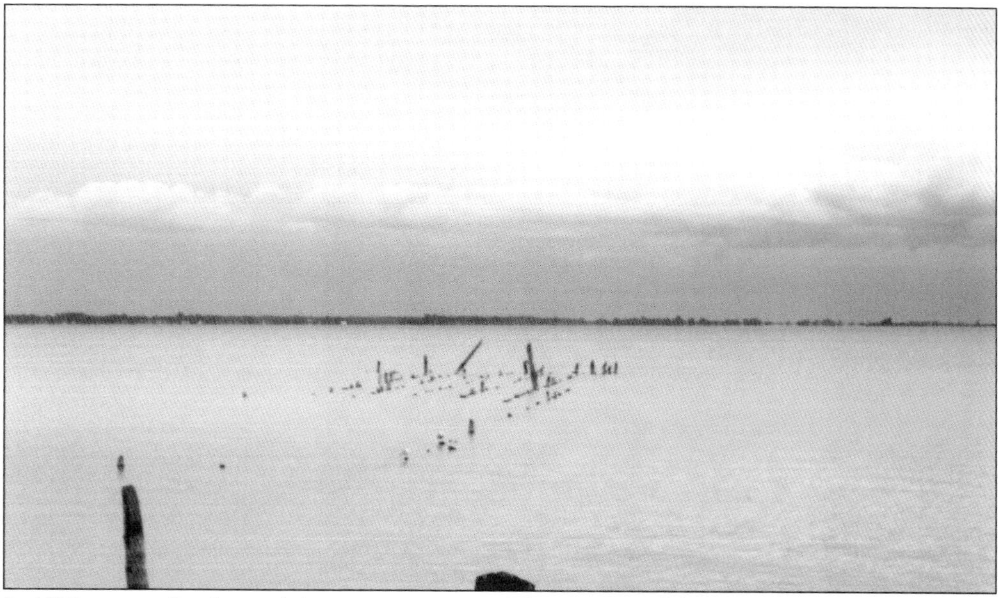

In 1929, a great flood wiped the entire pier away. The remains of the dock can still be seen at low tide. A far worse catastrophe, the Great Fire of 1870, destroyed more than two blocks of buildings on Washington Street from Alfred Street to Front Street. Reportedly started by children using a stove in a barn near the corner of Washington and Alfred Streets, the fire raged through the village. Unfortunately, most of the buildings at the time were constructed of wood, due to the area's recent lumber boom. At this time, the only firefighting available to the community was the bucket brigade, which was a very ineffective method. Although the fire damages were estimated at over $37,000, a figure that would be in the millions in today's dollars, leading citizen Gilbert Hatheway stepped up and provided much of the money to rebuild the business district. Soon, the townspeople voted 64 to 18 to establish a volunteer fire department and spend $1,000 on firefighting equipment. This purchased a horse-drawn, hand-pump engine and a two-wheel hose cart. The water tower can be seen in the view of Front Street below.

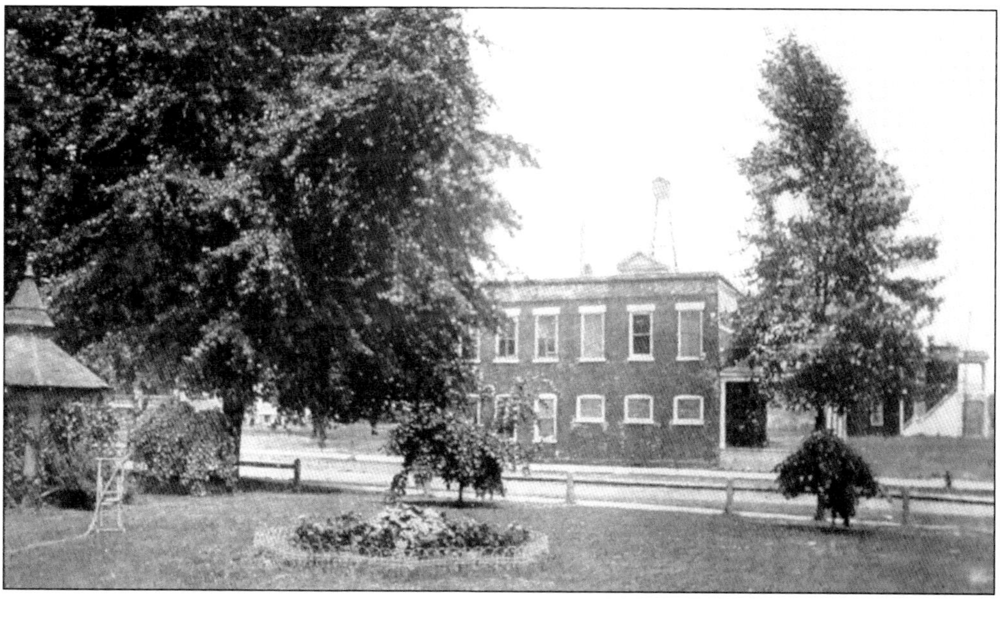

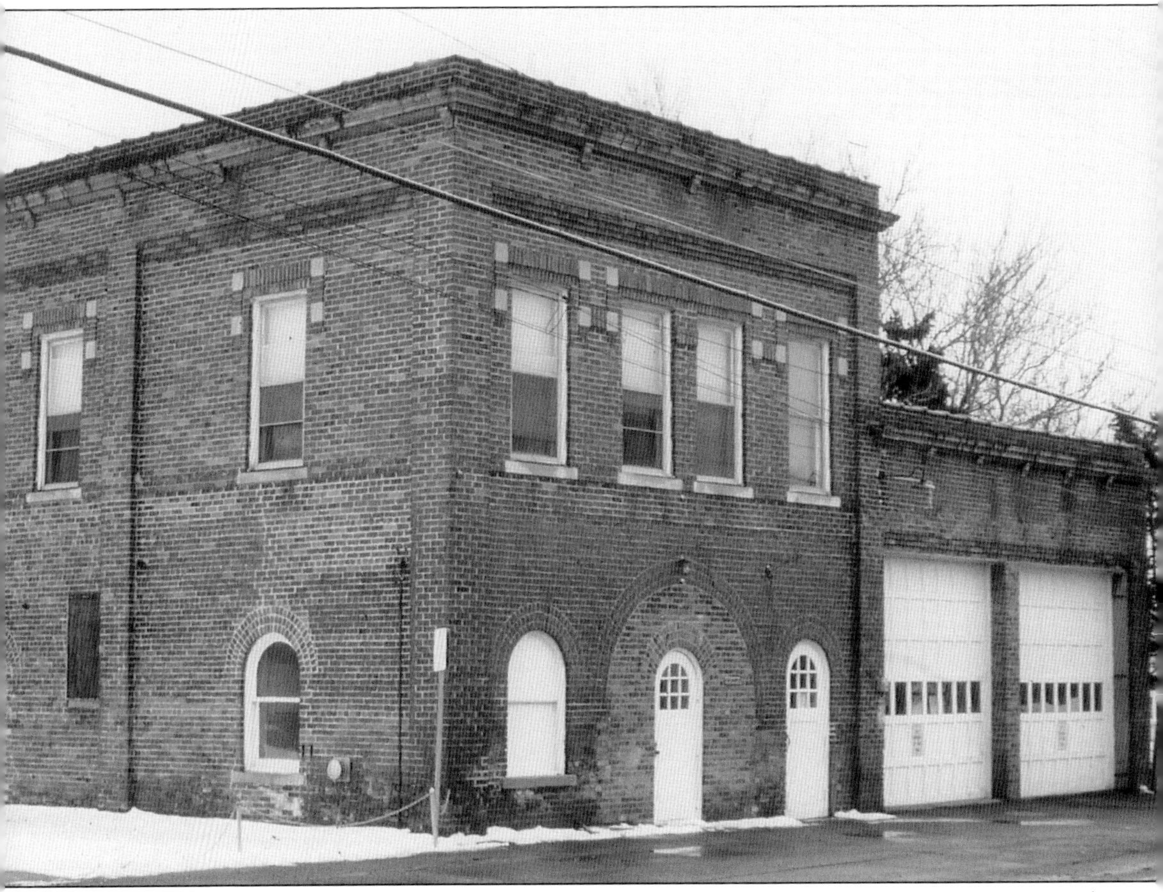

The village had four brick cisterns installed at various strategic points. The one at Washington and Green Streets was 15 feet deep and 10 feet in diameter. The addition of a water department was a boon to the city. A sewer and a sewage treatment plant were approved in 1917, and additional water lines and improvements were added over the years. The filtration plant was approved in 1935. The water department has been on Front Street since the early 1900s, near where the St. Clair Inn once stood. There have been two different buildings; for a time, the city municipal building and the police headquarters were located in the water department building.

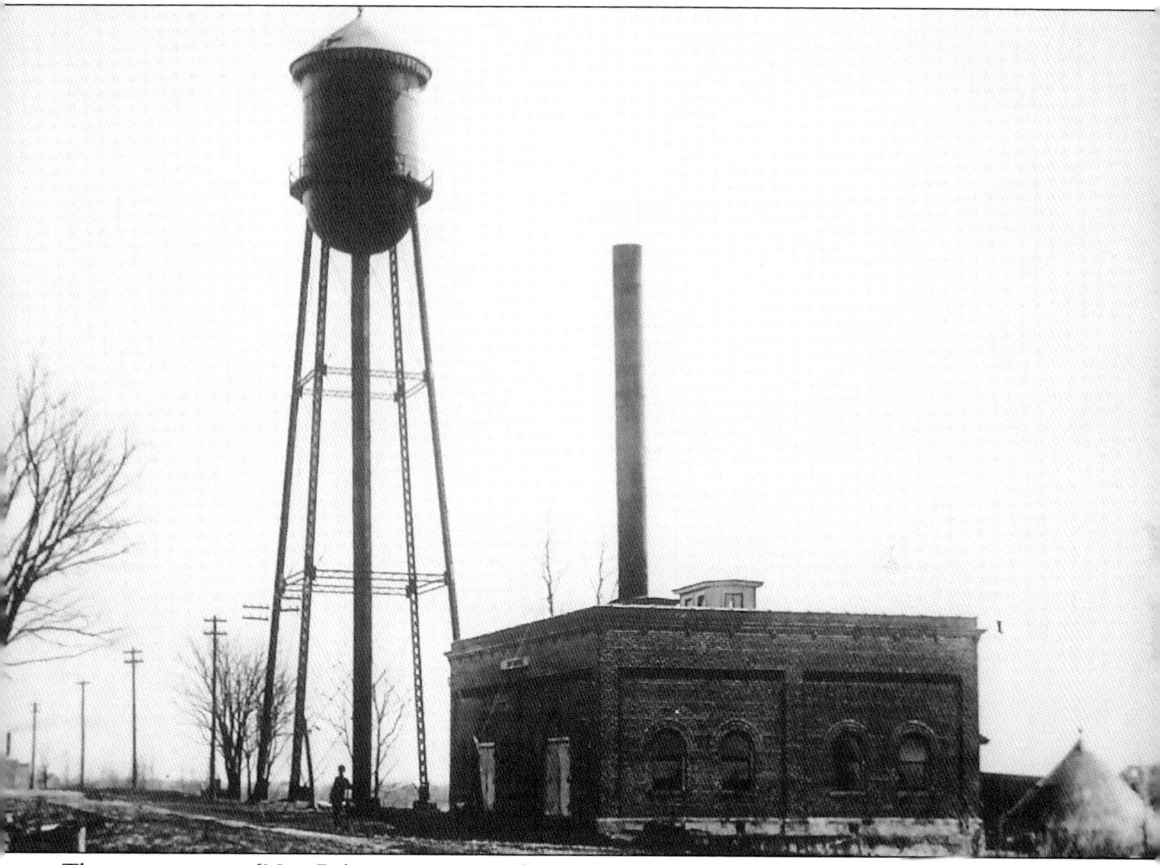

The water towers of New Baltimore, once used to store water, have also been a beacon for watercraft over the years. The present water tower is 147 feet high. When the first one, erected in 1902, was replaced by a more modern counterpart in 1949, both stood for 10 years, until the original water tower was torn down in 1958.

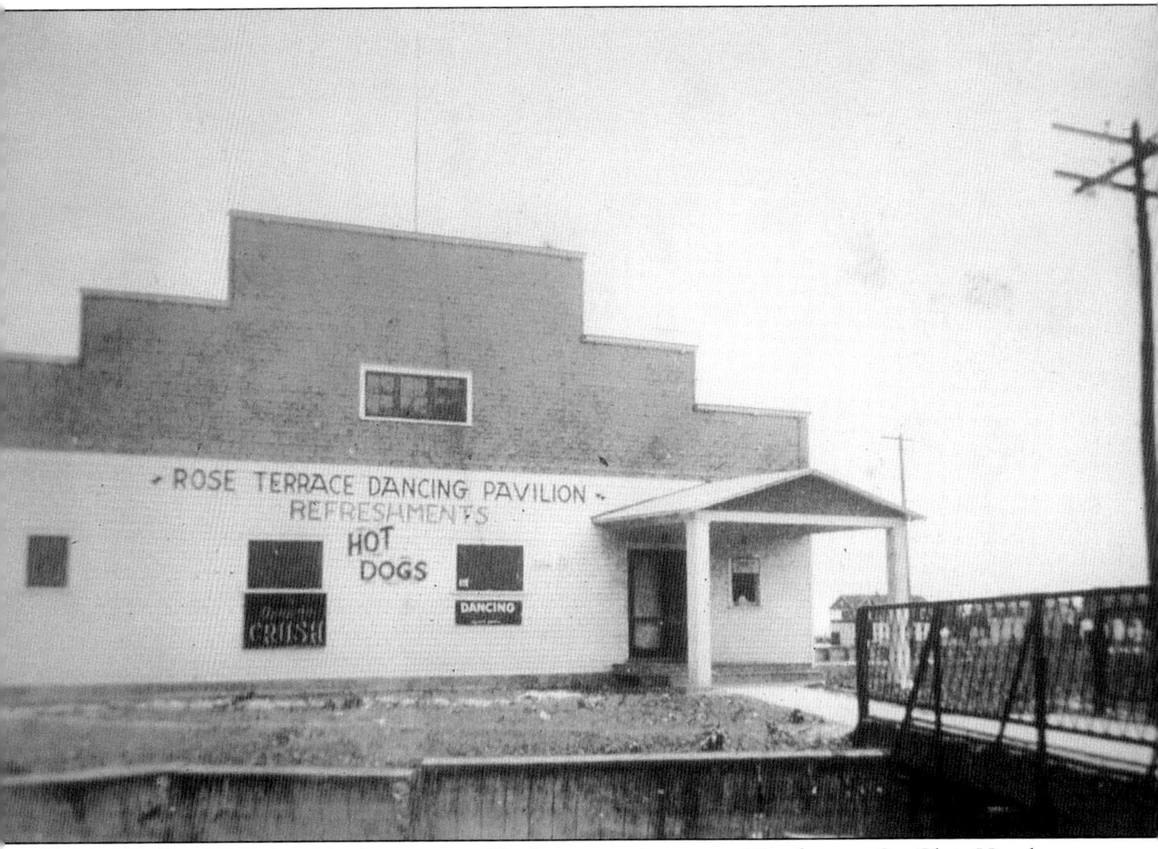

The fire department had many notable fires over the years. The famous St. Clair Hotel, near the city park's present location, caught on fire and was a total loss in December 1899. Arson was blamed, according to the Mt. *Clemens Monitor.* Arson was again suspected in the 1924 fire of the dance pavilion in the city park. In 1907, the hand pumper raced to County Line Road between Main and Green Streets to a giant fire at the grain elevator, which spread to the nearby roundhouse of the DUR.

Although there were notable losses over the years, the fire department was able to avoid more disasters like the Great Fire of 1870, in which multiple buildings were lost. The fire department was able to save the city's oldest church, the First Congregational Church, at Alfred and Base Streets, from a disastrous chimney fire in 1938. Two years later, firefighters performed the same service at the Bethel Temple Evangelistic Center on Base Street, the city's former opera house. In 1984, they prevented the First Baptist Church on Washington Street from being destroyed by flames. James Malane was 18 in 1938 when he and his friend Robert Goslyn saved six employees of the Iceolate Corporation—Iceolate was an artificial skate-surface material for ice-skating rinks—from a fire at their building near the corner of Bedford and Main Streets. In 1958, when St. Mary's Catholic Church burned down, Malane, a volunteer fireman, again braved the flames to rescue several sacred articles from the sacristy.

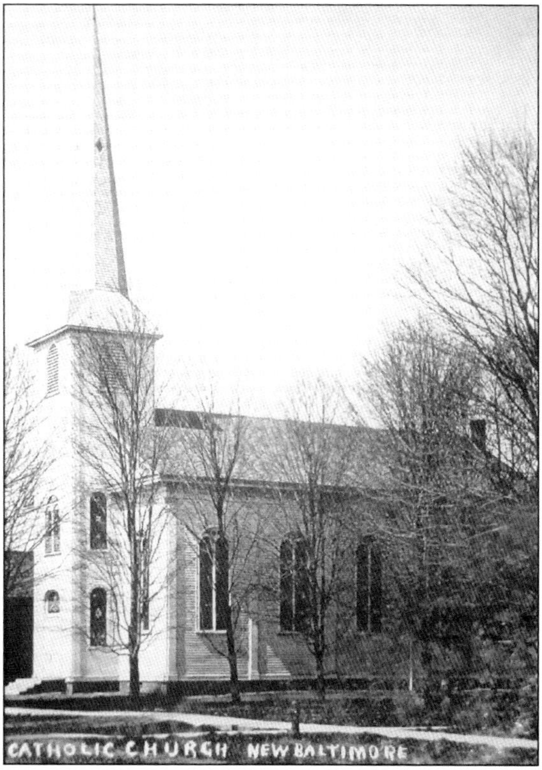

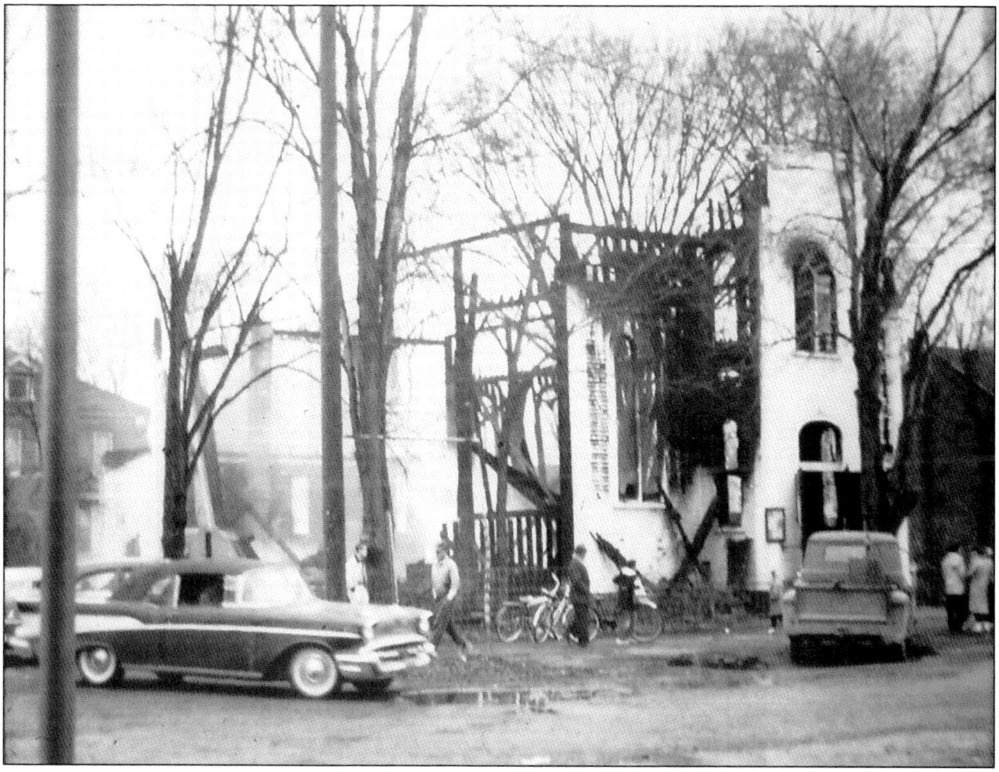

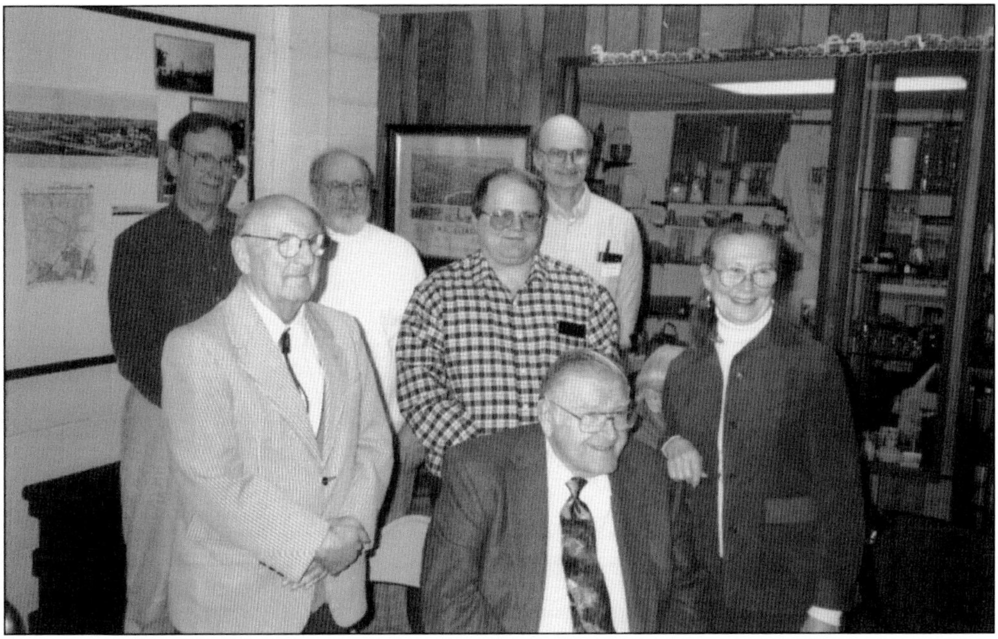

To keep alive the history of the city, the New Baltimore Historical Society was formed in 1975. In 1985, the members began negotiating to purchase the Grand Pacific House, which was repurposed into a museum with furnishings recalling its beginnings as a hotel. The historical society moved into the museum on January 26, 1987, moving the museum's collection from the city library, where it had been stored. The museum was opened to the public on June 14, 1987. Besides the annual history fair, New Baltimore also has the Bay-Rama carnival in the summer and a winter carnival featuring the polar plunge, sponsored by the New Baltimore Lions Club, proving once again that New Baltimore's most valuable resource is its people, who have unselfishly given their time and money in order to enrich the community.

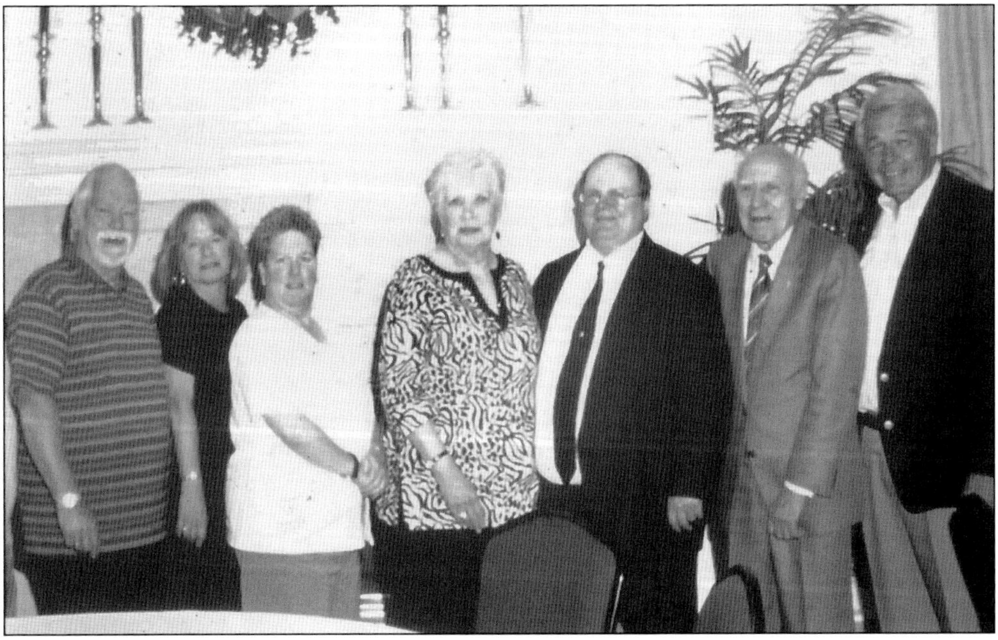

BIBLIOGRAPHY

Eldridge, Robert F. *Past and Present of Macomb County*. Chicago: S.J. Publishing Co. Inc., 1905.

Gonyeau, Richard. Various newspaper articles in the *Anchor Bay Beacon* and the *Bay Voice*, 1980–1996.

Ira Township Sesquicentennial Committee. *The Heritage of Ira: A Sesquicentennial History*. Algonac, MI: Reference Publications Inc., 1990.

Ira Township Sesquicentennial Committee. *Legends of a Legacy: Karl H. Schnoor – His Letters*. Algonac, MI: Reference Publications, 1987.

Leeson, M.A. *History of Macomb County, Michigan*. Chicago: self-published, 1882.

Naldrett, Alan. Images of America: *Chesterfield Township*. Charleston, SC: Arcadia Publishing, 2011.

Nellis Newspapers. *Pageant of Progress: Past and Present of Macomb County, Vol. VII*. Mt. Clemens, MI: Nellis Newspapers, 1928.

Pall, Karl Mark. *Amazing History of Macomb County*. Mt. Clemens, MI: Macomb County Historical Commission, Local History Spotlight Archive, 2007.

Romig, Walter. *Michigan Place Names*. Detroit: Wayne State University Press, 1986.

Rynearson, Dr. Elton James Jr. *The History of the Anchor Bay School System*. Unpublished, 1973.

Skinner, Grace C. and Elmer L. *History Stories of New Baltimore, 1845–1951*. Port Huron, MI: Kerr-Albert Office Supply, 1961.

Trinity, Bernard. *Many Yesterdays*. Dublin, OH: Trinity Enterprises, 1986.

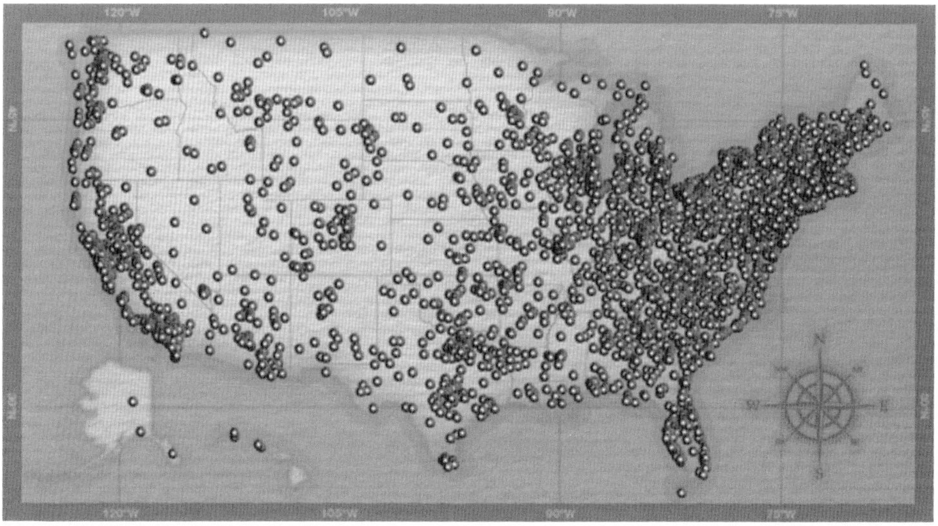